Medicine, Ethics, and the Third Reich: Historical and Contemporary Issues

Edited by
John J. Michalczyk

Sheed & Ward

Sheed & Ward™ is a service of The National Catholic Reporter Publishing Company.

Library of Congress Cataloguing-in-Publication Data

Medicine, ethics, and the Third Reich : historical and contemporary issues / [edited by] John J. Michalczyk.
    p.   cm.
    Includes bibliographical references and index.
    ISBN 1-55612-752-9 (alk. paper)
    1. Medical ethics—Congresses. 2. Holocaust, Jewish (1939-1945)—Germany—Congresses. 3. World War. 1939-1945—Atrocities—Congresses. 4. Human experimentation in medicine—Congresses. 5. Prisoners of war—Medical care—Congresses. I. Michalczyk, John J., 1941-
    [DNLM: 1. Ethics, Medical—congresses. 2. Physician's Role—congresses. 3. Holocaust—congresses. 4. Euthanasia—congresses. 5. Sterilization, Sexual—congresses. 6. Human Experimentation—congresses. 7. Political Systems—congresses. W 50 M48983 1994]
    R724.M3125   1994
    174'.2—dc20
    DNLM/DLC
    for Library of Congress   94-25916
                                                  CIP

Published by: Sheed & Ward
                 115 E. Armour Blvd.
                 P.O. Box 419492
                 Kansas City, MO 64141

To order, call: (800) 333-7373

Cover design by Gloria Ortiz. Cover photo: Defendants in the Nuremburg Doctors Trial. (UPI/Bettmann Newsphotos)

Contents

V. Jewish Doctors in the Shadow of the Reich

VI. Nuremberg's Legacy

VII. Into the Future

VIII. Conclusions

Appendix: Documents

List of Illustrations

Permissions

The following publishers have generously given permission to reproduce previously copyrighted materials.

For Francis P. Sullivan, SJ—
  a brilliant mind,
  a creative spirit,
  a sensitive soul.
           Merci

Acknowledgments

Conceived from the notion that the medical profession is one dedicated to healing and not destruction, as seen in the Third Reich, this project has found an outlet in a conference, the present text, and, eventually, a documentary film. It is the fruitful collaboration of a multitude of individuals and institutions.

Most notably generous has been Boston College, with its sponsorship of the conference. Here the Jesuit Institute, under the direction of Rev. Michael Buckley, SJ and with the assistance of Susan Rotondi, provided direction, funding, and technical help in bringing about the program. Sponsorship was also furnished by Dean J. Robert Barth, SJ, Dean Donald White, Rev. Joseph Appleyard, SJ, and Academic Vice-President William Neenan, SJ.

Also at Boston College, the Jesuit Community under the guidance of Rev. Joseph Appleyard, SJ assisted greatly in this endeavor. Mrs. Mary Carey and Mrs. Patricia Dolan of the Fine Arts Department and Honors Program respectively were there to take care of the countless financial and secretarial details that make up a conference and publication. Rev. James Bernauer, SJ, Rev. John Paris, SJ, and Rev. David Hollenbach, SJ and Prof. Rachel Spector, RN, offered their consulting assistance in the early development of the program.

Other departments at Boston College also assisted with the conference and gathering of the collection of essays, most notably Audio Visual, Theology, Media, as well as the O'Neill Library, The Office of Research Administration, the Honors Program, and the Faith, Peace and Justice Program.

Outside of the university, several institutions have been especially helpful, most notably Facing History and Ourselves, the *New England Journal of Medicine,* Legal Sea Foods, the National Center for Jewish Film, the Braun Holocaust Center of the Anti-Defamation League of New York, as well as the Israeli and German Consulates in Boston.

For their willingness to allow reprinting of key articles, I am indebted to the staff at the *New England Journal of Medicine,* the *Hastings Center Report, Dimensions* (especially Carol Perkins and Dr. Dennis Klein), *Health Matrix,* the Oxford University Press, and the Greenwood Press.

Other individuals were most gracious to offer their services such as Dr. Michael Resler (translations), Dr. Susanne Hahn of the German Hygiene Museum in Dresden (photos), Dr. Steven Cohen (chronology and proofreading), Dr. Susan Michalczyk (editorial assistance), Audra Kyrystofolski (bibliography), Prof. Donald Dietrich, Robert Drapeau (proofreading), Walter Krzastek (documents), and the Honors Program World War II seminar participants (exhibit and archival work).

Dr. Michael Grodin, MD, Dr. Robert Berger, MD, Dr. Joseph Alpert, MD, and Dr. Patrick Ross, MD served as medical consultants in the initial and intermediate stages of planning.

For her perseverance and invaluable commitment to the organization of the conference and publication of the proceedings, I am highly indebted to my assistant Gloria Backer. For his assistance with the many details of the project, especially the documentary, I am grateful to Ronald Marsh of the O'Neill Library.

At Sheed & Ward, Andy Apathy and Robert Heyer were sensitive guides in the many phases of publication. I am indebted to them for their professional assistance.

Finally, the value and burden of this publication rests on the shoulders of the authors of this collection of essays. These nationally and internationally respected experts have helped bring together stimulating material that will provoke us to think further about the integral connection of medicine and ethics. The format of their original presentation or publication has been repected in accordance with their wishes as well as their publishers. For their commitment to this project and to this relationship, I am most grateful.

John J. Michalczyk
Boston College

Preface

A half century has passed since the ashes of Auschwitz have cooled, the tribunals of Nuremberg have emptied, and the fragmented lives of survivors have been pieced together. Memory, however, keeps these moments of the Holocaust alive in our collective consciousness. Historical documents gathered in the wake of World War II, and those recently discovered at the Cold War's demise, assist us in reconstructing this period, a scar on humanity's soul. Oral testimony from the survivors who did not share the same tragic fate as the Six Million brings this history to a personal level and dramatically challenges the revisionist view that it never happened.

In the meantime, the daily news accounts of racial violence, national reports on hate crimes, and international government policies of war based on race and religion, reiterate the fact that the painful horrors of the past have come back to haunt us. The rise of the Extreme Right in America and Germany points out that anti-semitic and anti-foreign attitudes of the past have not been diminished by the tragedy of the gas chambers. At the outset of the Cold War, human experimentation in nuclear study resumed, perhaps not with the vigor and ruthlessness of Josef Mengele's experiments on twin subjects, but with an attitude that informed consent in life-threatening experiments was either a luxury or insignificant. In the former Yugoslavia, religion and politics bitterly divide the country, as "ethnic cleansing" recalls governmental procedures in Nazi Germany from the Nuremberg Laws to *Krystallnacht* and ending in the Final Solution.

Throughout the history of the western world the doctors and, by extension, the other members of the medical profession, were considered healers. The Hippocratic Oath became not only a symbolic but a real credo of the physician. In Germany's Third Reich (1933-1945), there was a crucial hiatus during which the medical profession no longer focused on the health of the individual, but on that of the State. Closely aligned with the Nazi Party, physicians and nurses aided and abetted the murder of millions of innocent people in the attempt to create a "clean" and "healthy" Germany. Ironically, theirs was a sincere but highly unethical belief in Germany as a "biocracy" that cried out for healing. By their orders, based on racial policies, Jews, homosexuals, Gypsies, Jehovah's Witnesses, and the mentally and physically handicapped, were sacrificed to create this "brave new world." These medical professionals only "did their job."

To respond to the need to confront these issues, the Jesuit Institute of Boston College sponsored a conference on "Medicine, Ethics, and the Third Reich: Historical and Contemporary Issues" on Oct. 28-29, 1993. From the papers presented by participating national and international scholars of various disciplines, and other authors, emerged the following proceedings. This publication, designed for ethicists, historians, Holocaust specialists, and medical professionals, as well as the general public, will raise our moral consciousness about provocative concerns in today's society.

The essays in this collection will not so much suggest the feasibility of History's repeating itself, as much as it will serve as a precaution that we understand the past in order to make more enlightened ethical decisions in the future. As will the subsequent documentary film made from conference interviews and materials, these papers touch upon human experimentation, euthanasia, forced sterilization, genetic engineering, and racial theory.

It is hoped that these proceedings will assist, in some small way, in the moral development of our society. If they can help us internalize what Prof. Jay Katz urges us to recall from *Genesis*—Cain's haunting rhetorical question, "Am I my brother's keeper?"—then they will have justified their existence.

John J. Michalczyk
Boston College

Medicine, Ethics
and the
Third Reich

Forty years ago, in his classic writing on the Holocaust, Leo Alexander, MD, a Boston psychiatrist who served on the staff of the Office of the Chief Counsel for War Crimes in Nuremberg, observed:

Whatever proportions these (German war) crimes finally assumed, it became evident to all who investigated them that they had started from small beginnings. The beginnings at first were merely a subtle shift in emphasis in the basic attitude of the physicians. *It started with the acceptance of the attitude, basic in the euthanasia movement, that there is such a thing as a life not worthy to be lived.* This attitude in its early stages concerned itself merely with the severely and chronically sick. Gradually the sphere of those to be included in this category was enlarged to encompass the socially unproductive, the ideologically unwanted, the racially unwanted and finally all non-Germans. *But, it is important to realize that the infinitely small wedged in lever from which this entire trend of mind received its impetus was the attitude toward the nonrehabilitable sick.*

—*Euthanasia: An Historical Overview*
Courtesy of Dr. Joseph Stanton, MD

I.

Laying the Groundwork

The Relevance of the Holocaust to Bioethics Today

Arthur Caplan

One of the most common arguments invoked in bioethics today is what might be termed the "Nazi analogy." This is a shorthand phrase that I will use to designate references made to the Holocaust, the conduct of Nazis or, to experiments, public health measures or euthanasia programs carried out by German doctors and scientists before and during World War Two. These references are made by those who believe that these events have a moral equivalent or parallel in contemporary conduct or policy.

The Nazi analogy is quite powerful. It is arguably the most serious charge that can be made in bioethics. Yet, there seems to have been little discussion or comment in contemporary bioethics about the appropriateness of invoking this most powerful of claims. And that is unfortunate, given the frequency with which the analogy appears in current discussions and debates.

For many years I have written a weekly syndicated newspaper column about ethical issues in medicine and science. It is not uncommon when somebody is mad about something I wrote for them to start a critical letter off by saying, "Don't you know what the Nazis did?" Or, if they are especially infuriated by some argument or claim I have made, they may say "you *are* a Nazi."

This sort of glib invocation of the Nazi analogy is not limited to those moved to write letters to columnists. It is not all that rare at an academic conference to hear a speaker invoke the Holocaust or mention the conduct of the Nazis in debates about euthanasia, gene therapy, abortion or the use of fetal tissue for transplant research. The Nazi analogy may be less common in academic writings than in letters to the editor, but if it is, it is not by a big margin.

Two or three years ago, Peter Singer, a philosopher from Monash University in Australia, went to Germany, having been invited there to give some talks at various universities. He was to speak, among other things, about his views concerning the termination of treatment for newborn babies in intensive-care settings. Singer has written many articles and books in support of the view that some newborns ought be allowed to die without any effort being made to treat their ailments or dysfunctions.

Singer is rather well known for his controversial views about the non-treatment of severely and hopelessly ill newborns. However, on this visit some people felt Singer should not be allowed to express his views. Demonstrators, including some with disabilities, came to his lectures to protest and shout him down. They argued vociferously that he should not be allowed to speak because he was echoing arguments that had been made by the Nazis. Many accused Singer of being a Nazi. Others complained to those who came to the lectures that Singer's views were similar to those held by the persons responsible for the Holocaust.

Singer found these attacks personally devastating. Here he was, a Jew, who had come to Germany to talk about his views concerning the use of contemporary medical technology in the care of newborns, being picketed and attacked as a Nazi. Of course, it may be true that someone who is a Jew espouses Nazi-like views. But, Singer felt the Nazi analogy was completely inappropriate as a response to his views. Was he right? Were those who disagreed with his views too quick or glib in invoking the Nazi analogy?

In 1993, the University of Minnesota's Center for Biomedical Ethics sponsored a conference that looked at the termination of treatment issues a number of families had faced in recent years. Among those who spoke were family members who had been involved in many of the most widely known cases such as Busalacchi, Quinlan, Delio, Wanglie and Brophy. Attempts were made to disrupt the conference by protesters who opposed euthanasia, and these protesters made many references to the Nazi analogy in their oral comments and the literature they distributed.

Joe Cruzan, the father of Nancy Cruzan, who had her food and water disconnected after a long court fight that went all the way up to the United States Supreme Court, was one of the speakers. His daughter had died just after Christmas in 1991. Joe Cruzan said that one thing he remembered with great anger about this experience was going to the hospital to say good-bye to Nancy, or Nan as he called her, and being yelled at by demonstrators who had encamped on the hospital grounds. They called him, Nancy's mother and her sister, Nazis. As Joe Cruzan reminded the conference audience even as protesters distributed literature invoking the Nazi analogy in the lobby of the conference hotel, the "Nazi analogy" has force, real bite, and can hurt.

The Nazi analogy is not confined to the street or picket signs. There are many references in print in books and learned journals. Let me offer by way of summary, paraphrases of common examples of the ways in which the Nazi analogy shows up in contemporary writings in law, religion, philosophy, medicine, and public policy. Typical of such invocations are "abortion is America's Holocaust," "Dr. Kevorkian will lead us, if unchecked, down the path to Dachau and Auschwitz," "The Germans started with the retarded and then moved to the senile and then . . ." with the inference left open about what the non-treatment or withdrawal of treatment from babies born with anencephaly means, and genetic engineering is a form of Nazi eugenics (Caplan, 1992).

Such analogies or arguments are global invocations of the Nazi analogy. They use the events of the Holocaust in a general, almost generic way. The idea behind this version of the analogy seems to be that the general history of that era has some vital lessons to teach about what is going on today.

But, the analogy can take more precise forms. For instance, germline genetic engineering, it is argued, is immoral because of its relationship to and precedent in the application of race hygiene in the Nazi regime to marriage laws. Or, as happened frequently during the debate in the late nineteen eighties and early nineteen nineties over the use of fetal tissue from elective abortions for transplant research, analogies were drawn between this research and the use of data from Nazi medical experiments in concentration camps. That specific analogy appears, for example, in the minority report of a special committee convened by the then Assistant Secretary of Health and Human Services, James Mason, to examine the issue. The advisory committee voted not to ban the Federal funding of such research or prohibit it, but the Bush Administration for many years maintained a ban partly on the basis of this sort of moral objection (Vawter and Caplan, 1992).

Another example of what might be called the specific or focused use of the Nazi analogy arose with reference to the case of Baby K. Baby K is a child, now more than a year old, who is in an intensive-care unit in a hospital in Virginia. The child was born with most of its brain missing and will not ever think or be conscious. The child's mother insisted that all efforts to keep the baby alive be undertaken. The hospital went to Federal court to obtain permission to stop life-sustaining care. Some critics of that action argued that stopping care would be morally akin to the secret euthanasia program undertaken at Hitler's orders in 1939 to eliminate children with disabilities. This precise opinion was put forward, for instance, in an opinion piece in *USA Today*, which argued that to allow Baby K to die despite the mother's wishes, would be doing precisely what had happened in the T4 euthanasia program in Germany.

Yet another focused invocation of the Nazi analogy is that experimentation on animals will someday be seen as akin to the experimentation done on concentration camp inmates. This analogy is fairly common in much of the animal rights literature.

When I spoke at Brandeis University in 1993, one person from the audience asked why blacks often do not see that the Tuskegee experiment is just like what happened to us, meaning "the Jews," in the concentration camps. Some people came up to me after my remarks and complained that they felt that some of the African-American panelists were being too adamant in their claims about the uniqueness of the Tuskegee experiment. The position of those making these points was that the Nazi analogy works. Blacks and Jews have something in common. They both suffered abuses in the name of science or at the hands of scientists. Why see differences, when in fact there is something exactly similar between what took place in the experiments done in the concentration camps and the Tuskegee study?

This is only a small sample of the uses of the Nazi analogy in bioethical debate. But they will suffice to show that the analogy comes in two forms—global and specific. And these examples will suffice to show that the Nazi analogy is one of the most powerful arguments mounted in bioethical discourse.

If you can persuasively invoke the Nazi analogy, it is taken for granted that you will win the moral argument. If you can make this charge stick, it has sufficient moral force to show that your opponent's position is simply not credible.

Arguments by analogy of this power deserve more comment than those in bioethics have given to them, for the Nazi analogy is not used with anything like the care and precision that it certainly deserves. Sadly, the requisite care is not much in evidence in the picketing about euthanasia and the withdrawal of medical treatment, in the letter to the editor about abortion, and in the rhetorical flourish about genetic engineering, in the comments of the pundit or TV talk show host who heats up the rhetoric by drawing facile analogies between the Holocaust and revelations about radiation experiments with retarded children in the United States in the 1950s, or in the scholarly literature which draws parallels between the use of fetal tissue in research and the use of data from hypothermia experiments at Dachau.

Part of the reason for the widespread appropriation of the Holocaust through the indiscriminate invocation of the Nazi analogy is the relative silence, until recently, in the field of bioethics about the Holocaust and the role played in it by Nazi medicine and biomedical science (Annas and Grodin, 1992; Caplan, 1992). It is only in the past few years that analyses have started to appear of the ethical issues raised by the brutal experiments in the camps and the creation of a genetically grounded euthanasia program. It is only within the past ten years that scholars such as Benno Müller-Hill, Robert Proctor, Michael Kater, Bill Seidelman and others have begun to do the historical work necessary to help us understand the role scientists, public health officials, nurses and physicians played in the Holocaust. Even with the emergence of this recent scholarship, the amount of attention paid to the questions of what did Nazi doctors do, what were the ethical rationales for concentration camp experiments, and what were the reasons and justifications that people gave for their conduct, is all still relatively unexamined terrain.

The scholarly examination of the Nazi analogy stands as equally unexamined intellectual terrain. There are very few articles on the subject in the literature of bioethics (Caplan, 1992).

Why is that so? Part of the reason is perhaps fear about the risks of discussing Nazi ethics. There is always a danger that in speaking of the ethical rationale used by the Nazis for their conduct and policies that the mere discussion of their views might confer moral legitimacy upon them.

There is also an aversion to taking a long hard look at what health professionals and scientists did during the years before and throughout the Holocaust. Medicine and science played such a prominent role in the Holocaust that it is hard for those who admire medicine and science to accept. We know that in the decades since the Second World War there have been many instances of large scale mass murder. Many of these more recent Holocausts have their roots in racism. But in Germany what took place not only had its roots in racism but in a racism that found boisterous support from mainstream biomedicine. And the consequences of that racism were implemented using scientific and engineering technology administered by doctors and healers. Whether it was building a gas chamber, running a transportation network, or selecting who would die based upon a psychological, physical, or anthropological examination, science permeates the Holocaust. And for those who see medicine and science as bound by a higher moral code, that is a very difficult fact to accept.

Still another reason to steer clear of an analysis of the Nazi analogy is uncertainty about how to respond to it. For many years when I heard the analogy made I didn't know what to say because I wasn't sure whether it was valid or not. If someone said that allowing the withdrawal of food, antibiotics or dialysis from a permanently comatose person is the first step on the road to what took place in Nazi Germany, I am not sure I could respond, because I didn't know if the analogy was right or wrong. I think that's still true for many in the bioethics field. Part of the reason for silence is that people don't know enough about history to know how to evaluate the analogy.

In one sense, all analogies are suspect, because they involve comparisons between events that are unique. Many survivors and students of the Holocaust maintain that the Holocaust is unique, and that the sufferings and experiences cannot even be described. Silence is the only possible response to events horrid beyond description.

Of course, even if one grants the uniqueness of the Holocaust, even the impossibility of accurately describing it, that does not place it beyond analogy. The magnitude of the horror of what took place may be beyond literary, cinematic or artistic depiction. It might only mean that great care and caution have to be used in making analogies. If the Holocaust is truly beyond adequate description, then what I have termed global or sweeping analogies may be by definition invalid. Those who invoke the Nazi analogy in a broad or general fashion are pressing the limits of valid analogy simply because the broader the scope of their reference, the harder it becomes to understand exactly what they think the Holocaust was, and thus why it is of moral relevance to a current issue.

If, however, the analogy is made in a more specific way, to a specific set of events such as the hypothermia experiments or to the T4 euthanasia program for demented elderly persons, then analogy might be possible and plausible. If so, what sorts of standards should be brought to bear in order to analyze these limited, more focused claims?

To answer this we need to know how people make analogies in other areas. By understanding what constitutes a valid analogy in other domains of life it may be possible to learn what ought to be expected to prove or justify the invocation of the Nazi analogy in bioethics.

Much has been written on the uses of metaphor, simile and analogy in literature. But analogy, metaphor and simile are not the same in poetry, drama, or theater, as in ethics. I think comparisons or analogies in the arts are meant to provoke, sometimes to puzzle. In other words, the arts use analogies to try and get people to recognize and think about comparisons and similarities that they might not otherwise have noticed.

Analogy does not often play this role in ethics. It is more akin, instead, to analogy as used in science. There comparison is used as an aid to exposition, as a heuristic, as a way to make you think about how to solve a problem in a way that you might not unless you've got an analogy that you can, so to speak, get your mind around. And sometimes analogy is used straight out as a way to explain something. Analogy, as Thomas Kuhn and others have argued, is used in science to ground paradigmatic problems that otherwise might be too abstract or unfamiliar. One place where this form of analogy abounds is in organismic biology.

Those who pursue the study of organisms in nature quickly learn of the importance of classification. In order to come up with generalizations or explanations for the natural world, scientists need to order their findings into categories so that others know to what they are referring. However, there is much dispute in biology about how best to classify animals and plants.

It is a commonly understood fact that many creatures have wings. Bats, birds, and flies all do. Even though each creature's musculature and bone structure may differ, scientists say they all possess wings because the things hanging off their bodies all let the creature fly through the air.

Now consider the hoof of a horse and of a zebra. They both, to remind those of you who have not looked at a zebra hoof lately, have sort of nails at the end, similar to our fingernails. They have one big toe, the other toes being pulled back into the leg, and they clearly have this hard substance on the ends of their toes to provide traction and a buffer. The hoof of the zebra is a lot like the hoof of a horse. They are pretty similar. The wings of a fly, a bat and a bird are also similar, because they all allow flight.

But biologists know that similarity in appearance is not always the result of common causes. Some traits or behaviors are similar because they perform the same function, and thus have similar properties. The fly wing, the bat wing, and the bird wing have some resemblance, not because of anything internal to the hereditary make-up of these animals, but because they all have to get through the air. Only certain shapes, as aeronautical engineers know, will get objects up into and through the air. In fact, some of the same physical requirements are present to move through water and other fluids, which is why a fish fin, a whale fin and a submarine fin are analogous to each other as well as to the wings of bats and birds. Biologists know that bird, fly and bat wings are analogous; there are real similarities between them. But the reason for their similarity is the demands made by the environment.

That is not true about the hoofs on the zebra's foot and on the horse. They are analogous but not because of external environmental pressures but because these animals are close biological relatives. Biologists call similarities due to common genetic ancestry homologies. Zebras and horses look like one another, just as do dogs and wolves, as a result of their common genetic make-up.

The biological understanding of similarity reveals something of importance about the Nazi analogy. When biologists make comparisons, they must first try to identify what is similar and what is different between organisms. The first step in any comparison is to examine closely the properties and traits to see if they are truly similar. The first task in making a comparison, in invoking an analogy, is to see what real similarities exist as opposed to what just appear on the surface to be similarities, but under closer inspection, are not.

The next step in making a comparison or analogy is to find out what factors are responsible for producing similarity. Some similarities, as my biological examples show, are accidental; they just happen to be that way because of some external force that makes things resemble one another, or they are merely due to chance, as when both I and my dog are covered in mud because we both fell into a marsh. Other similarities are rooted in biology. There is something about the very constitution of the creatures involved that makes them analogous or similar.

In using the Nazi analogy in bioethics, those who do so must identify exactly what it is that is similar. This means that it is most unlikely that any global invocations of the Holocaust will be valid. Then if there is real similarity between events from the past and today there still remains a question—why? Are things similar by chance or because of common causes? If analogies are made without this sort of care, then there is a very real risk of error in confusing what biologists would call homology with analogy, of mixing up traits that are similar but whose similarities are not the result of common or similar causes.

When I was a little boy I used to go up and visit a place called "the Old Man in the Mountain" in New Hampshire. This is a rock formation that looks like a face with a nose. I always wondered how God had made this sculpture. Later I learned that wind did it. Men can sculpt figures like this, too, but even though they are similar it would be a grave error to presume that the Old Man in the Mountain is a sculpture because it resembles statues artists have made.

Many, as I do, watch some of the "informative" shows on TV like Montel Williams, Sally Jesse Raphael or Geraldo Rivera. They often have people on who discuss paintings in the high deserts of Peru that they believe to be landmarks for UFO landing fleets, guidance systems for UFOs. Other people, who tend not to get the same exposure on tabloid TV programs say these are not markings for alien spacecraft but rather are pictures that were drawn by cultures for religious or symbolic reasons.

The "Old Man in the Mountain," the paintings on the high deserts of Peru and the bat, bird and fly wings are all examples where caution is in order if false similarities, analogies and homologies are to be avoided. The same is true of the Nazi analogy.

Certainly, the moral weight of the events of the Holocaust would seem to put an obligation on us to be very careful when invoking these experiences in current moral disputes. Those who invoke the analogy must be prepared to say precisely what properties or events they are talking about that they think are echoed or have parallels in the events of today. Those who invoke the analogy must be prepared to state how what took place in the concentration camp at Dachau, or in the construction of the specimen museum of Bolshevik Kommisar Jews, or in the race mixing laws prohibiting interracial sexual contact enacted during the early years of the Third Reich, is analogous to current events.

Those who are too quick and too facile in invoking the Nazi analogy, who hold up a sign and say, "You are a Nazi" whenever someone holds a view or takes a course of action they believe to be evil, risk both being wrong and demeaning the significance of the Holocaust. It is disrespectful and it cheapens the horror of the Holocaust not to understand that care and caution are obligatory where the invocation of this most powerful of analogies is concerned. Even if one rejects the view that the Holocaust is unique or the magnitude of evil involved so great as to be beyond description, there is a need for common sense and caution to prevail in referring to these events in moral argument. Those who see analogies must be specific about what they believe is similar between now and then. Blanket invocations such as "Abortion is today's Holocaust" or "euthanasia if legalized will lead to Nazi Germany," are to be avoided unless they can truly be supported in the scope of the claim being made. To do otherwise risks making the analogy stand as valid only by taking all of the moral force out of it.

Even if the similarities and the traits that are being compared between then and now are made explicit, more work remains to show the analogy is sound. Is the "Old Man in the Mountain" up there because the wind made him, or is he there because somebody went up and chiseled him out, like at Mount Rushmore? Does the wing of the bat resemble the wing of the bird because they have some genetic similarity, because they are responding to some environmental functional demand, or, is the resemblance just an accident? Things can appear similar because of many different reasons. Showing that the Nazis permitted and encouraged euthanasia or that forced sterilization was practiced on many camp inmates does not in itself show that there is any real or true similarity between these events and euthanasia or sterilization today.

If specificity and detail are crucial to the valid use of the Nazi analogy, then do we know enough to know when the analogy is false? Are there sufficient details available about particular instances of Nazi conduct, so that when an analogy is made it is certain that closer inspection shows the analogy to be valid?

I believe one such topic is the termination of treatment. Cases such as the Nancy Cruzan case, the Karen Ann Quinlan case, or the Paul Brophy case, all involve issues of stopping or foregoing life-saving medical care. Many critics of the actions taken in these and similar cases argue that, to paraphrase, people were starved to death in Nazi Germany, they were not fed, they were killed by the state as unworthy of life, and there was medical involvement in decisions not to give food such as happened to some of those in mental asylums.

It is true that German doctors allowed elderly, demented patients and the mentally ill to die for want of rations. People were in fact denied food when supplies got short. This form of social triage took place in Germany in World War I, as well as in World War II. But, the fact that these events took place, that they involved doctors not feeding those in their care, does not show that it is valid to draw an analogy with the decision of the Cruzan family to take a feeding tube away from their daughter and sister.

The overriding rationale for allowing people to die of starvation in World War II was racism. The decision was not to supply food to those who otherwise could have eaten it. And while doctors went along, they did so at the direction of the Nazi government (Caplan, 1992).

Joe Cruzan did not allow his daughter to starve to death because he thought she was an inferior biological being or a genetic threat to the health of his nation. He never viewed her as a threat to the public health. Nor could Nancy Cruzan have eaten without technological assistance. And the decision to remove her tube was made after much anguish on the part of her family with no influence or coercion by the government.

The similarities between the Cruzan case and Nazi policies of mandatory starvation of the insane or racial groups are either non-existent or nothing more than superficial. The Nazi analogy as cited with respect to the termination of treatment is not only false but, it is offensive simply because it obscures the motives and rationales for what took place in German concentrations camps, nursing homes and mental asylums (Annas and Grodin, 1992).

This is not to say the analogy is always false or invalid. When people warn that if we start to use formulas to determine the fiscal burdensomeness of people or groups on the state as a rationale for rationing health care away from them on the grounds that they see analogies between such arguments and claims in the writings of some proto-Nazis in the 1920s and 1930s, there may be parallels that are real.

However, most who invoke the Nazi analogy fail to do so with even a minimum of precision. The events of the Holocaust deserve to be treated as more than political rhetoric. Talk of "femi-Nazis" or doctors who perform abortions as Nazis, reveals a callous disregard for the millions who died and suffered at the hands of the Nazi regime. To use the Nazi analogy with abandon is to abandon history.

References

Annas, G.J. and M.A. Grodin, eds., *The Nazi Doctors and the Nuremberg Code*. New York: Oxford, 1992.

Caplan, A.L., ed., *When Medicine Went Mad: Bioethics and the Holocaust*. Totowa, NJ: Humana, 1992.

Vawter, D. and A.L. Caplan, "Strange Brew: the ethics and politics of fetal tissue transplant research in the United States," *Journal of Laboratory and Clinical Medicine*, Vol. 120, no.1, (1992): 30-35.

2

Biomedical Ethics
and the Shadow of Nazism

Peter Steinfels

Reasoning and argument often seem less conclusive in determining our ethical positions than certain basic or formative experiences. For individuals these may be professional experiences or family tragedies. For our culture as a whole they are major historical events, and no events loom so large in ethical discussion of biomedical science and technology as the actions of the Third Reich in the Europe of 1933-45. Such discussion, of course, is the very *raison d'être* of the Institute of Society, Ethics and the Life Sciences. And whether the topic be genetic engineering, prolongation of life, *in vitro* fertilization, behavior modification, organ transplantation, euthanasia, abortion, sterilization of the mentally incompetent, human experimentation, negative or positive eugenics, treatment of violent behavior, or societal interest in reproductive patterns, we find that the memory of the Nazi experience is evoked, often in a highly charged manner.

There are other instances of such seminal historical episodes. The Lysenko case pervades the literatures about genetic research. The Manhattan Project looms large in any discussion of technological development and political control. But no other historical experience has the place in our ethical discourse as the Nazi one. It is as though in a relativist and pluralist society this is our single absolute evil. A young Jewish professor of philosophy to whom I mentioned this fact commented bitterly that if there had not been a Hitler, we would have had to invent one. To him the use of the sufferings of Hitler's victims as examples by which to resolve our own moral dilemmas was but a final insult. His words should give us pause.

Still, there is another way of looking at the situation. It is out of our faithfulness to the victims that we keep their fate before us. It is in recognition of our own culture's involvement in this historical nightmare—for various strains of Western culture did to some degree invent Hitler—that we return to these events. Furthermore, these events have indeed been "used"—in the pejorative, manipulative sense of that verb—and that, too,

13

is one of the reasons for paying special heed to the significance of the Nazi experience. The casual, partisan, and polemical references we so frequently encounter are distressing. What moral currency is left us seems to be in the process of being cheapened.

At the same time, the serious literature in this area also returns to this historical moment, or departs from it. I cite two examples: Paul Ramsey's book, *The Patient as Person*, begins with a citation from the Nuremberg documents; Jay Katz says in the introduction to his casebook, *Experimentation with Human Beings*, that his interest in the subject began with his reading about the Nazi medical experimentation in the concentration camps.

It is not unusual to find both sides in current debates over biomedical issues making references to the Third Reich—those favoring and those opposing legal restrictions on abortion, for example. Reference to the Nazi experience is offered in support of scientific and technological innovations and in criticism of them, to characterize the drift of scientific and technological civilization, and to characterize the resistance to that drift. As long as people disagree about serious moral questions, it seems they will diverge in their appeals to this absolute standard. But the frequency and resonance of these allusions or analogies, however ambiguous or perhaps because of this very ambiguity, raises questions about not only the conduct of our discussion in this area, but about ethical discourse in our society generally.

It was with this in mind that the humanities program at the Institute [of Society, Ethics and the Life Sciences] sponsored a meeting on April 8, 1976. Participating along with Institute Fellows and Hastings Center staff were Lucy Dawidowicz, a noted historian of the Holocaust; Telford Taylor, chief counsel for the prosecution at Nuremberg; Milton Himmelfarb of the American Jewish Committee; and Joel Colton, historian of the interwar period and director of the humanities division at the Rockefeller Foundation.

The topic proposed for the discussion was: what is the proper use of the Nazi experience in our thinking about the ethical issues posed by modern medical science and technology? A number of questions were linked with this one: the uses of history in general, the particular place of the Nazi experience might or might not hold for the control of technology and the emergence of both scientific modes of thought. It was the premise of the discussion that obviously we cannot—we must not—forget or neglect this frightening revelation; but it is equally obvious that we must proceed with a certain caution and precision, not trivializing the experience which often seems like the sole common point of reference in our ethical discussion.

What I have referred to as the Nazi experience includes a number of different elements bearing on medicine, science, and technology. First and most strictly, the medical experiments carried out on prisoners of war and those in concentration camps. Second, the euthanasia and sterilization programs which preceded the Final Solution. Third, the Holocaust of European Jewry, which revealed the ultimate nature of the Nazi regime and which was based on a racism propped up by social Darwinism and other gleanings of popular scientism. Fourth, the complicated relationship between Nazi totalitarianism and modern science and technology: without the latter the reach of Hitler's will would certainly have been much shorter; and yet Nazism was in many respects an antimodern and antiscientific ideology. Fifth, the record of nonresistance and often enthusiastic cooperation on the part of the scientific and medical community in Germany. These are all elements to which reference is made on one side or another in current ethical debate. What in fact can we legitimately bring to these current debates from this historical experience? That was the question posed to our conference—and is now posed to our readers.

3

Contested Terrain:
The Nazi Analogy in Bioethics

Nat Hentoff

To say that certain contemporary bioethicists and members of the laity sometimes approach the solving of life-or-death problems as the Nazis did in no way means they are Nazis. It is possible, however, with the very best of intentions, to think and plan in a way that would bring about results that were also the goals of the Nazis—from different motivations.

For instance, beginning in 1933, the Germans began killing "defectives" of various kinds, in part because they were unproductive ("useless eaters") and therefore were costly to the society. The pragmatic, cost-benefit dimension to the murders was illustrated in the widely used high school mathematics text cited by Dr. Leo Alexander. The text, *Mathematics in the Service of National Political Education*, included such problems, Alexander noted, as "how many new housing units could be built and how many marriage-allowance loans could be given to newly wedded couples for the amount of money it cost the state to care for the crippled, the criminal and insane," ("Medical Science Under Dictatorship," *New England Journal of Medicine,* July 14, 1949).

Daniel Callahan readily admits that he wrote *Setting Limits* because of the acute and inexorably increasing problem of medical care costs, particularly with regard to the elderly. He does not advocate euthanasia for people past a certain age; but by having the state—through Medicare—refuse to pay for certain expensive life-extending procedures such as coronary bypass operations once that age has been reached, the result of his design is to shorten lives. For all that he talks about alleviating their pain and suffering and getting the society to provide them with decent home care or nursing home care, he is saying that the lives of the elderly are worth less—in terms of prolonging them—than other lives.

This is a variation, as I see it, of the Nazis' *lebensunwertes Leben*, "life unworthy of life." In this case, life unworthy of being extended, according to cost-benefit analysis, by procedures he believes ought to be more available to others in the society.

16

When Callahan is asked whether there is not a certain injustice in sorting out people by age as to whether they can get certain treatment—not counting the elderly who can afford whatever they want and do not depend on the government to stay alive—he admits there is an unfair economic bias to his plan. But, he adds, the resulting "injustice would not be for a very long time." A very long time by whose measure?

The comment, and cost-benefit designs for dying by others, recall something said by Milton Himmelfarb:

[I]s there not an argument that could be made . . . about a general coarsening of regard for life? There exists . . . a certain kind of accountant's mentality or an engineer's mentality in dealing with the questions of life. . . . While it has nothing to do necessarily with the specifics of Nazism, yet the Nazis too did not have the bias of awe toward life and dealt with life (certain kinds of life at any rate) as if they were dealing with mere things ("Biomedical Ethics and the Shadow of Nazism," *Hastings Center Report*, August 1976, Special Supplement).

In the Spring 1988 *Concern for Dying* newsletter, Dr. Ronald Cranford (Neurology Department, Hennepin County Medical Center, Minneapolis) is quoted as proposing that in the future, some instances of artificially shortening life—a most gentle euphemism—be exempted from charges of homicide. If someone, he adds, were in an irreversible persistent vegetative state, there is no "personhood." Without personhood, there could be no act of murder.

Aside from whether physicians are invariably correct in their diagnoses of "irreversibility," Cranford has gotten to the basic question in the similarities, if any, between some current physicians and ethicists and the Nazi doctors. Rosemary Anton puts it quite clearly in the March 18, 1988 *National Catholic Reporter:*

Fundamental to most bioethical problems are the questions: What does it mean to be a human being? Whom shall we admit into human society on an equal basis with ourselves, protected by the same rights, entitled to the same opportunities?

And who shall decide these irreversible matters? Will the decisions be subject to independent due process procedure?

Should someone in a persistent vegetative state be killed because a "person" is no longer there? The Nazis had no compunction about that solution. In this country, more and more bioethicists, and an increasing number of state courts, agree that it is permissible to end the feeding and hydration of permanently unconscious people. Is that not murder? Or is it okay because "personhood" has presumably disappeared?

The Hastings Center's 1987 *Guidelines on the Termination of Life-Sustaining Treatment and the Care of the Dying* say that in certain circumstances, nutrition and hydration can be "discontinued." (An accountant's or an engineer's way of saying "cut off" or "denied.")

German physicians who went along because of their peers—rather than out of intoxicating ideology—found that they were soon on the very definition of a slippery slope. And in dissenting from the food-and-water section and other parts of the Hastings' *Guidelines*, Leslie Steven Rothenberg warned of other slopes, American slopes:

> I fear these *Guidelines*, if widely endorsed, may be used to give a moral "imprimatur" to undertreating or failing to treat persons with disabilities, unconscious persons for whom accurate prognoses are not yet obtainable, elderly patients with severe dementia, and others whose treatment is not believed (to use the language [of another part of the report]) "costworthy."

No Nazis participated in that Hastings project, but the majority, overwhelmingly, decided that patients with certain conditions no longer had lives worth living and for their benefit—as well as that of our caring society—should leave us. If the Hastings *Guidelines* had been available at the time and I had been a defense attorney for the Nazi doctors at Nuremberg, I would have welcomed them.

With what has become nearly a rush to endorse the removal of nutrition and hydration for certain patients, the opposition of organizations of the handicapped—the Association for Retarded Citizens, the Association for Persons with Severe Handicaps, and the United Handicapped Federation—has been largely ignored.

What could they possibly fear anyway? The compassionate elimination of the handicapped for the good of the rest of society can't happen here.

4

The Healing-Killing Paradox

Peter J. Haas

How is it that the doctors, lawyers, and university professors, who formed the intellectual elite of Nazi Germany, came to participate in the destruction of European Jewry without remorse? The question is especially puzzling when it is directed to the medical profession, sworn as it was to the preservation of life.

Even if it were possible to comprehend how Nazi troops, trained for brutality, could carry out their crimes, it is startling to learn about the doctors' atrocities. In full control of their own laboratories and offices, they were not prey to anyone's hateful marching orders. It is these people, the cream of German society, who challenge us with crucial moral questions: What allowed these people to have been drawn into mass murder? How could they have enlisted their professional training to serve the Nazi state?

We instinctively expect more humanity from the medical profession. But the fact of the matter is that medical professionals in Nazi Germany acted no differently than other professionals. As a group, they acted no better or worse than lawyers, theologians, or teachers. There were those who fled and those who stayed and spoke out; there were those who took full advantage of the situation to further their careers.

To understand the "Nazification" of the medical profession, it is important to recall the incredible speed with which Hitler established an absolute dictatorship. According to Robert N. Proctor in his recent book, *Racial Hygiene,* over 10,000 physicians were forced from their jobs between 1933 and 1938. This number includes Jewish physicians plus those non-Jews who protested, resisted, or were thought too unsympathetic to Nazi policy.

However, not all medical professionals were frightened into accepting Nazism. Many exploited the Nazi state for their own purposes. A few, like Josef Mengele, made careers out of promoting the Nazi cause, rising in rank and stature. Many others used the euthanasia centers and the concentration camps as laboratories at the expense of Hitler's racial victims.

That physicians as a whole could coexist with Nazism is clear from Proctor's study of medical journals in Germany before, during, and after the Third Reich. Of the 200 journals and other publications examined, the overwhelming majority of those established before the Nazi era continued to publish throughout and beyond the Nazi period. Excluding Jewish publishers and presses, the advent of the Nazis seems to have caused little disruption in the professional lives of German physicians. In fact, some of these journals and periodicals eventually went on to publish data based on research done on concentration camp inmates. It was as if this was a perfectly normal and acceptable thing to do. As with most of the rest of the society, the medical profession in the aggregate absorbed the policies of the new Nazi regime with remarkably little resistance or disruption.

Many physicians, if not fully convinced of the scientific necessity of Nazi policies, accepted Nazi ideology nonetheless. This ideology claimed that Germans (or rather "Aryans") were engaged in a racial war against an enemy race. Their elimination was rationalized in the name of achieving a higher good.

Mere acceptance, or even toleration, of this ideology does not explain, however, the enthusiasm with which some doctors embraced the new regime and its ideology. To understand this, we have to look more closely at the nature of Nazi ideology, and especially at the component that would most likely attract medical scientists: the racial worldview.

Race was a major preoccupation of social, political, and scientific thinkers in Europe in the 19th century. One reason for this was their exposure to African and Asian "colonials" as well as to rising ethnic tensions in Europe. Europeans became convinced that people naturally broke down into a variety of races. These racial distinctions were regarded as vitally important. They believed each racial pool endowed its individual members with the capacity for constructing and sustaining a certain level of civilization. This had the useful consequence of explaining to "superior" Europeans why they had a natural right and obligation to rule over less-developed societies.

As a new science, racial theory sought to detect the innate characteristics of a group in every aspect of its communal life: language, art, literature, laws, religion, and so on. This led to an explosion of academic research in the West on the comparative standing of various groups. It was also understood that these characteristics only applied to the group as an aggregate. That is, even a primitive group could produce individuals of exceptional talent and intelligence.

Racial thinking promoted the idea that a group's characteristics could be genetically transmitted. If people from different races or nations interbred, the offspring would carry elements of both races. He or she, on average, would have greater potential than the "inferior" parent, but less than the "superior" one. In other words, national abilities would be "watered down" through interracial breeding.

Races, it was further believed, did not simply exist side by side, but were in fact engaged in a primal struggle for the control of scarce resources. Just as there was a "Darwinian" struggle in nature, in which only the fittest would survive, so was there a struggle for dominance among the human races of the world. For those who saw race in these terms (and in fairness to Darwin, this is not what he himself intended) the question of racial identity and racial relationships became a deadly serious game. Race and race relations for these people not only explained the past, but also accounted for the present and provided a blueprint for the future.

All of these speculations would become of interest to the medical profession—the health or weaknesses of a people, the question of genetic transmission, and the ability to prescribe a cure. The Nazis, by promoting research in their areas, were naturally alluring to practicing physicians.

Behind ascendant racial theory stood the most beguiling image of all. The Nazi theoreticians and policy-makers envisioned a beautiful world, one inhabited by healthy men and women free to carry civilization to new heights. What physician would not want a part in making a utopian world in which disease was controlled, poverty and oppression vanquished, and genetic flaws a thing of the past? In this grand endeavor, the medical profession would have a central role to play.

The acceptance of this vision did not automatically commit a doctor to support Auschwitz. As was true in so many other areas of the Nazi universe, matters began on a limited scale and, when protest failed to materialize, grew to gargantuan proportions. This is no less true of Nazi complicity.

The earliest level of medical cooperation with Nazi policy was in the field of euthanasia. Here is an area in which, at least on occasion, a moral argument supported ending a human life. Protest did eventually cause the Nazis to halt the euthanasia operation, or at least to send it underground. But by that time, the first compromise of the medical community had been made.

The campaign developed slowly at first, directed against infants born with severe mental or physical retardation. Hitler, himself, seems to have had a special interest in killing the handicapped. In fact, such programs were run out of an office established in the chancellery. Once this initiative had been taken, it was but a short step to talk about murdering the severely handicapped or terminally ill adults. As early as 1936, German medical journals were already discussing how best to manage wards of terminally ill patients slated for euthanasia. Within three years—by late 1939—the program acquired an intricate apparatus which was administered by medical professionals. Some 70,000 Germans were gassed under the auspices of this program before 1942, when the Wannsee Conference established the "Final Solution."

Once these initial steps had been taken, the rest of the journey toward Auschwitz was much easier. The Nazi conquest of foreign territories, with their "racially inferior" populations, expanded the practices of medical murder. When the ghettos became an unbearable drain on the army and the government, full of people who were deemed genetically inferior and dangerous, the Nazis "improved" on the euthanasia program. Using Zyklon "B" gas, they established more efficient, more insidious killing centers—the death camps.

To this point, German doctors seem to have acted largely as advisers. Somewhere along this line of development, however, they began to take on the role of active participants. This can be seen especially in the development and management of experiments in which camp inmates were used as "guinea pigs." Responding to Germany's growing military desperation, and seeing that camp inmates were targeted for death anyway, doctors devised experiments for what they believed was the ultimate good. These experiments included cold-water tests, in which inmates were immersed in icy water, in order to learn how to revive German pilots who were shot down over the ocean and retrieved.

By the end of the war, physicians were involved in hideous research projects. Concentration camp inmates at Auschwitz and elsewhere had simply become specimens of living tissue at the disposal of medical researchers. While it is true that the most vicious experiments on living human subjects were conducted at the camps, basic racial and hygienic research went on all over Nazi Germany, in 30 to 40 research centers in every major city. By 1944, medical professionals had become full accomplices.

The preliminary and sketchy information presented here gives us precious few answers and raises a number of important questions.

One question is why doctors were so easily (even willingly) co-opted. One possible answer suggests the moral myopia of medical training: Medical education in Germany prepared them only as technicians. Encountering a "Jewish problem," they were prepared to treat Jews only as a problem that needed to be solved. The blame, in this view, falls ultimately on the educational system that preceded the Nazis.

What we in fact find, however, is the fact that people, trained in the humanities and the liberal arts, conducted themselves in the same way. University professors, artists, theologians, people in all walks of life, fell in line in service to the Nazi ideology. The fault lies not with their education, but with something larger, perhaps the racial ethos of the time, or with something smaller, the individual who chose to conspire in the machinery of destruction.

We retain a certain trust in our institutions, particularly those that stand at the forefront of our value system: religion, law, medicine, and education. Can they resist another Holocaust from occurring? The experience of the medical profession in Nazi Germany offers an unsettling prospect.

II.

From Racial Hygiene Theories to Euthanasia and Sterilization

5

Human Genetics in Nazi Germany

Benno Müller-Hill

Human genetics is a peculiar field. When Mendel's work was rediscovered in 1900, it was immediately clear to many observers that the heredity of humans would be dictated by similar laws as Mendel had described for peas. It took just nineteen years until the first textbook of *Drosophila* genetics appeared.[1] With *Drosophila* extensive experimentation was possible. This work led to the construction of detailed genetic maps of three of the four chromosomes of *Drosophila*. A German animal geneticist, Hans Nachtsheim, translated Morgan's book into German in 1921.[2]

The same year, the first textbook of human genetics appeared in Germany.[3] The Baur-Fischer-Lenz, as it was called after its authors, was an excellent textbook. Hermann J. Muller who reviewed the English translation of the third edition in 1933 called it "the best work on human heredity" and Erwin Baur "the leading geneticist of Europe."[4] The Baur-Fischer-Lenz consisted of four sections. The first section written by Baur was a general introduction into genetics. The second section was written by Eugen Fischer. It was controversial. It dealt with races and genetic racial differences. The rest of the book was written by Fritz Lenz. It dealt with what is now the central aspect of human genetics, that is human genetic diseases. The description of the inheritance of physical diseases was straight forward. The section on the inheritance of psychic ailments such as low intelligence and psychiatric diseases such as schizophrenia was less well grounded. The last and most problematic part was on eugenics, or on race hygiene, as this subject was often called in Germany. Here

---

1. Morgan, T.H.: The Physical Basis of Heredity, Philadelphia and London, 1919.
2. Morgan, T.H.: Die stöffliche Grundlage der Vererbung. Translated into German by H. Nachtsheim. Verlag von Gebrüder Bornträger, Berlin, 1921.
3. Baur, E., Fischer, E. and Lenz, F.: Grundriss der menschlichen Erblichkeitslehre und Rassenhygiene. J.F. Lehmanns Verlag, München, 1.ed. 1921, 2.ed 1923, 3ed. 1927, 4.ed. 1936.
4. Muller, H.J.: Human Heredity; Birth Control Review *17*, 19-21, 1933. Reprinted in: H.J. Muller: Studies in Genetics. The Selected Papers of H.J. Muller. Indiana University Press, Bloomington, Ind., 541-545, 1962.

Lenz tried to describe the social and political consequences of human genetics and proposed political action based on the knowledge of human genetics and on a particular value system.

We have to recall that human genetics differs from animal or plant genetics in that breeding experiments cannot be done. The human geneticist observes the phenotypes in families and comes to his conclusions according to this pedigree analysis. I also have to recall that the nature of the genetic material was unknown until it was unravelled first in bacteria by Avery in 1944.[5] It took thirty more years until DNA could be sequenced, synthesised and manipulated at will. Thus, human genetics was, until about 1980, predominantly a field for experts in human phenotypes. Medical doctors, trained in internal medicine, dealt with physical, psychiatrists or psychologists with mental ailments. Thus, in order to become a human geneticist, one first had to become a doctor in internal medicine or psychiatry.

One branch of human genetics which these days is (yet) of little importance was a prominent part of the Baur-Fischer-Lenz. That is the branch which deals with genetic differences between races or ethnic groups. The human geneticists who dealt with such problems were anthropologists or ethnologists by training. In general, they had a medical training too. Eugen Fischer who dealt with this topic in the Baur-Fischer-Lenz was an anatomist who was interested in anthropology and race. He had published his *magnum opus* in 1913,[6] a book in which he summarised his analysis of the descendants of white males and black women in one of the German African colonies, now Namibia.

Right from the beginning, the interest of the German human geneticists was not concentrated on single persons or patients. Their interest was centered on the entire population. The German geneticists asked the question how large was the section of the German population that carried deleterious mutations? Or to word it differently, how large was the group that carried "inferior" genotypes in regard to physical diseases, intelligence or psychiatric diseases?

In countries where a large percentage of the citizens belonged to different races like the US or which housed different races in their colonies like Great Britain or pre-WWI Germany, the following question was raised: Were the sometimes substantial differences in culture between the various races due to differences in genotype? A leftwing, communist geneticist like Hermann Muller proposed that this question could only be answered when equal opportunities were available to everybody as they

5. Avery, O.T., MacLeod, C.M. and McCarthy, M.: Studies on the Chemical Nature of the Substance Inducing Transformation of Pneumococcus Types. J.Exp.Med. *79*, 137-158, 1944.

6. Fischer, E.: Die Rehobother Bastards und das Bastardisierungsproblem beim Menschen. Verlag von Gustav Fischer, Jena, 1913.

would be presumably in due time in the Soviet Union. But the majority of geneticists thought that the question could be answered right then: They simply assumed there were major genetic, and racial differences which determined cultural and intellectual differences. It was the habit at that time to put values on presumed intellectual genetic differences. The German psychiatrists routinely called schizophrenics "inferior." The anthropologists called the African Blacks similarly "inferior." These value statements were the basis for the rise of science-based racism, in Europe and the U.S.

The rise of Science and the decline of Christian religion had already led in the nineteenth century to a new type of antisemitism. Until then antisemitism was linked to Christian religious creed, *i.e.* the Jews were seen as the unrepentant descendents of those who had murdered Jesus Christ. Conversion to Christian creed and expropriation were then considered sufficient to accept Jews in the Christian society. This happened only rarely. But around 1800 many Jews began to leave their religion and converted seriously or *pro forma* to Christianity. At that time Christianity itself was no longer as accepted as before. Thus, a new type of antisemitism was rising. The new antisemites claimed that it was race and not religion which was important. For the new antisemites the change of religion was irrelevant since race could not be changed. These thoughts got fresh ammunition when genetics began in 1900. For the new antisemites it was then easy to say that Jews and their way of thinking were defined by genes and not by belief. I should add that then, as today, there is no evidence whatever for such statements.

Their statements on race connected the German human geneticists with the Nazis. Hitler discovered this link between antisemitism, general racism and science in 1924 when he served his one-year jail sentence for the failed *Putsch* in 1923. The publisher of the Baur-Fischer-Lenz, Julius Lehmann, an early and ardent supporter of Hitler, sent him a copy of the second edition of the textbook while in jail. Lenz later reviewed *Mein Kampf* and claimed that Hitler had incorporated parts of the textbook in his book.[7] This was the official statement of mutual interest and the beginning of cooperation between the German human geneticists and the Nazis. The Nazis were the only party that was seriously interested in eugenic measures. I should add here that most German human geneticists called eugenics "race hygiene." This alluded to the fact that most of them were more or less racists and antisemites.

The German human geneticists wanted eugenic measures. They were worried by population studies which indicated that the genetically "inferior" bred faster than the genetically "superior." To avert cultural disaster,

---

7. Lenz, F.: Die Stellung des Nationalsozialismus zur Rassenhygiene. Archiv für Rassen- und Gesellschaftsbiologie *25*, 300-308, 1931.

they wanted to stop the breeding of the "inferior." The only efficient possibility they saw was involuntary sterilisation. But no party of the Weimar Republic with exception of the Nazis was willing to pass such a law. Some other parties were indeed considering in 1932 to pass a law which allowed sterilisation but only with informed consent.

The Nazis saw the race concept and expropriation of the Jews as their central political aim. They knew that antisemitism was not so much the product of scientific reasoning but an irrational gut feeling. But they were eager to get scientific support of the scientific race specialists. And these were the human geneticists. And so an alliance grew between the Nazis and the German human geneticists which was kept intact until the last days of the war. The human geneticists profited: they got the law they wanted, allowing them to sterilise the feeble-minded, the schizophrenics, the manic depressives, the genetically deaf or blind, the carriers of Huntington's chorea, the epileptics and the chronic alcoholics.[8] This law led to the sterilisation of about 350,000 to 400,000 persons from 1934 to 1939.[9]

On the other hand, the German human geneticists applauded and confirmed the anti-Jewish measures as measures which were necessary for efficient race hygiene. It was an accident, but a highly symbolic accident, that the rector of Berlin University who followed the orders to fire his Jewish colleagues in 1933 and 1934 was Eugen Fischer. He had been voted in as rector just before the Nazis gained power. He had not been their candidate but the candidate of the conservatives, his antisemitism was not outspoken enough. Yet Fischer fired all his Jewish colleagues. In his rectorial speech in the summer of 1933, he mentioned this as a painful but necessary act of race hygiene.[10]

The German human geneticists got more than the sterilisation law. They got chairs for human genetics, or for race hygiene, as this field was then called, in all German universities. There was one thing they wanted dearly but they did not get, and that was a law allowing the sterilisation of about one million Germans they considered to be genetically "antisocial," *i.e.* involved in petty or serious crime.[9] This law was phrased and proposed but never passed. It said that two medical doctors and one police officer would decide upon sterilisation and confinement to a concentration camp. The Secretary of Justice was adamantly against this law which was favoured by the Secretary of the Interior. The reason for the

---

8. Gütt, A., Rüdin, E. and Ruttke, F.: Gesetz zur Verhütung erbkranken Nachwuchses vom 14. Juli 1933. J.F. Lehmanns Verlag, München, 1934.

9. Müller-Hill, B.: Murderous Science. Elimination by Scientific Selection of Jews, Gypsies and Others, Germany 1933-1945. Translated from the German by G. Fraser. Oxford University Press, Oxford, New York, Tokyo, 1988.

10. Fischer, E.: Der völkische Staat biologisch gesehen. Junker und Dünnhaupt Verlag, Berlin, 1933.

discontent of the Secretary of Justice was obvious. This law would have undermined the position of all judges.

I have to add here that two groups of people were illegally sterilised with the help of human geneticists: First, all German coloured children who were born from fathers of the French army in the early twenties;[9] then, many Gypsies. They actually were part of the group to be sterilised according to the law dealing with "antisocial" persons that was never passed. Of the thirty thousand German Gypsies, twenty thousand were sent to Auschwitz in the spring of 1943. Most of them died there from hunger and infections. The last group of women and children were murdered there in the gas chambers in the fall of 1944.[9]

The Nazis relied on the propagandistic help of the human geneticists when they introduced their antisemitic measures. It helped their argument when the German human geneticists said and wrote that they saw the Nuremberg Laws as a scientific necessity of race hygiene. This cooperation is best summarized in the words of Eugen Fischer. In the spring of 1943, he had just retired as director of the Kaiser Wilhelm-Institute, and he published an article from which I quote: "It is a rare and special good fortune for a theoretical science to flourish at a time when the prevailing ideology welcomes it, and its findings can immediately serve the policy of the state. The study of human heredity was already sufficiently mature to provide this when, years ago, National Socialism was recasting not only the state but also our way of thinking and feeling (*Weltanschauung*). Not that National Socialism needed a "scientific" foundation as a proof that it was right—*Weltanschauung* is formed through practical experience and struggle rather than created by laborious scientific theoretizing—but the results of the study of human heredity became absolutely indispensable as a basis for the important laws and regulations created by the new state."[11]

Human genetics had incorporated ideology in its reasoning and thus became a mixture of science and ideology. This made it attractive for charlatans of all sorts. Moreover, the fact that it had become a national science undermined its foundations. Science is cosmopolitical and its peers are international. This was negated in Germany. Human genetics as it was performed in Germany had the appearance of science on the outside. Internally, it was rotten to the core.

What went wrong with the German human geneticists and how could it happen? The question is of interest as human genetics is about to become a most important part of medicine in the next century.[12] The Human Genome Program and modern genetics will produce solid knowledge

---

11. Fischer, E.: Erbe als Schicksal. Deutsche Allgemeine Zeitung vom 28.3.1943.

12. The Code of Codes. Scientific and Social Issues in the Human Genome Project. Ed. by D.J. Kevles and L. Hood. Harvard University Press, Cambridge MA, London, UK, 1992.

where the German human geneticists could only guess. Let us look at some examples:

- Until recently only those who were already severely ill could be diagnosed in the case of Huntington's chorea. There was no way to predict who was a carrier of the defective gene and who was not. Since 1992, carriers can be diagnosed easily.[13] Then the human geneticists diagnosed the family members often against their will. Now informed consent is necessary and information is nondirective. Yet this simple process is not without problems even when no possible disadvantage in insurance or employment is connected.

  Huntington's chorea was typical then and is typical now for diseases for which there is no effective treatment. Today much hope is sold that treatments for so far untreatable genetic diseases are around the corner. Time will tell. It should be remembered that the absence of treatment eased the abandonment of the psychiatric patients in Germany. It is typical that Lenz called euthanasia, *i.e.* the murder of the psychiatric patients in 1940, "a humanitarian and not a eugenic act":[14] The patients had all been sterilised and had not the slightest chance to procreate. From the eugenic point of view they were indeed already dead.

- The feeble-minded were not asked whether they wanted to be sterilised. They were sterilised. Even now there is no solid genetic knowledge for most cases of feeble-mindedness. We should keep in mind that the German geneticists knew very well that they were not sure in every case whether feeble-mindedness was hereditary. They argued that the well-being of the German population as a whole demanded sterilisation also in doubtful cases. The German human geneticists had abandoned the single German patient for the putative well-being of the German population, the *Volk.* To quote Konrad Lorenz, subsequently a Nobel Prize winner: "For us the population (*Volk*), the race is everything, the individual almost nothing."[15]

  I have to add here that the social democratic government of Sweden introduced a law in 1934 which allowed the sterilisation of the feeble-minded if they or their parents, *etc.* agreed. This law led to the sterilisation of 62,888 persons between 1935 and 1975.[16] As two recent books indicate,[16,17] the pressure upon the patients was often enormous.

---

13. The Huntington's Disease Collaborative Research Group: A Novel Gene Containing a Trinucleotide Repeat. Cell *72*, 971-983, 1993.

14. Lenz, F.: Introduction to the dissertation of W. Stroothenke: Erbpflege und Christentum, Fragen der Sterilisation, Aufordnung und Euthanasie. Berlin, 1940.

15. Lorenz, K.: Nochmals: Systematik und Entwicklungsgedanke im Unterricht. Der Biologe *9*, 24-36, 1940.

16. Bromberg, G. and Tyden, M.: Oönskade i folkhemmet. Rashygien och sterilisering i Sverige. Gidlunds, Värnamo, 1991.

17. Lindquist, B.: Fördälade svenskar-drömmen om att skapa en bättre mäniska. Alfabeta Bokförlag, Falun, 1991.

Many Gypsies were among the victims of this Swedish law. Sterilisation against the will of the feeble-minded was most efficient. But their sterilisation after informed consent, letting them choose between some form of confinement or liberty, was a violation of human rights.

• All the examples and arguments for genetic differences of races in regard to intelligence stood then as now on very, very weak ground. The German human geneticists simply regarded this assumption as common sense. Many international geneticists expected then racial genetic differences in intelligence. The German human geneticists went further by preferring in their value system what they called the Nordic race which was, of course, the same preference as the preference of the Nazis.

It is interesting to follow how the international and German geneticists thought of this problem after WWII. UNESCO produced in 1952 a statement on race and inheritance.[18] Its central, controversial points were the following: "Available scientific knowledge provides no basis for believing that the groups of mankind differ in their innate capacity for intellectual and emotional development." And: "There is no evidence that race mixture produces disadvantageous results from a biological point of view. The social results of race mixture whether for good or ill, can generally be traced to social factors."[18] It is of interest to note that the German human geneticists were officially asked to comment on the UNESCO document. Nachtsheim signed it. Lenz, Fischer and two of their students objected to the statements. This may be assumed. But one should keep in mind that many international geneticists, among them Hermann J. Muller, also objected in carefully chosen words: "To the great majority of geneticists it seems absurd to suppose that psychological characteristics are subject to entirely different laws of heredity of development than other biological characteristics."[18]

It is to be expected that human genetics will eventually answer these questions unambiguously in the next twenty or thirty years. Then we will know whether there are psychic genetic differences between races and whether they do or do not exist. Those who claim that such differences exist will have to predict statistically the behaviour of people from their relevant genotype alone. Then we will know whether alleles of genes exist which predetermine for schizophrenia, manic depression, alcoholism and various grades and forms of intelligence. I imagine that such knowledge can be sound.

But I have serious doubts whether such knowledge will be equally sound in the case of alleles of genes which supposedly determine criminal or violent behaviour.[19] Here genes supposedly determine good and bad,

18. The Race Question in Modern Science. The Race Concept—Results of an Inquiry. UNESCO, Paris, 1952.

19. Stone, R.: HHS "Violence Initiative" Caught in Crossfire. *Science 258,* 212-213, 1992. For the latest claim for a gene determining male violence, see: Angier, N: Is Violence Hereditary? A New Finding. *International Herald Tribune,* October 23-24, 1993.

i.e. ethical behaviour. Here genetics amalgamates with values (ideology, religion) and that is deleterious for genetics and values: Genetics turns into an evil religion, which makes morals and values disappear. If the majority of peers will agree with this process, human genetics will enter a deep crisis.

The German human geneticists were carried away by their early successes in the twenties. They guessed where only half a century later such knowledge is about to appear. They abandoned their patients to criminal politicians. I think that is the worst accusation one has to say about those German human geneticists. Can it happen again? Certainly not the way it happened then. But I think there is another, more modern way to abandon patients. If genetic differences lead to drastic differences in insurance rates and employment, the human geneticists who have discovered those genotypes and all other geneticists will be accused of not having stopped this process to create a genetic "underrace." Certainly the circumstances will differ drastically from those in Germany. No *Führer* will be responsible. It will be the market place with all its participants that will possibly create such an outrage.[20]

---

20. Müller-Hill, B.: The Shadow of Genetic Injustice. Nature *362*, 491-492, 1993.

6

Racial Hygiene: The Collaboration of Medicine and Nazism

Robert N. Proctor

At the end of the 19th Century, German Social Darwinists, fearing a general degeneration of the human race, set about to establish a new kind of hygiene—a racial hygiene *(Rassenhygiene)*—that would turn the attention of physicians away from the individual or the environment, towards the human "germ plasm." In the eyes of its founders (Alfred Ploetz and Wilhelm Schallmayer), racial hygiene was supposed to complement personal and social hygiene; racial hygiene would provide long-run, preventive medicine for the German germ plasm by combating, for example, the disproportionate breeding of "inferiors."

In 1918, Hermann W. Siemens identified racial hygiene as "a political program that stands above all parties." After all, racial hygiene was based on "the facts of inheritance and variability." Inheritance taught that "man owes the essential part of his character, good or bad, physical or spiritual, to his genetic material *(Erbmasse)*." Variability taught that "men differ substantially in their genetic value *(Erbwert)*," and that "there are men who are genetically fit, and men who are genetically unfit." It follows, Siemens argued, that if those who are fit breed less than those who are inferior, the quality of the race will decline. The goal of a "positive racial hygiene" was to ensure that the fit leave more offspring than the unfit. If we failed in this, "all other earthly strivings will be in vain." More specifically, Germany would collapse in the face of an "Asiatic triumph."[1]

Anti-Semitism played a relatively minor role in early racial hygiene. In fact, for Ploetz, Jews were to be classed along with the Nordics as one of the superior, "cultured" races of the world.[2]

---

1. Hermann W. Siemens, "Was ist Rassenhygiene?" *Archiv für Rassen- und Gesellschaftsbiologie*, 12 (1916/1918), pp. 281-282.

2. Alfred Ploetz, *Die Tüchtigkeit unsrer Rasse und der Schutz der Schwachen* (Berlin, 1895).

However, by the mid-1920s, when the right-wing faction of the racial hygiene movement merged with National Socialism, this had changed. The conservative, anti-Semitic J. F. Lehmann Verlag took over the publication of the *Archiv für Rassen- und Gesellschaftsbiologie* (the main racial hygiene journal) shortly after World War I, setting the stage for Nazi ideologues to incorporate eugenics rhetoric into their discourse.

In 1929, a number of physicians formed the National Socialist Physicians' League to coordinate Nazi medical policy and purify the German medical community of "Jewish Bolshevism." The organization was an immediate success, with nearly 3,000 doctors, six percent of the entire profession, joining the League by January 1933—that is, *before* Hitler rose to power.

In fact, doctors joined the Nazi party earlier and in greater numbers than any other professional group. By 1942, more than 38,000 doctors had joined the Nazi party, representing about half of all doctors in the country.

Racial hygiene was recognized as the primary research goal of two prestigious institutes: the Kaiser Wilhelm Institute for Anthropology in Berlin (1927-1945) and the Kaiser Wilhelm Institute for Genealogy in Munich (1919-1945). Both institutes performed research in the fields of criminal biology, genetic pathology, and what we today would call human genetics. Both also helped train SS physicians and helped construct the "genetic registries" later used to round up Jews and Gypsies. Twin studies, aimed at sorting out the relative influence of nature and nurture, were among the leading preoccupations of these and other racial hygiene institutes. This was to become one of the major priorities of Nazi medical research. In 1939, Interior Minister Wilhelm Frick ordered all twins born in the Reich to be registered with Public Health Offices for purposes of genetic research.

The largest such institution was the Frankfurt Institute for Racial Hygiene, with 67 rooms and several laboratories. Here Josef Mengele did his doctoral research on the genetics of the cleft palate. Mengele was stationed at Auschwitz, from where he provided "experimental materials" to the Kaiser Wilhelm Institute for Anthropology in Berlin (eyes, blood, and other body parts) as part of a study on the racial specificity of blood types.

Scientists, in other words, were not simply pawns in the hands of Nazi officials. But without a strong state to back them, racial hygiene research was relatively impotent. It was not until 1933 and the triumph of Hitler that the programs of the pre-Nazi period gained the support of governing officials willing to move aggressively in this area.

Three main programs formed the heart of the Nazi program of medicalized "racial cleansing": the sterilization law, the Nuremberg Laws, and the euthanasia operation. These programs (especially euthanasia) cleared the path for subsequent mass killings.

The 1933 Sterilization Law (the Law for the Prevention of Genetically Diseased Offspring) permitted the forcible sterilization of anyone suffering from "genetically determined" illnesses, including feeblemindedness, schizophrenia, manic-depressive insanity, genetic epilepsy, Huntington's Chorea, genetic blindness, deafness, and "severe alcoholism." The measure was drawn up in July 1933 by several of Germany's leading racial hygienists, including Fritz Lenz, Alfred Ploetz, Ernst Rüdin, and Gerhard Wagner, "Führer" of the National Socialist Physicians' League.

In 1934, 181 Genetic Health Courts and Appellate Genetic Health Courts were established throughout Germany to adjudicate the sterilization law. The courts were usually attached to local civil courts and were presided over by two doctors and a lawyer, one of whom had to be an expert on "genetic pathology." According to the provisions of the law, doctors were required to register every case of genetic illness known to them. Physicians could be fined for failing to register anyone who was "genetically defective." To help physicians determine who should be sterilized, the German Medical Association founded a journal, *Der Erbarzt* (the genetic doctor). The journal also described the latest sterilization techniques.

Estimates of the total number of people sterilized in Germany range from 350,000 to 400,000. In some areas more than one percent of the total population was sterilized. Compared with the demands of some racial hygienists, even this was considered inadequate: Lenz, for example, believed that as many as 10 to 15 percent of the entire population were defective and ought to be sterilized As a consequence of the law, sterilization research and engineering rapidly became one of the largest medical industries. Medical supply companies (such as Schering) designed sterilization equipment. Medical students wrote more than 180 doctoral theses exploring the criteria, methods, and consequences of sterilization. In 1943, the gynecologist Carl Clauberg announced to Heinrich Himmler that, with a staff of ten men, he could sterilize as many as 1,000 women per day.

At the same time that forced sterilization and abortion were instituted for individuals of "inferior" genetic stock, sterilization and abortion for "healthy" German women were declared illegal and punishable (in some cases by death) as a "crime against the German body." (Bavaria's official medical journal declared abortion a form of "treason.") Access to birth control in all forms was also severely curtailed—except, of course, for Jews, for whom birth control was generally available, and encouraged.

The Nuremberg Laws, which Hitler ratified in the Fall of 1935, excluded Jews from citizenship and prevented marriage or sexual relations between Jews and non-Jews. A further measure, the Marital Health Laws, required couples to submit to medical examination before marriage to detect and avoid the possibility of "racial pollution."

The Nuremberg Laws were considered public health measures and were administered primarily by physicians. In early 1936, when the Marital Health Laws went into effect, responsibility for administering the laws fell to marital counseling centers, which were established in the Weimar period. The centers, renamed "genetic counseling centers," were greatly expanded in 1935 and were attached to local Public Health Offices. The Nuremberg Laws, along with the sterilization law, were two of the primary reasons expenditures and personnel for public health actually expanded under the Nazis.

In early October 1939—a month after World War II began—Hitler issued orders that certain doctors be commissioned to grant "a mercy death *(Gnadentod)* to patients judged incurably sick by medical examination." By August 1941, more than 70,000 patients from German mental hospitals had been killed in an operation which provided the stage rehearsal for the subsequent destruction of Jews, homosexuals, communists, Gypsies, Slavs and prisoners of war.

The fundamental reason given for forcible euthanasia was economic: euthanasia was justified as a kind of pre-emptive triage to free up beds. This was seen as especially important in wartime. In fact, the euthanasia operation was consciously timed to coincide with the invasion of Poland. The first gassings of mental patients occurred in Posen, in Poland, on October 15, 1939, just 45 days after the invasion of that country.[3] In Germany itself, after the end of the first phase of euthanasia in August 1941, euthanasia became part of normal hospital routine: handicapped infants were regularly put to death; persons requiring long-term psychiatric care and judged "incurable" suffered a similar fate. After bombing attacks on Germany made space short, psychiatric institutes were cleared out (*i.e.*, their patients were murdered). In at least one instance, a home for the elderly was emptied in this fashion—its inhabitants sent to Meseritz-Obrawalde (in Poland), where they were killed.[4]

The euthanasia program was planned and administered by leading figures in the German medical community. When the first experiments to test new gases for killings took place in Brandenburg Hospital in January 1940, Viktor Brack, head of the operation, emphasized that such gassings "should be carried out only by physicians."

The "Jewish question" was commonly cast as a public health problem—in fact, the official journal of the German Medical Association *(Deutsches Ärzteblatt)* published a regular column during the war years called "Solving the Jewish Problem." One of the leading research priorities in this period was to study the racial specificity of disease (*e.g.*, by means of blood group research). In 1935, when Gerhard Wagner addressed the Nuremberg Party Congress, he claimed that various "diseases," includ-

---

3. Institut für Zeitgeschichte, *Medizin im Nationalsozialismus* (Munich, 1988), pp. 24-25.
4. Ibid., pp. 25-26.

ing homosexuality, insanity, feeble-mindedness, hysteria, suicide, gall-stones, bladder and kidney stones, neuralgia, chronic rheumatism and flat feet, were more common among Jews than non-Jews. In the same speech in which he proposed the destruction of the mentally ill, Wagner declared that "Judaism is disease incarnate."

The medicalization of deviance continued into the war years. The first Nazi-administered Jewish ghettos in Poland, for example, were justified in terms of a "quarantine"; permission to enter or leave the ghettos was granted only by medical authorities. Medical journals in the early 1940s denounced the Jewish "race" as a diseased race, and were able to invoke statistics on typhus levels in the Warsaw ghetto to prove this.[5]

In the course of the late 1930s, German scientists proposed a number of different solutions to the "Jewish question." Philip Bouhler proposed sterilizing all Jews by X-rays. Brack recommended sterilization of the two to three million Jews who could be put to work in Germany's factories.

The ultimate decision to gas the Jews was based on the fact that the technical apparatus already existed for the destruction of the mentally ill. In the fall of 1941, with the completion of the bulk of the euthanasia operation, the gas chambers at psychiatric hospitals were dismantled and shipped east, where they were reinstalled at Majdanek, Auschwitz, and Treblinka. Doctors, technicians, and nurses from these hospitals often followed the equipment. There was a continuity between the destruction of the "lives not worth living" in Germany's mental hospitals and the destruction of ethnic and social minorities.[6]

Many physicians were proud of the fact that their profession had supported the Nazis earlier and in greater strength than any other professional group. Why?

To begin with, the medical profession was quite conservative. Prior to 1933, the leadership of the profession was dominated by the *Deutschnationalen*—a German nationalist party that subsequently supported Hitler. Not all physicians, of course, were conservative. The Socialists and Communists, however, were always a minority in the German medical community. By the end of 1932, the Nazi Physicians' League was twice as large as the Association of Socialist Physicians (3,000 vs. 1,500 members).

Apart from this conservatism, there was an ideological affinity between the profession and Nazism. Many physicians were attracted by the importance given to race in the Nazi view of the world. Race was gener-

5. After the war, the Nazi chief of police for occupied Warsaw (Arpad Wigand) defended shooting several thousand Jews attempting to leave the ghetto on the grounds that the area had been quarantined.

6. Compare also, Henry Friedländer, *The Origins of Nazi Genocide: From Euthanasia to the Final Solution* (Chapel Hill, 1995).

ally considered a medical or anthropological concept (most anthropologists were trained as physicians). Physicians were intrigued by the Nazi effort to biologize or medicalize a broad range of social problems, including crime, homosexuality, the falling birth rate, the collapse of German imperial strength, and the "Jewish and Gypsy problems."

The Nazis, in turn, were able to exploit the intimacy of the traditional physician-patient relationship. Doctors routinely performed "selections" of people to be killed in the concentration camps. Himmler recognized the special role of physicians in this regard: on March 9th, 1943, the Reichsführer of the SS issued an order that only physicians trained in anthropology could perform selections at concentration camps.[7] Medicine also served to disguise mass murder: in Buchenwald 7,000 Russian prisoners of war were executed in the course of "medical exams," victims of a device disguised as an instrument to measure height.

There was yet another factor behind the collaboration of medicine and Nazism. The rise of the Nazis coincided with what was widely believed to be a crisis in modern science due to its increasing specialization and bureaucratization. The Nazis promised to restore Germany to a more natural (*biologische*) way of living, to rejoin once again the separate sciences for "the laboratory and the bedside."

For doctors who sympathized with Nazism, the Jews were to blame for transforming medicine from a "calling" into a "trade," from an "art" into a "business." Jews were a convenient scapegoat given the long tradition of anti-Semitism and the fact that Jews were prominent in the profession (60 percent of Berlin's physicians, for example, were either Jewish or of Jewish ancestry).

Despite the banishing of Jews and Communists from the profession, the overall number of practicing physicians increased under the Nazis. Physicians also achieved a higher status in the Nazi period than any time before or since. For example, during the 12 years of Nazi rule, the office of *Rektor* (president) at German universities was occupied by physicians 30 percent of the time in contrast to 19 percent for the decade prior to the rise of the Nazis, and 18 percent for the two decades following the Nazi period. Doctors also prospered financially under the Nazis. In 1926, lawyers earned an average annual salary of 18,000 RM, compared with only 12,000 RM for physicians. By 1936, doctors were earning 2,000 RM more than lawyers.

Scientists were not bystanders, nor even pawns. Many helped to construct the racial policies of the Nazi state. It is probably as fair to say that Nazi racial policy emerged from within the scientific community as it is to say that it was imposed upon the scientific community.

---

7. Benno Müller-Hill, *Murderous Science: Elimination by Scientific Selection of Jews, Gypsies, and Others, Germany 1933-1945* (Oxford, 1988), p. 18.

It took a powerful state to concentrate and unleash the destructive forces within German medicine, and without that state, science would have remained politically impotent. In the midst of a war engineered by a brutal expansionistic state, Nazi ideologues were able to turn to doctors and scientists to carry out programs that even today stand as unparalleled examples of evil.[8]

8. Note: Earlier versions of this article have appeared in *Dimensions* and George Annas and Michael Grodin, eds. *The Nazi Doctors and the Nuremberg Code* (New York, 1992), and elsewhere. For a more elaborate discussion, see my *Racial Hygiene: Medicine under the Nazis* (Cambridge, MA, 1988).

7

Sterilization, "Euthanasia," and the Holocaust—The Brutal Chain

Daniel Nadav

In February 1932, Julius Moses, a Jewish physician and politician, who perished later in Theresienstadt, published the following lines in an article appearing in the periodical *Der Kassenarzt* (edited by Moses himself): "Everything that was considered until now as the holiest obligations of medicine—to care for the sick without paying attention to their race, to deal in the same way with all diseases, to help ill men everywhere and ease their pain—all this is viewed by the National-Socialists as sheer sentimental stuff which should be thrown away. The only matter of importance in their eyes is leading a war of annihilation against the less worthy (*Minderwertige*)—the incurable patients." Moses warns in another passage: "If this line of thought will win the upper hand the German medical profession will lose its ethical norms [. . .]. the physician will act as a killer, the doctor will become a murderer."[1]

Those prophetic words of Moses, the spokesman of the Social Democrats in the Reichstag in medical matters,[2] were not the one and only warning heard against the deteriorating ethical standards in German medicine under Nazi rule. There were others who let their negative attitude be known right at the beginning of the road leading to the so-called "Euthanasie" program in 1940—killing by gas people whose life was labeled by so-called experts "Lebensunwertes Leben" (life not worth being lived), or "Ballastexistenzen" (an existence which is considered a burden

---

1. "Der Kampf gegen das 'Dritte Reich'—ein Kampf für der Volksgesundheit" *Der Kassenarzt*, IX No. 5 (27.2), (1932), pp. 1-4. The periodical appeared in Berlin from May 1924 to March 1933, when it was closed down by the NS authorities.

2. Moses served in the Reichstag from 1920 to 1932. He was one of the devoted activists in the political arena for the realization of Social-hygienic theses. For more details see my book: *Julius Moses (1868-1942) und die Politik der Sozialhygiene in Deutschland.* (Schriftenreihe des Instituts für Deutsche Geschichte—Universität Tel-Aviv, 8), Gerlingen, 1985.

for the society). Worse was still to come, culminating in the genocide of the Jews (and the Gypsies). The first sign in the road was already put in July 1933, when a law was formulated, which enabled mass sterilization of people judged hereditarily ill. This law was greeted by most of the eugenic specialists and race hygienists, not all of them Nazi sympathizers. We should not forget that German Race Hygiene, beginning with Alfred Plötz and Wilhelm Schallmayer, and European Social Darwinism already had a history of two generations which we cannot elaborate here.[3] We know also that similar laws existed long before in other countries, including many states in the USA, but those were restricted mainly to sexual offenders. The difference was both in scope and in numbers. The German definition of the hereditarily sick included even chronic alcoholics, besides schizophrenics, manic-depressives and five other categories of considerable or alleged hereditary character, like epileptics. Hundreds of thousands of men and women were operated on, 95% against their will, in the next seven years.[4]

Besides the numbers (and expenses) directly involved, there were other indications of the importance the Nazi regime accorded to the scheme and its potential perspectives. A bureaucratic machinery of sifting and judging people according to their racial, social and hereditary qualities was set up in different parts of the country. Millions of Germans, mainly those whose families had a "black sheep" of some sort, were questioned and registered in an ever widening network of card files and genealogical trees. Men like Walter Scheidt from Hamburg dreamt of a complete roundup of the whole German people even in the pre-computer era.[5]

In a little known periodical *Internationales Ärztlisches Bulletin* printed by émigré German and foreign anti-Nazi doctors in the thirties, first in Prague and then in Paris, left-wing authors headed by Ewald Fabian tried to warn their colleagues against the forced attempt of the Nazi authorities to shape a "better race" in Germany.[6] There existed indeed a close relationship between the eugenic characteristics of the operation and its racial traits. From the Nazi point of view, hereditary problems were not only of individual character or involving this or that family.

---

3. See, for example, Sheila F. Weiss, *Race Hygiene and National Efficiency. The Eugenics of Wilhelm Schallmeyer*. Berkeley, 1987.

4. No exact numbers are available. The best discussion is in Gisela Bock, *Zwangssterilisation im Nationalsozialismus*, Opladen, 1986. pp. 230-31.

5. Karl Heinz Roth (ed.), *Erfassung zur Vernichtung: Von der Sozialhygiene zum "Gesetz über Sterbehilfe."* Berlin, 1984, esp. pp. 57-100.

6. The periodical was reprinted in Berlin, 1989. It appeared there as volume 7 of the series "Beiträge zur nationalsozialistischen Gesundheits-und Sozialpolitik." Relevant articles appeared for example in IV(1937), No. 4/5, pp. 45-56 ("Eugenik und Rassismus") and No. 6/7 of the same year, pp. 77-80. ("Zur Anthropologie der Preussen")

They saw those health problems as a collective risk for the whole German-Aryan people or "Volksgemeinde," in their language. The threat of degeneration of the German people at large, through the claimed accelerated rate of birth between the "Minderwertige" was a constant theme in Nazi propaganda and served as an ideological justification for the sharp measures taken.

Even in Germany itself there were some dissenting and skeptical voices staying aloof from the euphoric expectations of Nazi administrators and race hygienists to wipe out hereditary illness in a generation or two. This was possible as some attempts were made to keep the image of a serious scientific consideration of the problem, continuing the public discussion of the matter during the twenties and earlier.[7] In a survey made one-and-a-half years after the law became reality, for example, 106 directors of mental institutions were asked to define the duration of time needed to measure the effects of the law upon their institutions. Summing up the 56 completed questionnaires in a scientific periodical, its editor Johannes Bresler noted that three directors did not anticipate any reduction in the admittance of the hereditary ill into their institutions in the future. Others spoke of two or three generations. Not less than 28 directors declined to make any estimate at all.[8]

But what was the conclusion drawn by Bresler and reflected in the article's title? It was not to stop the brutal and risky sterilization which cost many lives (mainly of women), but on the contrary—widen its scope and dedicate more funds to Race Hygiene and Eugenics in order to locate even more people who carry some undesirable hereditary traits, real or imagined, which should be wiped out in future generations.

This was indeed the path chosen by Nazi policymakers—defining an ever widening circle of so called "Minderwertige" including at a later stage "asocial" types, such as Gypsies and homeless people, hard-core criminals and even homosexuals who did not seem fit to be included in the half-utopian, half-propagandistic "Volksgemeinde." In July 1940, an official circular of the ministry of the interior divided the whole German nonjewish population into eight hierarchical categories. This division was based on racial, biological and social criteria. It went down from the "most valuable" which should be encouraged by the state through "positive eugenics" (including financial subsidies to large families), to the undesired "Minderwertige" whose increase in numbers should be stopped by "negative eugenics."[9] The circular did not specify how this could be done,

---

7. Hans-Walter Schmuhl, *Rassenhygiene, Nationalsozialismus, Euthanasie; Von der Verhütung zur Vernichtung "lebensunwerten Lebens" 1890-1945.* Göttingen, 1987. esp. pp. 99-105.

8. "Deutsche Erbforschung in grösster materiellen Not!," *Psychiatrisch-Neurologische Wochenschrift* (Halle), XXXVI (1934), pp. 625-634.

9. The circular of the interior Ministry carries the date 18.7.40.

but we can make a guess: All the "Minderwertige" ought to be identified and registered, sterilized or even murdered when circumstances proved ripe and expedient to go that far. The murder was actually in full swing when the circular was being published.

I mean of course the murder of the "uncurable"—an idea which was not new in the intellectual climate of Germany even before the rise of Nazism. The best known formulation was put into print in 1920 in a pamphlet written by the physician Alfred Hoche and the lawyer Karl Binding. Its title read: "The Sanctioning of the Destruction of Life Unworthy of Living"[10] and needs, I think, no further explanation. One has to admit, however, that the main emphasis was put (especially by Binding) on reducing the suffering of the acutely ill and their next of kin. It has very little in common with the cynical and vicious use of the same motive in the infamous directive Hitler wrote to his medical henchmen after the outbreak of war. The Führer enabled them "to grant mercy-death [*Gnadentod*] to incurable patients after a serious review of their situation according to the best of human knowledge."[11]

Under the guise of care for the suffering stood the express wish of Hitler to kill as many of the "uncurable" as possible. The outbreak of war fulfilled the necessary precondition to realize a plan which Hitler confided to a few of his inner circle, long before, of getting rid of those coined "Nutzlose Esser"—those who only eat and are useless.[12] In the late thirties, here and there appeared some articles in Nazi periodicals like the S.S. publication "Der schwarze Korps" which suggested killing the "Minderwertige," but those were not endorsed publicly, and even condemned, by Nazi functionaries.[13] The military turn of events changed the atmosphere. One could camouflage, for example, the transfer of patients from some institutions for the mentally ill or retarded people with "war needs"—making place available for the war-wounded and so on. To stress the "emergency character" of the matter Hitler's secret directive, read before, was dated September 1, 1939—the day of the attack on Poland—although it was actually signed a few months later.[14]

The relatively far away provinces of occupied Poland made it possible now (autumn 1939) to begin with the killings themselves. This was

---

10. K. Binding und A.E. Hoche, *Die Freigabe der Vernichtung lebensunwerten Lebens. Ihr Mass und ihre Form*. Leipzig, 1920.

11. The document was first brought to our attention in the Nuremberg physicians trial 1946/47 and was printed also in the pioneer work of A. Mitscherlich and F. Mielke, *Wissenschaft ohne Menschlichkeit*. Heidelberg, 1949.

12. This idea was expressed often to Hermann Rauschning, for example.

13. A useful introduction to the developments in the Nazi era can be found in the first part of the book by Robert J. Lifton, *The Nazi Doctors: Medical Killing and the Psychology of Genocide*. New York, 1986.

14. R.J. Lifton, *The Nazi Doctors*, p. 63.

done with the help of willing S.S. doctors and other S.S. personnel who cooperated in the execution of some thousands of Polish and German mental patients in institutions located in East Prussia and Pomerenia. The killings were done by shooting in the style of the "Einsatzgruppen" used later in Russia. The German patients were not murdered in large groups, however, as was done in Babi Yar and many other places, two years later, but led individually on a "walk," chatting with seemingly friendly guards, and then being shot in the back in a sudden way. This was a troublesome and a slow procedure which did not satisfy the authorities in Berlin—located in the meantime in a nice building confiscated from a Jew at Tiergartenstrasse 4 at Grünwald (this address was shortened to "T4" which served as the code name for the whole "euthanasia" action). With the help of the technical department of the S.S. a new method of killing—more sterile and not necessitating direct contact with the victims—was sought.

The method chosen—gas—first carbon monoxide (CO) and then exhaust gas used in the gas vans,[15] could not come as a complete surprise. Actually, it is one of the important links between some aspects of the brutal chain which led from the poisonous gas warfare in the First World War up to the Holocaust. Adolf Hitler, who was blinded for a while in this method of war, looked for revenge and was easily convinced to turn it against those who were represented as a burden or a risk to the German people.

Seen in this perspective, sterilization seemed an almost logical way to accustom the German people to honor the need expressed in *Mein Kampf* of discontinuing the proliferation of persons deemed "unfit." Additional steps were taken including the obligation to get a health certificate in order to marry. No allowance was granted, needless to say, to marriage between Christians and Jews after The Nuremberg Laws of September 1935. This was another striking illustration of the similar attitudes towards racial and hereditary problems which were put together by Hitler under the rubric of "Rassenhygiene"—not always with the consent of the academic race hygienists who were not necessarily rabid antisemites. A few killings of retarded children like the famous "Knauer kid" of S.S. members who could not stand the "shame" of caring for their "minderwertige" offspring, took place even before the war began. This also signaled the widening scope of the planned action—not only the hereditarily sick but also misfortunate children and grown ups who were born retarded or invalids without an hereditary background—all of whom were doomed to die now.

One of the amazing (and, one may add, depressing) aspects of the whole "Euthanasia" action was indeed the extent of readiness of renowned

---

15. Christopher Browning: *Fateful Months: Essays on the Emergence of the Final Solution.* New York, 1985, especially chapter 4.

men of science to endorse and participate in the murderous action. More than that—they were eager to make use of the opportunities opened now before them to follow new and doubtful, not to say criminal, avenues of research. To name just one example: Prof. Julius Hallervorden from Kaiser Wilhelm's Brain-Research Department in Berlin who was happy to be supplied with hundreds of brains cut from victims murdered in the nearby Brandenburg "Euthanasia" Institute. He was not ashamed to publish "interesting cases" based on this peculiar "material" even after the World War ended. It is the great achievement of Benno Müller-Hill who brought the sordid details to our attention based on thorough documentation and archival work.[16]

Euthanasia proposals were discussed with leading physicians, admittedly hand-picked by S.S. doctors headed by Ernst Grawitz, even before the war started—in the summer months of 1939. Most of the cooperative doctors were convinced they were doing what was needed in the context of a new order of values—Nazi ethics—which put aside the Judeo-Christian heritage and the Hippocratic Oath. They cherished the needs of the state as defined by Nazi ideologues. If some of the doctors had sporadic pangs of conscience they were easily put aside with an often expressed mechanism of rationalization. This was based on the old assumption, expressed already by Binding, and supported by some empirical evidence also collected in the twenties,[17] that most of the victims and their relatives were suffering and should, as a matter of fact, be grateful to be delivered of their continuous ordeal.

On the other hand, material incentives were offered. The specialists were called upon to participate for a pay in the bureaucratic procedure of selecting the candidates to be gassed. This process was compartmentalized, by the way, to lessen the individual moral inhibitions. Questionnaires were sent, for example, to all mental institutions and their directors were called upon to list their patients including their evaluations for their future. They were not told anything about the real aim of this inquiry. The directors also had to report on the work of those patients occupied in the framework of the institution—in the kitchen garden, for example. Those patients who proved "useful" could be saved sometimes from the lot of their less profitable comrades. Götz Aly and others demonstrated in recent years[18] with somewhat determined zeal, the growing importance of the

---

16. His book in German which appeared in 1984 was translated into English: *Murderous Science.* New York, 1988. Hallervorden's deeds are described mainly on pp. 66-67. It is still worthwhile to look at the pioneer work: Max Weinreich, *Hitler's Professors: The Part of Scholarship in Germany against the Jewish People.* New York, 1946.

17. Ewald Meltzer, *Das Problem der Abkrüzung "lebensunwerten" Lebens.* Halle, 1925.

18. G. Aly and S. Heim, *Vordenker der Vernichtung.* Frankfurt/M., 1991.

economic factor in all the developments discussed here. After the questionnaires were sent back to Berlin, the specialists went over the lists and decided who should be killed. A plus sign with a pencil was sufficient to send the patient to his death. This checking was rarely done in a serious way. The pay was very modest—8 to 20 Pfening for every formular—this was the value of a human life (even an "Aryan" one!) in Nazi Germany.[19] Many of the so called specialists went over hundreds of formulas daily. Sometimes their wives and spouses lent a helping hand, too. . .

After the lists were approved in this summary way (only rarely were cases brought to a final judgment of expert "Obergutachter" like Herbert Linden from the Ministry of Interior or the psychiatrist Max De Crinis) the process of murder itself began. The condemned patients were transferred from their former institutions to six annihilation centers located in different parts of the Third Reich, including Austria. There they were photographed and registered. Afterwards, they were told to remove their clothing in order to be disinfected and washed. They were led naked into a room which looked like a shower-room but actually hid the gas installation. When enough people (usually 70 to 80) were compressed in the small room a steel door closed behind them, and the physician responsible for the action let the bottled carbon monoxide flow into the room, watching the results through a small glass hole in the door. After approximately a quarter of an hour, everybody was dead, and the corpses were carried over to a nearby crematorium to be burned, but not before the gold teeth of the victims had been pulled out.

The awful procedure which cost the lives of some seventy thousand Germans in 1940/41 reminds us in all its dreadful details of the murder of millions in the gas chambers in Auschwitz and elsewhere some years later. This is of course not a coincidence. The so-called "Euthanasia" program served not only the criminal end of getting rid of the "undesired" between the Germans but also proved to be the major training ground of the personnel who put the first death camps in to action in the next years.

Seen from this perspective, the official "stop" of the "Euthanasia" action in August 1941[20] was not only a gesture to the church for people like Bishop von Galen of Munster and a few others such as Friedrich von Bodelschwingh from the "Beth El" Institutions, protested loudly and courageously against it. The summer of 1941 also witnessed the invasion of the Soviet Union. The swift German victories of this summer brought into Nazi control densely populated regions where millions of Jews lived. The "Einsatzgruppen" were called in to kill hundreds of thousands. It was proved this time, too, that their shooting technique was not the right way

---

19. R. Winau in *Medizin im Nationalsozialismus*. Munchen, 1988, p. 37.
20. The action was continued till the end of war, but the patients were killed now mainly by other means, and not by gas.

to deal with the task ahead—the systematic annihilation of European Jewry which Hitler decided upon and combined now with the realization of his other dream, "Lebensraum," in Russia.

In an analogous way to the events a year or two before, a better "industrial" system of murder was sought after, and the gas specialists of the "Euthanasia" program were willing to offer their expertise. Medical killing became a pilot scheme for the "Final Solution."[21] The close connections which already existed between the management of "T4," the SS and the Gestapo made this process easier. Many if not most of the "Euthanasia" doctors were actually members of the SS themselves. Some of them, like Friedrich Mennecke participated in the "14f13" action and selected so called "sick" Jews in the older concentration camps (not yet equipped with gas chambers) to be gassed in the remaining gas installations not needed anymore for the "Euthanasia" of the Aryans. He did his job with the cynical joy of a convinced man-hunter which was reflected in the many letters he wrote to his wife.[22] Men like Dr. Irmfried Eberl, who led the "Euthanasia" institute in Brandenburg, and Stangel, who was stationed in Hartheim—another gassing center—were sent at the end of 1941 to advise and supervise the construction and successful operation of gas installations in the first death camps of Chelmno, Belzec, Sobibor and Treblinka. Eberl and Stangel actually served as the first directors of Treblinka and Sobibor camps where a million Jews at least, from Warsaw and the eastern part of Poland, were gassed from the spring of 1942 on.

The participation of the "Euthanasia" doctors in the Holocaust was the last step in dehumanizing medicine in the Third Reich. The doctor with his classic mission to save life became a mass-murderer, well integrated in the genocide machinery and fulfilling Julius Moses' somber prophecy written a decade before. Robert Jay Lifton's demystification of the SS physicians in the camps[23] does not ease the moral issue involved. On the contrary, I agree with Michael Kater[24] that if Mengele, Rascher (from Dachau) and others were not demons, our task of explaining the past and preventing similar occurrences from happening again in the future becomes even more complex and demanding.

21. Paul Weindling, *Health, Race and German Politics between National Unification and Nazism, 1870-1945.* Cambridge, 1987. pp. 548 ff.

22. See also the citations from a diary of another doctor, Hans H. Kremer, which Peter J. Haas printed in his book: *Morality after Auschwitz: The Radical Challenge of the Nazi Ethic.* Philadelphia, 1988.

23. *The Nazi Doctors.* op. cit.

24. *Doctors under Hitler*, University of North Carolina, 1989, p. 9.

8

Nazi Eugenics: Adaptation and Resistance among German Catholic Intellectual Leaders

Donald Dietrich

1.

Varied explanations have been offered to help explain the growth of the eugenics environment in Europe generally and in pre-Nazi Germany more specifically. A biologically oriented cultural climate rooted in new theories of human development had emerged during the late nineteenth century as a hygienic paradigm based on social engineering. By finally severing God's hand from nature, eugenicists in general saw human engineers as those with the responsibility for the species. These eugenicists may have differed sharply in their racist emphases, but the implications for individuals were far reaching, whichever biological/eugenic concept would be adopted (Weiss, 1987; Proctor, 1988; Schmuhl, 1987; Bolle, 1962; Graham, 1977). Professional eugenicists began to perceive medicine as a tool with a social function, which from their perspective should nurture a political responsibility for maintaining a "good" genetic pool. This concern with "social hygiene" encouraged an active interventionist outlook. These professionals tried to offer a scientific solution to social and, in some cases, "racial problems." Some scholars have recently noted that for these men eugenic practices were to be introduced into the national consciousness as a new religion (Kater, 1989; Zmärzlik, 1963; Proctor, 1988, 29, 46-47).

In particular, eugenicists were worried about the degeneration of the species, which they attributed to a decline in the birthrate of the dominant social groups, which seemed inevitably to be leading to the increase in the proportion of "inferior" genetic specimens within the population. Social and eugenic superiority were equated from the start (Kaup, 1913). World War I with its devastating casualties increased concern about the declining number of births, as well as about their quality, and prompted renewed interest in negative eugenics, *i.e.*, in sterilization and euthanasia (Binding and Hoche, 1920; Lenz, 1921; Blasberg, 1932). Both the negative eugenics program to improve German racial hygiene and the policy of scientific antisemitism ultimately were derived from the foundational perspective which viewed humanity and society in biological terms. As a result of this extensive eugenic debate, illness was transferred from the private to the public or communal sphere. To be sick became an infraction against the body politic, which appeared to be deprived of valuable labor resources (Mann, 1973; Webster, 1981; Dörner, 1977).

After World War I, German Catholics, along with the rest of their fellow citizens, were faced with acute political problems in a defeated nation. Making the theological and political situation particularly complex was the fact that the Nazi nationalist and anti-Marxist assault on Weimar could be supported by varied individuals and groups across a broad spectrum. This was true even though the Nazi radical racist eugenic theories might well be anathema to most Catholics who were concerned with such brutal threats to the integrity of the human person. Most Catholic bishops and theologians opposed the compulsory negative eugenics proposals of the Nazis and their predecessors, when, as representatives of the church, they interpreted these initiatives as intrusions into the private spheres of human relations and as an unnatural interference with God's creative plans. By using moral casuistry, however, Catholics who were determined to remain good Germans could adapt even to the Nazi Sterilization Law of 1933. A minority, including Hermann Muckermann and Joseph Mayer, represented the view that scientifically guided sterilization as an example of negative eugenics could morally be embedded into an all-inclusive program of positive eugenics under the correct conditions. Ultimately, Mayer would even extend his moral analysis into a justification of euthanasia as well (Dietrich, 1988; Lilienthal, 1979; Amir, 1977; Fassbinder, ch. A, II, 5.b).

2.

During the 1920s and early 1930s, the scientist and Jesuit who left his order, but remained a priest, Hermann Muckermann, had taken a position in several works, which opposed Nordic and biological racism. But while his publications and professional activities indicate that he opposed this antisemitic *Weltanschauung*, he did not seem to understand that the simple grouping of individuals can psychologically help create the grounds for discrimination and also reinforce a "softening of the conscience" in those supporting a eugenics solution to socio-economic problems. To be anti-racist and pro-eugenic in the context of 1928-1945 may have been intellectually possible, but such an approach did not provide a secure intellectual position from which Hitler's biological politics could be resisted. Muckermann's scientific posture, naively conceived in light of what occurred in the Third Reich, helped reinforce the eugenic values that could be co-opted into Nazism. He maintained, at least until *Casti Connubii* (Pius XI's encyclical on marriage) and the subsequent clarification by church authorities, that he could support sterilization as well as positive eugenics, which were qualitatively distinct, he insisted, from Nordic or biological racism. Like so many other Germans, he failed to see that academic discourses on eugenics and the traditional antisemitism of his culture and church served to reinforce the radical biological racism of the Nazi leaders (Weiss, 1987; Anonymous, 1930; Tajfel, 1981).

Racial hygienists and eugenicists judged individuals according to their social productivity; those deemed a national liability—people, who in the words of Muckermann, "cannot be brought back to work and life"—were to be institutionalized as cheaply as possible. Certainly, their tainted germ plasm was not to be passed on to future generations. Only *Vorsorge* (foresight) in the form of eugenics could prevent generations of increased *Fürsorge* (welfare) (Weiss, 1987, 151-53; Muckermann, "Illustrationen," 1931, 42). Muckermann insisted that no conflict need arise between racial hygiene and Catholicism as long as racial hygiene was applied to the human species as a whole with all of its races without differentiating between inferior and superior races (Muckermann, 1932; Proctor, 1988, 46-47; Müller-Hill, 1988, 84).

In his own work, Muckermann emphasized the *Volkswohl* (welfare of the people) and the *Volksgesundheit* (health of the people) as his research focused on issues of procreation and degeneration. In this, he bore similarities to eugenicists in both the United States and the major European nations. Only in light of the disasters of the Third Reich does the "slippery slope" he was descending become apparent. As he developed his position, he distinguished between "positive" and "negative" eugenics. Like the Catholic church itself, he found that he could support positive eugenics, that is, healthy procreation strategies based on Christian principles that stressed education and avoided physical intervention into the natural processes. The issues of negative eugenics, that is, sterilization, abortion and euthanasia, were more problematic (Muckermann, 1932, 157-62; Muckermann, 1920, 98-115; Muckermann, 1928; Lilienthal, 1980, 426-36; Hare, 1988, 417-418).

Muckermann, of course, repudiated euthanasia, and, in fact, very little in his work refers to this issue. His basic position was that God is the author of life, and so individuals do not have any ultimate power over life and death. Since at the moment of conception he felt that a person existed, abortion was also not a viable ethical possibility. He felt, however, that one could intervene before conception to prevent degeneration. To forbid marriage, and presumably procreation, to those who were afflicted with mental or physical disabilities, had been discussed in scientific and religious circles, but no universally accepted consensus had emerged. This issue was particularly sensitive to Catholic leaders who felt that the ultimate goal of marriage was to procreate (Muckermann, 1918, 339-44; Muckermann, 1921, 12-25; Muckermann, "Die Enzyklika," 1931, 339-410). As a basic human right, marriage should not, many Catholics felt, be legally restricted. This right to marriage among those with so-called genetic disabilities should not simply be eliminated, since it could be controlled to avoid degeneration through procreation. That is, birth control was available.

As Muckermann observed the debates swirling around social and eugenic issues, he sought to develop a position that he felt was consistent with Christian values. In the eugenics debate, one of the themes persistently voiced was the ultimate cost of controlling births when dealing with the mentally or physically impaired, since traditional institutionalization demanded the expensive separation of the sexes. Sterilization seemed to be a cheaper option. Contemporary laws had already been established in the United States where legislators attempted to stop criminals and the feeble-minded from reproducing. Initially, Muckermann did not find himself torn on this issue between his Catholic allegiance and his scientific professionalism (Muckermann, 1933, 160; Muckermann, 1934, 20; Müller 1985, 35, 43).

The ecclesial situation changed abruptly in 1930 with the promulgation of the papal encyclical, *Casti Connubii*, in which compulsory sterilization for eugenic reasons was forbidden. Arguing from a very narrow technical perspective, Muckermann asserted that sterilization as an eugenic intervention was still ethically an unresolved issue, since the criteria applicable to the sterilization of an individual person were distinct from those that would be applied to a group (hygienic class) and since the scientific import of the issue was not really understood by the pope. In other words, all the data was not in, and so a state of doubt existed. Thus, the law did not bind, since the pope did not understand eugenics as social management. Pius XI had stressed the ideal for the individual without understanding genetic and social reality. Muckermann departed from the literal text of the encyclical by suggesting that voluntary, as opposed to compulsory, sterilization might be licit, although it would be difficult to determine how in future Nazi legal situations this distinction might save a person from compulsory surgery (Muckermann, 1920, 163; Grosch-Obenauer, 1986, 49).

Until 1930, then, as a scientist Muckermann viewed sterilization as an ethical duty to enhance the common welfare. He had initially dissented from *Casti Connubii*, saying that the last word had not been spoken, even though the document had to be considered as one articulating a properly authorized teaching. While initially disappointed in the magisterium, he admitted by 1933 that "the decision of Rome binds each child of the Church." With the onset of racial politics in the Third Reich, moreover, he began to see the sterilization issue from the perspective of the basic rights of the individual and not just as an issue of a medically and politically defined common good or as an exertion of the Catholic church's authority (Gottlieb, 1932, 466-7; von Verscheuer, 1932, 462-66; Muckermann, 1934, 125). Increasingly, he de-emphasized sterilization in line with the church's teaching and stressed eugenic education for the common welfare and for the individual's own development.

As a Catholic, he opposed Nazi racist paganism, but as a scientist he found that he still had to support the social management policies of the eugenics movement. On 3 April 1936, for example, in St. Martin's church in Bamberg, Muckermann reminded his audience that the Catholic faith discouraged marriage between congenitally diseased persons and that the church definitely supported genetic health, which was a gift from God. Christian parents, therefore, should exercise all possible care to support and multiply the *Heimrasse* "Ethnic/Native Race" through such positive eugenic approaches as education focused on genetic health (Witetschek, 1967, 2:90).

Under pressure from *Casti Connubii*, he distanced himself from negative eugenics and refused to support sterilization as a Nazi racist policy, since such an affirmation would have meant support of the Nordic race as the superior race. His use of the term *Heimrasse*, however, indicates a desire for a national eugenics policy, since that was the arena in which he operated. Unfortunately, *Heimrasse* was also a Nazi term loaded with connotations of racial superiority. The obvious dangers in Muckermann's position have become apparent in hindsight and have led to an on-going debate on the concept of the slippery slope. In hindsight, it is clear that his discussion of genetically healthy individuals as necessary for the common good and the distinction that he drew among peoples helped reinforce Nazi racist values, even though that was not his intention as he championed eugenic policies. His viewpoint tended to weaken the official Catholic policy on scientific eugenics.

3.

Along with sterilization, euthanasia had also been debated among Catholics long before the advent of the Third Reich. The parameters of the debate were shaped by two issues: voluntary and involuntary mercy killing. Classical Catholic ethical speculation opposed both forms. But scholastic philosophy broke with this classical tradition by rejecting suicide (voluntary euthanasia) when the purpose was solely to preserve individual dignity. Group survival was considered to be a mitigating condition. The fundamental development emerging in the Medieval era was that "quality" of life was applied to the group and became normative in making ethical as well as societal determinations. The private criterion of the dignity of the individual became more prominent initially during the

Enlightenment. The eugenics movement opened new dimensions to the ongoing discourse in the modern period by insisting that the welfare of the group superseded that of the individual.

In the 1920s, Joseph Mayer had taken his first tentative steps on this path by defending sterilization and abortion (Amir, 1977, 4-5; Niedermeyer, 1937, 357-84; Niedermeyer, 1949-52, 222; Just). During the 1930s, Mayer's position on the varied aspects of the eugenics issue remained consistent with his earlier opinions and were a source of confusion to those who looked to the Catholic church for the articulation of guiding moral principles. His views on negative eugenics were consistent with those of the regime, and he seemed as obsessed with the "good" of society as were his Nazi contemporaries. That such a prominent theologian was not explicitly and publicly corrected by the church certainly added to the confusion of German Catholics. Opposing such Catholic professional colleagues as Franz Hürth during the 1920s, Mayer had also argued against the principle point promoted by his opponents in the 1933 sterilization controversy, who contended that those sterilized, according to canon law, would not really be capable of a proper marital relationship, since the essence of marriage, they insisted, was procreation (Mayer, 1927; Dietrich, 1988, ch. 7; Mayer, 1933; National Archives, RG I-FIR/123, 9 January 1947, 61).

Even during the 1920s, Mayer had felt that marriage was not a union designed exclusively for procreation, but could also be accepted as a relationship instrumental in sanctifying the souls of the partners. The only question, Mayer asserted, that could realistically and logically be asked was whether sterilization intended either an individual or a societal moral good. He concluded that neither private morality nor the moral world order was endangered through the sterilization of the mentally ill. The medical health of the marital and societal community, he concluded, was more important than the physical integrity of the individual. In his scholarly treatises, he asserted that it would be licit for the state to enforce sterilization for eugenic reasons (Mayer, 1927, 113, 121, 124-25, 128, 352, 373-86, 422; Mayer, 1929, 137-62; Mayer, 1933, 887-88).

In 1939-40, Albert Hartl of the SD (*Sicherheitsdienst*) commissioned a memo from Mayer, which would offer a Catholic justification for euthanasia. The memo, "Euthanasie im Lichte der katholischen Moral und Praxis," under the name Erich Warmund and thought to be lost has been discovered in the Nürnberg Archives (Dietrich, 1992, 589-91). The memo exposes the extent that *völkisch* and Nazi values had permeated theological circles, even though the Catholic church had repeatedly denounced euthanasia (Dietrich, 1987, 19-46). Mayer's memo, frequently disjointed, offers a good example of moral theology tailored to a diseased, political milieu. His speculation also suggests that under specific conditions there could be a logical development from sterilization to euthanasia to Auschwitz. Mayer offered a memo of 110 pages offering a survey of western culture in which the common good outweighs individual welfare. From antiquity to the Enlightenment, the support of the common welfare or public good rather than private needs had been a foremost consideration (Mayer, "Euthanasie," 3-15). In principle, for example, Christ, who talked about casting out devils, had the same goal as Plato – to free the community of the unhealthy. Both wanted to cleanse the community of sickness in body and soul (Mayer, 1939-1940, 28, 32-39, 40-43, 47-48).

Mayer pointed out that medieval thinkers wanted to expurgate the insane and thus maintain the holistic integrity of the community (Mayer, 1939-1940, 62-63). From this point, Mayer could and did develop the theme that the individual person should exist for the good of the community according to Platonic as well as Christian thought (Mayer, 1939-1940, 70-72). The church, he insisted, had historically supported the political authorities in the elimination (*Ausmerzung*) of mentally ill adults and children. From the perspective of current medical advances, they were innocent. But theologians in the thirteenth century declared that they were guilty through their parents. Only in modern times has the medical profession denied the so-called demonic possession of the mentally ill. This enlightened opinion resulted in charitable Christians accepting "idiot" children, epileptics, and the mentally ill (Mayer, 1939-1940, 93-94). Since the nineteenth century, according to Mayer, moral theology had opted for the absolute protection of the lives of those who were insane and had rejected euthanasia as its instrument to protect the community. Thus, Mayer insisted, opinions seem to change in accordance with historical circumstances, and so euthanasia could not really be condemned by the Catholic church, which had hardly followed an historically consistent policy.

Theologians, Mayer asserted, had tailored theology to accord with modern thought, just as they had always done. Basically, the current, enlightenment ideal was to save and lengthen human life. The mentally ill and physically impaired were to be nursed in the family and in the *Volk* community, even though such individuals had lost the true essence of a rational life and so had ceased to be human. What formerly nature had allowed to be destroyed, modern science was now trying to save. With this attitude and the rise of social hygiene and care, the artificial prolongation of life became in the nineteenth century a universally accepted norm. Thousands of insane persons had been kept alive, Mayer insisted, who in past centuries would have been eliminated. More food and better medicine made all this possible. Given the number of current inmates in institutions, for example, Germans were supporting, Mayer wrote, an additional 1.2 million "labor years" of these mentally dead and vegetable-like persons (Mayer, 1939-1940, 98-100).

According to Mayer, the Enlightenment and the current church itself seemed to be stressing the absolute value of the individual human life, which resulted in an irresponsible invasion into the corrective goals of the natural processes of selection, which in less sentimental times had been used by the church and state to preserve the organically healthy *Ordo*. Not Christianity, but enlightened rationalism had, at least initially, caused this perversion of nature. Thus, the common good had apparently lost its preeminence to private individualistic rights. Historically, the principles of Christianity, he maintained, had opposed this until the nineteenth century. On the basis of historical precedent, then, Mayer insisted that the health of the *Volk* should again become the controlling principle guiding the political community (Mayer, 1939-1940, 102-103; Proctor, 1988, 15). According to Mayer, the Catholic church, which has consistently adapted to the culture in which it has been embedded, should not now insist that it alone enunciates *the* eternal and unchangeable norms or it will be mauled by the wheels of history. Theologians concerned with the evils wrought in the name of religion, Mayer insisted, should clarify their basic principles, which had developed historically over centuries and supported the *Volk* rather than individual rights until the Enlightenment, before they try again to claim that they have the right to act as the conscience of the world and to assume *the* responsible role of a moral arbiter in German society (Mayer, 1939-1940, 108-109). Thus, Mayer contended that euthanasia could be supported by Catholic moral theology.

The euthanasia program itself was a logical escalation of the sterilization law. Once a human hierarchy was established and the scientific exclusion of the *Untermensch* from procreation was decided, the next logical step was an exclusion from life and additionally for the Jew to be viewed as a sick or diseased creature (Wagner, 1935, 432; Günther, 1929). The views that Muckermann and Mayer espoused in the moral and scientific context of the time were not necessarily supportive of racist extermination, but were congruent with the elements of the Nazi *Weltanschauung*, which were devoted to the welfare of the *völkisch* group and characterized the "softening of the conscience," which many in that generation displayed. Some theologians, however, saw the threat more clearly.

4.

From 1933 until 1935, German theologians who prided themselves as patriotic nationalists tended to adapt to the Nazi New Order (Dietrich, 1987, 22-29). Naturally, given the Nazi transformation of societal values in part under the aegis of Social Darwinism, Catholic theologians felt compelled to reassert the meaning of Christ in history as well as the traditional precepts of morality. Fritz Tillmann's Christocentric moral theology, for example, was not merely a combination of natural ethical norms and the demands of grace, which resulted from the supernatural determination of man. Over and above this abstract approach, Tillmann relied on Christ's personal injunction, "Follow me." His moral theology was rooted in historical, scriptural events. Not simply the avoidance of sin, but rather the positive virtue of love stands as the focal point of moral obligations (Tillmann, 1934; Müncker, 1934).

Concerned with Nazi eugenic policies, Max Pribilla urged that morally orthodox and not racist marriage manuals, for example, should be developed for the moral guidance of the faithful. In 1939, as the world approached war and as eugenic enterprises became more intense, Pribilla expanded his concern to the very survival of the Catholic church and to the moral decisions being made by Catholics. The church itself, he asserted, had an unchangeable essence, and the crisis facing Christianity was only the most current in a long series. Christians had no right to be fatalists but should shape their era, since humans are social creatures and so need the help of society to develop properly. A good society was thought to form good persons (Pribilla, 1935, 53-56; Pribilla, 1939, 169-75).

Focusing on the dangers of Nazi racism, Anton Artweiler also insisted that race was not absolute, but rather was limited by its very essence. All humans belong to one community, since all persons are Man. Within this all-inclusive category, there were also such communities as the family and nation. The state was the organized form of the *Volk*, which merely stressed connection by blood. Every community, however, was derived from God. Indeed, the church was the community (*Gemeinschaft*) most closely approximating God's idea (Artweiler, 1938, 8-10, 36, 152-53, 157-60). Artweiler emphasized the Catholic church as a union closely reflecting God's intended order and certainly more worthy of adherence than Hitler's *Volk*.

In 1939, Otto Schilling as well tried to clarify some of the issues that Catholics were facing. To de-emphasize the organic notion of the common good being promulgated by the Nazis, Schilling stressed that the basis of social justice was that the community has to give to the individual what was necessary for personal development. In essence, then, the individual was at the alpha and omega of the social order. Law was to have its basis in natural law, not in the will of the Führer. Harking back to the solidarist position, he reminded his readers that social justice and the organic principle would both belong to the traditional Christian pattern of thought and implied that only from this *Weltanschauung* was it possible to mediate values seemingly at odds with one another (Schilling, 1939, 198, 201).

In light of Mayer's line of thought, the common and individual goods also had to be delineated if human dignity were to be preserved. Peter Lippert saw the truly Christian community as the highest form of human interaction. Communities of two or three or several hundred million, such as the church, overflow with power and fullness. Each person receives his or her anchoring from the community. He could agree with the Nazi slogan: *Gemeinnutz geht vor Eigennutz* (common need before the individual need), at least for specific socioeconomic dimensions of community life. Such an approach was not valid, however, where a specific good had the individual as its referent focus, *i.e.*, all such values of the spiritual person as religious truth. The "common good" could not be decisive in a matter of conscience. Values proper to the person were to be defended against the political society (*Gesellschaft*), since the well-being in a community was love, not hate. Ultimately, the essence of the true community was to be the individual giving to those in need (Lippert, 1935, 361-76).

By 1938, Ivo Zeiger's defense of the Catholic church had also evolved into a defense of human persons. All discussion on the issue of morality and moral doctrine ultimately had to be referred back to anthropology, *i.e.*, to the human person as the image of God. The moral law was peculiar to the human race. Hence, humans were only truly human when they obeyed moral precepts, clearly a notion that differed radically from Nazi philosophy, which had historically opted for a morality rooted in race. Although he did not discuss or even mention race, Zeiger insisted that revelation is God speaking to humans and affirms the existence of a personal being. God speaks to humans through creation and has established a universe in which obedience to the human's true nature as a creature of God is his natural law. Natural morality was verified in revelation. Natural moral law, which was designed to help humans reach the ideals originally created by God, opposed Nazi morality rooted in the *Volk* or in Hitler as its representative (Zeiger, 1938, 298-307). For Zeiger, Catholic morality was not based on speculative abstractions, but was rooted in the living church. Imitating Christ was to reveal the ultimate principles of morality (Zeiger, 1938, 149-50). Such ideas as those briefly highlighted above seem to suggest that by the end of the 1930s, an array of theologians were losing even their limited enthusiasm for an acceptance of the New Order. They seemed to be strengthening traditional doctrinal fortifications as they prepared for the siege.

5.

The Nazi experience as well as contemporary genetic developments suggest some of the questions and issues that should be pondered today when the maintenance of human dignity is even more in jeopardy. Do particular eugenic or biological alterations enhance the dignity of the human person or do they establish additional external criteria useful in evaluating humans? Is human dignity a function of a person's success in society? Does a particular biological enhancement support personal freedom? Such questions can help focus attention on the value intrinsic to the individual subsisting in centralized and technologically oriented nation-states. Unfortunately, these were not questions asked frequently enough until after the disasters of 1933-45, and the real power of the modern state could be observed in operation. The eugenic theories that helped rationalize the Third Reich's policy toward the ill and those "unworthy" to live stand as a frightful warning both against the application of "valueless science" to social problems and against the rationalization of social prejudices by using science and moral theology. Despite the fact that some Catholics contributed to the culture that nurtured Nazi racism, others saw the dangers to humanity when the dignity of the person was not held sacrosanct. Theologians aware of the crucial value of human dignity to the functioning of a moral community have taught a lesson with implications for today as well.

References

Amir, A. "Euthanasia in Nazi Germany," Ph.D. dissertation. New York: SUNY-Albany, 1977.

Anonymous. "Geleitwort." *Eugenik*, 1930.

Artweiler, Anton. *Unter Glaube. Christliche Wirklichkeit in der heutigen Welt*. Munich: Kösel Pustet, 1938.

Binding, Karl and Hoche, Alfred. *Die Freigabe der Vernichtung lebensunwerten Lebens, Ihr Mass und Ihre Form*. Leipzig: E. Strache, 1920.

Blasberg, J. "Ausländische und deutsche Gesetze und Gesetzentwürfe über Unfruchtbarmachung." *Zeitschrift für die gesamte Strafrechtswissenschaft*, 52, 1932, 488-97.

Bolle, Fritz. "Darwinismus und Zeitgeist." *Zeitschrift für Religions- und Geistesgeschichte*, 14, 1962, 143-78.

Dietrich, Donald. *Catholic Citizens in the Third Reich: Psycho-Social Principles and Moral Reasoning*. New Brunswick, NJ: Transaction Books, 1988.

Dietrich, Donald. "Catholic Eugenics in Germany, 1920-1945: Hermann Muckermann, S.J. and Joseph Mayer." *Journal of Church and State* 34, 1992, 575-600.

Dietrich, Donald. "Catholic Theologians in Hitler's Reich: Adaptation and Critique." *Journal of Church and State* 29, 1987, 19-45.

Dörmer, Karl. "Nationalsozialismus und Lebensvernichtung." *Vierteljahrshefte für Zeitgeschichte* 15, 1977, 121-52.

Fassbinder, M., ed. *Des deutschen Volkes Wille zum Leben*. Freiburg: Herder, 1917.

Gottlieb, Theodor. "Eugenik, Papst und Muckermann." *Flugblatt der Erneuerung Deutschlands* 16, 1932, 466-71.

Graham, Loren. "Science and Values: The Eugenics Movement in Germany and Russia in the 1920s." *American Historical Review* 82, 1977, 1133-64.

Grosch-Obenauer, Dagmar. "Hermann Muckermann und die Eugenik." Inaugural Diss., Mainz: Johannes Gutenburg Universität, 1986.

Günther, Hans F.K. *Rassenkunde des jüdischen Volkes*. Munich: Eher, 1929.

Hare, Peter. "The Abuse of Holocaust Studies: Mercy Killing and the Slippery Slope." in Rosenberg, Alan and Myers, Gerald, eds., *Echoes from the Holocaust: Philosophical Reflections on a Dark Time*. Philadelphia: Fortress Press, 1988.

Just, Karl. *Eugenik und Weltanschauung*. Berlin: Reichert, 1932.

Kater, Michael. *Doctors under Hitler*. Chapel Hill, NC: University of North Carolina Press, 1989.

Kaup, L. "Was kosten die minderwertigen Elemente dem Staat und der Gesellschaft." *Archiv für Rassen und Gesellschaftsbiologie* 10, 1913, 720-27.

Lenz, Fritz. *Menschliche Auslese und Rassenhygiene (Eugenik)*. Munich: J.F. Lehmann, 1921.

Lilienthal, Georg. "Rassenhygiene im Dritten Reich." *Medizinhistorischen Journal* 14, 1979, 114-32.

Lilienthal, Georg. "Rheinlandbastarde, Rassenhygiene und das Problem der rassenideologischen Kontinuität." *Medizinhistorisches Journal* 15, 1980, 426-36.

Lippert, Peter. "Der Gemeinschaftsmensch." *Stimmen der Zeit* 128, 1935, 361-70.

Mann, Günter, ed. *Biologismus im 19. Jahrhundert. Vorträge eines Symposiums von 30. bis 31. Oktober 1970 im Frankfurt am Main*. Stuttgart: Ferdinard Enke, 1973.

Mayer, Joseph. "Euthanasie im Lichte der katholischen Moral und Praxis." Staatsarchiv Nürnberg, KV-Anklage Dokumente Nr. ZZ266 Rep. 502, 1, 1939-1940.

Mayer, Joseph. "Eugenische Sterilisierung?" *Schönere Zukunft* 34, 1933, 814-15, 837-39.

Mayer, Joseph. *Gesetzliche Unfruchtbarmachung Geisteskranken*. Freiburg: Herder, 1927.

Mayer, Joseph. "Sexualprobleme zur Strafrechtsreform." *Theologie und Glaube* 21, 1929, 137-62.

Mayer, Joseph. "Vorschläge für ein eugenisches Aufbauprogram." *Schönere Zukunft 37*, 1933, 887-88.

Muckermann, Hermann. "Die Enzyklika 'Casti Connubii' und die Eugenik." *Ethik* 8, 1931, 339-400.

Muckermann, Hermann. *Eugenik.* Berlin: Dümmler, 1934.

Muckermann, Hermann. "Eugenik und Katholizismus." In Günther Just, ed. *Eugenik und Weltanschauung.* Berlin: Alfred Metzler, 1932.

Muckermann, Hermann. "Illustrationen zu der Frage: Wohlfahrtspflege und Eugenik." *Eugenik* 2, 1931, 40-44.

Muckermann, Hermann. *Kind und Volk.* 3rd ed. Freiburg: Herder, 1920.

Muckermann, Hermann. "Um das Leben des Ungebornen." *Stimmen der Zeit* 94, 1918, 339-44.

Muckermann, Hermann. *Vererbung und Entwicklung.* 2nd ed. Bonn: Dummler, 1947.

Muckermann, Hermann. "Der Wert von Strafgesetzen zum Schutz des keimenden Lebens." *Stimmen der Zeit* 100, 1921, 12-25.

Muckermann, Hermann. "Die Wirkungen des Alkoholgenusses auf die Nachkommenschaft." In Johannes Thiken, ed. *Die Alkoholfrage in Wohlfartspflege und Sozialpolitik.* Vol. 1. Berlin: Neuland, 1928.

Muckermann, Hermann. "Wohlfahrtspflege und Eugenik." *Caritas* 11, 1932, 157-62.

Müller, Joachim. *Sterilisation und Gesetzgebung bis 1933.* Husum: Matthias Verlag, 1985.

Müller-Hill, Benno. *Murderous Science: Elimination by Scientific Selection of Jews, Gypsies, and Others: Germany, 1933-1945.* New York: Oxford University Press, 1988.

Müncker, Theodor. *Die psychologischen Grundlagen der katholischen Sittenlehre.* Düsseldorf: L. Schwann, 1934.

Niedermeyer, Albert. "Die Bedeutung der Enzyklika 'Casti Connubii' für Eugenik in Wissenschaft und Praxis." In K. Kleineidam and O. Kuss, eds. *Die Kirche und die Welt. Beiträge zur christlichen Besinnung in der Gegenwart.* Salzburg: Pustet, 1937.

Niedermeyer, Albert. *Handbuch der spezieller Pastoralmedizin.* 6 vols. Vienna: Herder, 1949-1952.

Pribilla, Max. "Christliche Haltung." *Stimmen der Zeit* 135, 1939, 169-79.

Pribilla, Max. "Ehe und Familie." *Stimmen der Zeit* 134, 1938, 53-56.

Proctor, Robert. *Racial Hygiene: Medicine under the Nazis.* Cambridge, MA: Harvard University Press, 1988.

Schilling, Otto. "Von der sozialen Gerechtigkeit." *Theologische Quartalschrift* 120, 1939, 197-205.

Schmuhl, Hans-Walter. *Rassenhygiene, Nationalsozialisimus, Euthanasie: Von der Verhutung zur Vernichtung 'lebensunwerten Lebens,' 1890-1945.* Göttingen: Vandenhoeck and Ruprecht, 1987.

Tajfel, H. *Human Groups and Social Categories.* Cambridge: Cambridge University Press, 1981.

Tillmann, Fritz. *Die katholische Sittenlehre. Die Idee der Nachfolge Christi.* Düsseldorf: L. Schwann, 1934.

von Verscheuer, Othmar. "Die Eugenik des Hermann Muckermann." *Flugblatt des Erneuerung Deutschlands* 16, 1932, 462-66.

Wagner, G. "Unser Reichsärzteführer spricht." *Ziel und Weg* 19, 1935, 432.

Webster, Charles. *Biology, Medicine, and Society: 1840-1940.* Cambridge: Cambridge University Press, 1981.

Weiss, Sheila. *Race Hygiene and National Efficiency: The Eugenics of Wilhelm Schallmayer.* Berkeley: University of California Press, 1987.

Witetschek, Helmut, ed. *Die kirchliche Lage in Bayern nach der Regierungspräsidentenberichten, Vol. II, 1933-1943, Regierungsbezirk Ober–und Mittelfranken.* Mainz: Matthias Grünewald Verlag, 1967.

Zeiger, Ivo. "Katholische Moraltheologie Heute." *Stimmen der Zeit* 134, 1938, 143-53.

Zeiger, Ivo. "Werde, der du Bist." *Stimmen der Zeit* 133, 1938, 298-307.

Zmärzlik, Hans-Günter. "Der Sozialdarwinismus in Deutschland als geschichtliches Problem." *Vierteljahrshefte für Zeitgeschichte* 11, 1963, 246-73.

9

Euthanasia in Nazi Propaganda Films: Selling Murder

John J. Michalczyk

In the Third Reich, the medium of propaganda film was utilized to disseminate diverse Nazi policies. While *Triumph of the Will* (1935) and *Baptism of Fire* (1940) revealed the strength of the military and political arm of the Reich, *The Eternal Jew* (1940) and *Jud Süss* (1940), depicted virulent anti-semitic views, especially of the Slavic races.[1] From the mid-thirties through the early forties, the Reich also exploited film to promote its euthanasia program. These policies, promoted under the hereditary health law, are graphically presented in the recent documentary *Selling Murder: The Killing Films of the Third Reich*.[2] An analysis of the film with an accompanying commentary, will provide some insights into the inhumane and unethical euthanasia policies of the Nazi government.

Selling Murder opens and closes with a profound spiritual memorial in June 1991 for those who died under the Nazi euthanasia program. It takes place at one of the more infamous euthanasia centers, Hadamar. This center, along with others, such as the Hartheim Castle near Linz, operated as an integral part of a program for the systematic elimination of the handicapped. In order to build a "clean" and "healthy" Germany, certain "sickly" elements had to be removed. At Hadamar, the mentally and

---

1. For a further discussion of the propaganda value of film in Nazi Germany see David Stewart Hull, *Film in the Third Reich* (New York: Simon and Schuster, 1973), and on *Ich klage an!*, pp. 200-203. Erwin Leiser, in *Nazi Cinema* (New York: Collier Books, 1974), is much more detailed. Leiser includes an analysis of several of the euthanasia films, a lengthy excerpt from *Ich klage an!*, and various responses to the work.

2. *Selling Murder: The Killing Films of the Reich* (1991) was produced by Stewart Lansley, directed by Joanna Mack and written by Michael Burleigh. The film was produced by British Channel 4 and Domino Productions, using extensive historic footage from the Koblenz and Berlin film archives, among other sources. One significant sequence in the film *Architecture of Doom* (1991) by Peter Cohen, covers some of the same general medical ground as *Selling Murder* with a central thesis of the "aesthetic cleansing" of Germany.

physically disabled, considered "Life unworthy of life," were processed "mercifully" to carry out the government orders.[3] In creating a new and healthy Germany, more than 200,000 handicapped people were eliminated through starvation, gas, or lethal injection. The film asks rhetorically, "What sort of people were capable of doing such cruel deeds?"

With a determined attitude to record and preserve, the Nazi government documented via film the several stages of the euthanasia program as it laid the groundwork for the Final Solution. Ironically, this documentation would later be critical in sentencing the participating Nazi officials at the Nuremberg Doctors' Trial in December 1946.[4]

Two early films of the thirties provide the racial and biological theory necessary to justify mercy killing, theories that already appeared in seminal form in *Mein Kampf.* These prototypes were created as so-called educational films. Despite their technically amateur production, they furnish in seminal form the historical and scientific bases upon which the euthanasia program was constructed. These films expose the apparent tragic state of the hereditarily ill by deliberately stigmatizing their situation. Although much of the incriminating evidence was destroyed by the Nazis once defeat became imminent, scripts and footage were at times discovered, as was the case in Potsdam.

The two silent documentaries depict images of the most severely mentally handicapped patients—*Was du erbst* (What You Inherit), and *Erb Krank* (The Herditarily Ill, 1935).

These films, with frequent staged scenes of degradation, were primarily destined for Party members and Nazi supporters. More scientifically developed were two other more professional documentaries, *Opfer der Vergangenheit* (Victims of the Past, 1937) and *Das Erbe* (The Inheritance). As an integral part of the "enlightenment" or propaganda program, *Opfer der Vergangenheit* was produced under Hitler's direct order and shown by law in all 5,300 German theatres. It relied heavily on 19th Century hereditary studies, primarily Darwinian theories of natural selection. Modern discoveries in medicine help keep seriously ill people alive, the propaganda film argues. This is, however, against the basic principles of Nature. The chronically ill and the handicapped lead unproductive and meaningless lives and thus burden our society. The economic rationale for euthanasia is then proposed—If these unhealthy individuals were removed from society, how much money could be saved to house healthy people?

---

3. For an illustrated account of the euthanasia program displayed at the U.S. Holocaust Museum, see "Murder of the Handicapped," in Michael Berenbaum's *The World Must Know* (Boston: Little, Brown and Company, 1993), pp. 64-65.

4. For more detailed results of the euthanasia program as connected with the medical crimes against humanity, see George Annas and Michael Grodin, eds. *The Nazi Doctors and the Nuremberg Code* (New York: Oxford University Press, 1992).

The biological rationale offered here further maintains that the hereditarily ill, if allowed to multiply, would become a genetic threat to the health of Germany. Compulsory sterilization would prevent this disaster. This would be one of the first steps in the "healing of the State." Statistics recorded indicate that between 1933 and 1939, 350,000 individuals were sterilized based on this premise.

The second film, *Das Erbe* (The Inheritance) develops the same Darwinian struggle for survival in a more dramatic manner. Using fiction and documentary footage, the film reinforces the Darwinian principle that the strongest survive through natural selection. The medical and scientific authority figures in the film attempt to apply the inferior/superior analogy from the animal kingdom to the human realm. The juxtaposition of weak animals with mental patients in asylums reinforces the message that the weakest, by Nature's law, should not be allowed to survive. Not unlike the spirit reflected in *Triumph of the Will*, the film jubilantly concludes with images of the pure Aryan—strong, healthy, and vigorous. A healthy national community is in Germany's best interest. The viewer draws the conclusion that in order to build a healthier country, the weak must be eliminated. *Selling Murder* then focuses on the step-by-step program of euthanasia, noting the program's formal initiation in October 1939, when Hitler authorized children, then adults, to be processed. His letter to Reich Leader Philip Bouhler and Hitler's personal physician, Dr. Karl Brandt, back-dated to 1 September 1939, charges them with

> "the responsibility to broaden the authority of certain doctors to the extent that (persons) suffering from illnesses judged to be incurable may, after a humane, most careful assessment of their condition, be granted a mercy death."[5]

After diagnoses, the "incurables" were transported to centers such as Hadamar. Eyewitnesses from the town recall that thirty or forty mental patients would arrive by train. In one or two postal buses with covered windows, they would be driven to the center atop the hill, and then totally disappear. As a normal procedure, these patients would be herded into areas designated as showers. Sixty at a time would be gassed. An orderly at the time, Paul Reuther, was allowed by the medical official in charge, Dr. Corgass, to witness the procedure through a peephole in the iron door. He graphically describes how the victims were gassed with carbon monoxide. The bodies were then disentangled and burned. Fake death certificates indicating their death by advanced pneumonia, lung collapse, or other serious complications, were then issued to the families along with a letter of condolence.

---

5. A copy of the letter is found in the U.S. Holocaust Museum's exhibit "Murder of the Handicapped," and in Berenbaum's publication *The World Must Know*, pp. 63-64.

This systematic "purification" of the Aryan race was supervised by Philip Bouhler, Chief of Hitler's chancellery, and commonly referred to as the AKTION T4, an operation named for its Berlin address, Tiergartenstrasse 4. As part of the program, doctors, psychiatrists, and nurses were integrated into the plan of mercy killing and often indoctrinated through films, training sessions, and later detailed procedures. In hindsight, sociopsychologists raise the same issues of obedience to authority in an unethical situation as does Stanley Millgram in his classic study *Obedience*.[6]

Following Hitler's letter to Philip Bouhler in October 1939, T4 commissioned two films *Dasein ohne Leben* (Existence without Life) and *Geisteskrank* (Mentally Ill). The films were designed to reassure those involved in the euthanasia program that this was an ethical and humane procedure. Although the film *Dasein ohne Leben* was destroyed at the end of the war by Germans as evidence of their unethical activity, the script testifies to the means of justification of death by mercy killing.

In a dramatic recreation of the script written by T4 psychiatrists, an honest-looking and serious professor offers a lecture on racial theory to an auditorium of captivated youths. It is billed as a human question that concerns us all. An occasional Nazi uniform can be seen in the audience. Graphically interspersed in the lecture is actual footage that was used in the documentary. As the professor clinically describes the masses of 400,000 German patients in mental asylums, images of the helpless wards punctuate his words. Schizophrenics, Down's Syndrome adults, and epileptics populate these asylums. The footage is shot so as to accentuate their disabilities in a dramatic manner, purposely suggesting an almost demonic aura about them. Close-ups of behavior considered abnormal, rolling eyes, and unusual grins, haunt the viewer. "Mental illness is a hereditary evil and the greatest danger to the health of the nation," the professor exclaims. The care of this burden on society is extensive, he further argues. It unjustifiably consumes the lives of 2,000 doctors and 40,000 nurses. In a pseudo-humane tone, the lecturer uses religious language of mercy killing to help "liberate" these creatures, while simultaneously denying these individuals their humanity. How cruel it would be to maintain these spiritually dead people as "living corpses." It is a sacred demand of charity that we eliminate the suffering of these helpless individuals, the film advocates. To show how humane this process is, the lecturer concludes by confessing that if he were struck down by a crippling disease, he himself would opt for mercy killing.

---

6. See Stanley Millgram's critical study of "Obedience" based on his 1962 experiments at Yale University released as a film by Penn State University in 1965. For a study of more current issues, see Herbert C. Kelman and V. Lee Hamilton, *Crimes of Obedience: Toward A Social Psychology of Authority and Responsibility* (New Haven: Yale University Press, 1989).

The second film, *Geisteskrank* appears to have been a more classi-
fied documentary. The film apparently no longer exists, but the script was
recently discovered in the East German Stasi files at the close of the Cold
War. The film argues that electro-shock can help certain mentally disabled
patients, but there are many others that are incurable. Its thesis reiterates
the fact that these incurables would be left to vegetate without a purpose
in life. Implied is the necessity to eliminate them in a merciful way.

The script offers a step-by-step description of the mercy killing of
those suffering from Down's Syndrome, schizophrenia, severe deafness or
blindness, and others listed as "incurable." They were selected on the basis of their unproductive state or the failure of relatives to visit them. The
bureaucratic T4 staff, paid on a piece-meal basis, seldom saw the patients,
and only cursorily looked at their files before the victims were sent to
their deaths. These files were given a scientific appearance, heavily documented with intelligence tests, medical records, and psychological reports,
as if to justify the staff's actions.[7] Once sent to the chambers, carbon
monoxide gas "delivered" them from their debilitated state. In the film,
Elvira Monthey, slated for the chambers, was spared at the last minute
and testified to the inhumane process.

The townspeople near the Hadamar center suspected something by
the arrival of trainloads and busloads of patients. The dark, pungent
smoke cloud from the center's chimney provided a further clue to what
was occurring. The citizens felt helpless to act since everything was secre-
tive about the mercy killings. The Bishop of Munster, Count von Galen,
however, protested the euthanasia in a pastoral letter dated 3 August 1941.
It stated that this was morally wrong, and that the perpetrators were guilty
of murder. One citizen, Paula Sarach, also exhibited too much interest in
these activities and spent six months at the Ravensbrück concentration
camp as an example to the citizens of Hadamar of what would happen to
dissidents.

The last propaganda film treated in *Selling Murder* is *Ich klage an!*
(I Accuse, 1941), based on the novel *Sendung und Gewissen* (*Mission and
Conscience*) by T4 doctor and writer Helmut Unger. The full-length, melo-
dramatic yet provocative work advocating euthanasia was directed by a
leading filmmaker, Wolfgang Liebeneiner, for Tobis Studios, and had a
completely professional and commercial quality to it.

Hanna Heyt, an established pianist, is married to Thomas, a prominent scientist. Her former suitor, Bernard Lundt, is a close friend and
family doctor. When she begins to deteriorate physically from multiple
sclerosis, she is adamant that she does not want to live out her life in a

---

7. Robert J. Lifton in *The Nazi Doctors* (New York: Basic Books, 1986),
discusses the medical bureaucrats who signed the euthanasia orders as "desk
criminals." These were normally senior physicians, while the doctors who were
obliged to carry them out were often younger and less experienced.

vegetative state. After consultation with Bernard, her husband provides her with an overdose of medication which kills her. The subsequent court room drama is intense, as Thomas accuses the law of not helping in the case of his wife's suffering. The defense concludes that the law must be changed to allow mercy killing for humanitarian reasons. The film ends by putting the verdict in the hands of the audience.

Ich klage an! was a popular means of rationalizing mercy killing by challenging the current legal status. It was viewed by 15 million Germans and won a prize at the Venice Biennale Festival. Catholics, however, did not agree with the conclusion of the film, feeling that it was anti-Catholic in principle and used propaganda to justify murder. The film nonetheless clouded the mercy killing issue, failing to distinguish between voluntary euthanasia and the State-sanctioned policy of eliminating any unwanted sector of society. The director, Wolfgang Liebeneiner, in 1965, stated that this was "no propaganda film but on the contrary a document of humanity in an inhuman time."[8]

In early 1942, following the Wannsee Conference, mass euthanasia programs formally ceased. Euthanasia, however, was still allowed to continue on a private basis. The knowledge and experience gained from the euthanasia program, nonetheless, would now be used in the Final Solution in the East, for example in Chelmno, Poland, to provide "Special Treatment" to Jews, Gypsies, and political prisoners.[9]

In May 1945, U.S. Army film crews documented the mass murders for the Nuremberg War Crimes tribunal.[10] More than eleven thousand bodies were found in mass graves in Hadamar. These were individuals believed by the doctors and the medical staff to represent "Life unworthy of life," neither patients nor human beings.

As the film concludes, he memorial bell at Hadamar tolls a warning not to allow this to happen again.

Selling Murder: The Killing Films of the Reich is a powerful testimony to the Nazi euthanasia policies based on hereditary health laws. Through the interviews with witnesses, graphic footage of the mental patients, and the recreation of a film-lecture justifying the policy, the film provides an unsettling look into the mechanisms that drove the Nazis to sterilize or eliminate hundreds of thousands of German citizens who had no rights in this bio-centric State. *Selling Murder* furnishes the viewer with a keen insight into the rationale behind these decisions, normally

---

8. Leiser, p. 149.

9. Lucy S. Dawidowicz offers a succinct glimpse of the evolution from the euthanasia program to the extermination camps, in *The War Against the Jews 1933-1945* (New York: Bantam, 1975), esp. pp. 131-135.

10. Extensive U.S. Army footage from the camps can be viewed through the National Archives in Washington, D.C., as well as the National Center for Jewish Film at Brandeis University.

based on economic fears and pseudo-racial threats to the well-being of Nazi Germany. With provocative images, it reveals the specific, systematic plan to eliminate the severely handicapped, the lack of any consent in sterilization, and the complete deception or cover-up to avoid detection of the immoral policies. The film, however, does not develop in depth the psychology of the euthanasia mass murderer so as to answer the question raised at its outset about the cruelty of these physicians. Nevertheless, it provides the historical setting and processes that are crucial in understanding the collaboration of Third Reich politics and medicine.

Fifty years after T4 attempted to carry out its master plan for a genetically safe Germany, the issue of euthanasia has been at the center of heated debate. Although current controversies most often focus on the patient's right to die, the role of the doctor becomes a crucial element in the debate. The physician, committed by the Hippocratic Oath to the healing of a patient, becomes linked with the death of a patient, and in current cases, one in a terminally ill condition. Contemporary society raises the questions about the morality of euthanasia not so much to draw graphic parallels with Nazi policies that we see carried out in this documentary, but to help establish the dignity of the dying patient and the moral integrity of the physician. Sadly, when there is a threat to either or both, one has the ominous feeling that the past has unfortunately caught up with us.

III.

Human Experimentation:
"Am I My Brother's Keeper?"

10

The Concentration Camp Experiments: Their Relevance for Contemporary Research with Human Beings[1]

Jay Katz[2]

In writing this essay I have asked myself, more insistently than ever before, one question: Were the concentration camp experiments so unique in the history of medical experimentation with human beings that they can teach us little, if anything, about the conduct of research in the Western world? Generally, they have been viewed as a singular aberration and, therefore, of little relevance for research practices, past and present. The utterly inhumane, totally expendable ways in which the subjects had served purposes of research, reminiscent of the cruelest animal experimentation, led to this judgment and precluded any comparative analysis of what transpired at Auschwitz and other concentration camps in the name of science.

I shall contend, however, that the Nazi experiments are relevant for our time and that their uniqueness resides in one aspect of what transpired at Auschwitz, an aspect which, to begin with, was extraneous to the concentration camp experiments: The Final Solution. It envisioned the eventual total extermination of certain "lives not worth living"[3] and thus facili-

1. I want to express my thanks to Irene Adams, Amy Goldminz, Sally Katz, Dori Laub, Peter Mostow, Howard Needler, Tony Perry, Ernst Prelinger, Katherine Weinstein and Alan Weisbard for their insightful comments on earlier drafts of this essay. I am particularly indebted to my wife Marilyn Katz for her critical wisdom which is reflected throughout this essay.

2. Elizabeth K. Dollard Professor Emeritus of Law, Medicine and Psychiatry, and Harvey L. Karp Professorial Lecturer in Law and Psychoanalysis, Yale Law School.

3. For a historical account of the idea of the destruction of "lives not worth living," beginning with the Nazi extermination of handicapped children and psychiatric patients and ending with the destruction of racial and ethnic minorities, see Robert Proctor, *Racial Hygiene—Medicine under the Nazis*, Cambridge, Mass:

tated the inflicting of deliberate pain, sadistic torture and intentional death as integral aspects of the research design. The inevitable and understandable reluctance to sort through this debris of barbarism and agony has made its own contribution to the dismissal of the Nazi experiments as irrelevant to an understanding of research practices in the Western world.

Yet, the conviction that these experiments have nothing to teach us about the conduct of research has other, perhaps deeper roots: an unwillingness to acknowledge that the concentration camp experiments illuminate in starkest form the impact of the ethos of science in its relentless search for truth on the treatment of human beings as research subjects. Scientists' commitment to the morality of acquiring knowledge for the benefit of mankind can all too readily lead to the disregard of another moral imperative: not to use human beings as means for others' ends. For although it has been asserted, and with some plausibility, that the objects of scientific knowledge (such as gravity) do not possess moral status, the same cannot be said of scientific inquiry, which, as the case of Galileo demonstrated, is always a moral and social enterprise. And when the objects of scientific investigations are human beings, both the objects and the inquiry have moral dimensions.

I shall also comment at some length on the Allied Military Tribunal's Nuremberg Code for human research. It has been considered of limited relevance for medical research in a civilized world, even though the judges believed that they were only setting forth "basic principles [that] must be observed in order to satisfy moral, ethical and legal concepts,"[4] principles which they thought the scientific community had embraced long before the Nazi era. This assumption was incorrect. The judges nevertheless left us a legacy which deserves more careful thought than the scientific community has given it so far.

To illustrate my contentions about the relevance of the concentration camp experiments and the Nuremberg Code for contemporary research, I begin with four stories from the history of human experimentation both contemporaneous with, and subsequent to Auschwitz, in order to identify some of the problems inherent in all scientific research with human beings which seeks to advance knowledge for the future benefit of humanity:

1. *The U.S. Armed Forces Chemical Defense Research Program*: During World War II "at least 4,000 U.S. servicemen participated in tests conducted with high concentration of mustard agents or Lewisite in gas cham-

Harvard University Press 177-222 (1988).

4. *Trials of War Criminals Before the Nuremberg Military Tribunal*, Volumes I & II, The Medical Case, U.S. Government Printing Office, Vol. II, at 181 (1948) [hereinafter *Trials of War Criminals*].

bers or open field exercises."[5] The subjects were either told little about the nature of the experiments or deceived about the purpose of the studies. Although it had been known for years that exposure to mustard gas caused long-term debilitating health problems requiring medical attention, the subjects were "sworn to secrecy" and told to reveal nothing about their participation, even to their physicians.

When in the early 1990s the secret could no longer be contained, the Department of Veterans' Affairs asked the Institute of Medicine (IOM) to appoint a committee to "assess . . . the association between exposure to [mustard gas] agents and the development of specific diseases, identify gaps in the literature and recommend strategies and approaches to deal with the gaps found."[6] When I appeared before the committee, I urged that it go beyond its limited scientific charge and condemn the ways in which the experiments had been conducted.

In the Preface to its Final Report, the IOM Committee commented on the abuses perpetrated by the military and its scientists. It noted that not only the World War II experiments but also similar experiments conducted from 1950-1975, years after the revelations at Nuremberg, "demonstrated a well-nigh ingrained pattern of abuse and neglect. Although the human subjects were called 'volunteers,' it was clear from the official reports that recruitment of the World War II human subjects, as well as many of those in later experiments, was accomplished through lies and half-truths."[7] In support of this conclusion, the Committee included in the appendix to its Report a revealing document:

> The fact that has been most obvious throughout these experiments is that when the men first began the work they should not be told too much. If they are, it sets up a fear reaction that remains for varying lengths of time and definitely affects their "virgin" runs in the chamber. . . .
>
> Occasionally there have been individuals, or groups, who did not cooperate fully. A short explanatory talk, and, if necessary, a slight verbal "dressing down" has always proven successful. There has not been a single instance in which a man refused to enter the gas chamber. . . .
>
> No man is sent into the chamber without the Medical Officer's approval. Occasionally at this point, malingerers and psychoneurotics are discovered. These cases have all been handled so far by minimizing their symptoms and then sending them into the chambers.[8]

---

5. Constance M. Pechura and David P. Rall, eds.: *Veterans at Risk—The Health Effects of Mustard Gas and Lewisite*, Washington, D.C., National Academy Press 1 (1933).

6. *Ibid.* at vi.

7. *Ibid.* at vii.

8. *Ibid.* at 346-47.

"Most appalling," the committee went on to observe, "was the fact that no formal long-term follow-up medical care or monitoring was provided . . . Although the experiments began in a wartime climate of urgency and secrecy, it was clearly a mistake . . . to continue the secrecy after the conclusion of the war . . . Further, these men were ordered to keep their participation secret. They did so for 50 years in some cases, despite serious disabling diseases . . . There can be no question that some veterans, who served our country with honor and at a great personal cost were mistreated twice—first, in the secret testing and second, by the official denials that lasted for decades. . . ."[9]

2. *The Tuskegee Syphilis Study*: From 1932-1972 the U.S. Public Health Service (USPHS) conducted research on 400 African-American men in Macon County, Alabama, to study the natural history of untreated syphilis from its inception to death.[10] Their syphilitic condition had been discovered during a demonstration project on the incidence of syphilis in the South, initially designed also to provide treatment once their condition was diagnosed. However, when money for treatment became unavailable, the USPHS physicians seized the "golden opportunity" to conduct research with persons considered inferior, lives not worth respecting. The subjects were apprised neither of the nature of their illness nor of what could and could not be done for them therapeutically. They were not informed that their yearly physical checkups were in the service of research and not treatment. When in the early 1940's effective treatment became available, penicillin was deliberately withheld from them, even though it was known that in the absence of treatment, some of the subjects would suffer premature death and many more would be exposed to the cardiovascular and cerebral ravages of tertiary syphilis.

3. *Research with Patients Suffering from Alzheimer's Disease*: Recently the Institutional Review Board (IRB) of the National Institute on Aging (NIA) asked me to respond to the following question: "Should patients suffering from Alzheimer's disease who are incompetent to give their consent be used for purposes of research that both exposes them to greater than minimal risks, and provides no therapeutic benefits for them?" This was not a new question. NIA had raised it ten years earlier, when it appointed a Task Force "to design a set of guidelines that might be of help to researchers as well as to those who formulate and review research protocols . . ."[11] Four members of that Task Force subsequently published an

---

9. *Ibid.* at vii-viii.

10. U.S. Department of Health, Education and Welfare, Public Health Service: *Final Report of the Tuskegee Syphilis Study Ad Hoc Advisory Panel* (1973); Alan M. Brandt: Racism and Research—The Tuskegee Syphilis Study, 8 *Hastings Center Report* 21-29 (Dec. 1978).

11. Vijaya L. Meinick, Nancy N. Dubler, Alan Weisbard and Robert N. Butler,

article which set forth "guidelines that resulted from [its] deliberations."[12] With respect to the question once again posed to me, the task force had concluded:

> . . . It may be that in at least some instances, the importance of research may ethically justify interventions posing greater than minimal risk on a willing subject who lacks the capacity to grant legally effective informed consent, even in the absence of any realistic probability of direct therapeutic benefit to the subject. Such a conclusion *must rest on a thoroughgoing assessment of the risks involved and of the scientific importance of the research.* When the local IRB believes these conditions are met, the sensitivity and the public importance of the issue strongly indicate the advisability of further definitive review of the particular protocol by a national ethics advisory body whose decisions shall be made in the course of a public process. . . .[13]

The article, in its entirety, was carefully crafted and included a number of judicious statements on the lengths to which investigators should go to seek approval for such research. The national body proposed by the authors, however, however, has not yet been established by Congress and given *the authority not merely to advise but to make such fateful decisions, subject to Congressional review.* Therefore, I argued that such research cannot yet be conducted, and my answer to the question posed by NIA was "no." Since such research transgresses our deep commitment to the inviolability of personal autonomy and, instead, uses human beings without consent for our benefit, an explicit societal mandate is required before physician-investigators should be allowed to proceed. If approval is granted, investigators will, of course, conduct such experiments infinitely more humanely than did the Nazi physician-scientists, but this may still be a step taken down their road.

4. *The University of California, Los Angeles /UCLA/ Schizophrenia Project*: During the 1980s and early 1990s a series of experiments were carried on at UCLA with recovered schizophrenic patients, all on antipsychotic medication.[14] The project was designed to take these patient-subjects off medication in order to determine who would relapse and to what level of psychotic disorganization. The research design anticipated, at least

---

Clinical Research in Senile Dementia of the Alzheimer Type, 32 *J. of the American Geriatric Society*, 531 (1984).

12. *Ibid.*

13. *Ibid.* at 535. The article leaves unclear how a person "who lacks the capacity to grant legally effective informed consent" can be deemed a "willing subject."

14. Jay Katz, Human Experimentation and Human Rights, 38 *St. Louis University Law Journal* 7, 41-15 (1993)/Hereinafter *Human Experimentation/*. *See* also James Willwerth, Tinkering with Madness, 42 *Time* 41-42 (August 30, 1992).

in some instances, a relapse to the severest levels of psychosis, and some of the subjects did regress to such levels. The informed consent agreement, approved by UCLA's Institutional Review Board, was utterly deficient in warning the subjects in clear, understandable and explicit language of the great risks which their participation entailed. I can only mention in passing that in 1993 similar concerns about the adequacy of consent agreements were raised about two National Institutes of Health research projects, one of which was designed to explore the benefits of various hormone-replacement regimens to reduce the incidence of breast cancer,[15] the other to study the benefits of a new drug for the treatment of Hepatitis B.[16]

I present these four examples to illustrate that questionable research is still being conducted in civilized, democratic societies. To be sure, such research does not descend to the barbarism and sadism with which the concentration camp subjects were treated. That, as I have already suggested, was unique. Not unique is the proclivity and power of medical science to condone victimization in the name of science.

In this essay, I shall not recount the concentration camp experiments which, in the words of the Allied Military Tribunal "were conducted with unnecessary suffering and injury and . . . very little, if any, precautions . . . to protect or safeguard the human subjects from the possibilities of injury, disability, or death."[17] These experiments are well-known: the high altitude, the sea water, the malaria, the typhoid, the phosgene gas and many other experiments as well. At the Nuremberg Trial the Nazi physicians defended them on grounds of national necessity, *i.e.,* the need to learn as quickly as possible how to protect their own military and civilian populations from the ravages of disease and death during war time conditions. They also asserted that many of these experiments went beyond these most pressing immediate concerns and made important contributions to the advancement of science for the benefit of all mankind.[18]

Similar claims were advanced by the investigators of the four experiments I have presented: The necessity to conduct research in order to advance knowledge and to protect mankind against the ravages of disease and death. These claims identify ethical problems common to human experimentation both inside and outside of concentration camps: (1) The existence of a "national emergency" that led to the Nazi experiments and the

---

15. Warren E. Leary, Questions Raised on Drugs Used in Breast Cancer Study, *The New York Times* A23 (Oct. 23, 1993).

16. Lawrence L. Altman, Fatal Drug Trial Raises Questions about "Informed Consent," *The New York Times* B7 (Oct. 5, 1993).

17. *Trials of War Criminals, supra* note 1, Vol. II at 183.

18. For a more detailed discussion of the controvesy over the scientific status of the concentration camp experiments, see the articles by Robert S. Pozos, Robert L. Berger, Jay Katz and Pozos, and Katz in Caplan, A.L. *When Medicine Went Mad.* Totowa, N.J.: Humana Press 95-108, 109-33, 135-139, 233-270 (1993).

American experiments which, beyond mustard gas studies, extended to research with Native Americans on the effects of Uranium poisoning,[19] designed to provide better protection against atomic attacks; or with schizophrenic patients in reputable psychiatric hospitals on the effects of LSD and other mind-altering drugs[20] in order to learn more about brainwashing techniques that our enemies were then developing. (2) The need to extend the frontiers of knowledge for the sake of reducing human suffering which can readily lead to less than forthright disclosures as in the cases of women with breast cancer or patients suffering from hepatitis B, to mention only two of countless examples.

These experiments illustrate the terrible consequences which human experimentation can entail: the pain, suffering, abandonment and cruelty which the human subjects in the American army mustard gas experiments had to endure; the likelihood of premature death or severe physical disabilities to which the Tuskegee subjects were exposed; the exploitation for the benefit of future patients of Alzheimer's disease patients whose consent is unobtainable not because of political but because of biological status; the suffering to which schizophrenic patients in the UCLA experiments were exposed not of their own free choosing but by manipulation of their consent as evidenced in the agreement they signed.

All these studies share in common a disregard of the human subjects' dignitary interests, albeit for the noble scientific purpose of alleviating the pain and suffering of other human beings. The socially and economically deprived as well as the racially and ethnically disfavored are all too frequently recruited for human research and precluded from exercising their rights to free and fully informed choice. The history of human experimentation with prostitutes, men and women afflicted with syphilis, gonorrhea, or tuberculosis, and children who are mentally retarded, attests to all this.[21] And so does in today's world the ubiquitous recruitment of persons from Third World countries for the testing of new contraceptive devices and other innovative treatments. In recent decades, matters have improved, but not sufficiently so.

The concentration camp experiments, as I have already noted, were unique in one respect only: they were embedded in a national policy of total extermination of despised and "dangerous" racial, ethnic and political groups whose lives were not considered worth living and who were condemned to eventual death. Participation in research was at best only a temporary respite on the road to extinction. Yet, uniqueness in torture and brutality notwithstanding, the link between the concentration camp ex-

---

19. *Begay v. United States* 663 F.2d 1226 (3rd. Cir. 1981).

20. *Barret v. United States* (1987).

21. Jay Katz, *Experimentation with Human Beings.* New York: The Russell Sage Foundation 284-291, 957-964 (1972).

periments and current unethical research is there to be seen: persons and groups who occupy a lower station in society all too often bear the brunt of experimentation. The recent revelations about the radiation experiments[22] demonstrate "that scientists take their guinea pigs (retarded children, Native Americans, prisoners, the poor, the aged) where they find them, and they find them just where society and social prejudice leaves them."[23] The African-Americans of Tuskegee to be sure were also disrespected, deprived of decent housing, jobs and medical care. All this and more made many of them syphilitics, untreated ones at that and, thus, ready victims for an "experiment in nature" which, however, was not ordained by nature but by a white society that did not care. And, some of these subjects would die or become severely disabled because the physician-investigators had made common cause with a racist society that tolerated such outcomes by superimposing a medical, experimental dimension on such a fate.

The Holocaust was different, however. Unlike Jews and Gypsies, the State did not relegate all African-Americans to eventual extinction. It was the convergence of assigning human beings to categories marked for political, racial, ethnic and biological discrimination *and* for death which led to torture on an unprecedented scale. The horror of the Holocaust, its call for the Final Solution, and the research practices it then spawned, however, should not blind us from recognizing smaller scale examples of unpardonable human abuse in the conduct of research. It occurs, as my stories seek to illustrate, when such convergence is not so total; *i.e.,* when persons are reduced to the status of objects as a result of racial discrimination, are demeaned because of their social status, are discounted because of their terminal illness, or are stripped of their autonomy, as patients too often are, by virtue of the imputed incompetence which being ill supposedly engenders. Human beings then readily can become means for our ends, aided and abetted by other justifications, so compellingly rational that we overlook what we are doing to them.

If we put aside the torture for a moment, the lessons to be learned from the concentration camp experiments are these: the obvious one that the ethics of medical research should never permit experiments on persons whose lives the State considers expendable. The misuse of human beings is then an inexorable consequence. For that reason proposals to use prisoners condemned to death for experimental purposes have never gained much favor.

---

22. Gary Less, U.S. Should Pay Victims, O'Leary Says 800 Were Deliberately Exposed to Radiation; David Armstrong, Energy Chief Reveals, *Washington Post* A1 (Dec. 29, 1993); State Expects Further 1940s-50s Revelations, *Boston Globe* 1 (Dec. 29, 1993). Keith Schneider, Anguish on Both Sides in Human Experimentation, *The New York Times* A12 (March 2, 1994).

23. Peter Mostow, Personal Communication (1994).

Beyond this obvious lesson lurk more hidden lessons to be learned: Auschwitz can shed light on Tuskegee by teaching us that the mere availability of persons "imprisoned" by society to remain syphilitics and altogether condemned to live under degraded conditions should frustrate and preclude their use for experimental purposes. Dachau can shed light on the Armed Forces mustard gas experiments by teaching us that the availability of soldiers, subject to the chains of command, should not allow their participation in research unless the greatest care is taken not to exploit their subservient status by manipulations of their free consent. Ravensbrück can shed light on research in hospitals and Third World countries by teaching us that those afflicted by disease, terminal illness, biological accidents, or those degraded in status by social and political conditions, should not be used lightly, if at all, for others' purposes. These grave moral problems have not been squarely confronted and, therefore, I want to put what I have already said more challengingly: the concentration camp experiments ought to teach us that the use of patients so readily available as subjects for research raises profound questions of when and how they can be invited to participate in research because their situation at times makes manipulation of consent so inevitable, so tainted by anxiety, fear and coercion.

The historian Mario Biagioli pleaded that we need "to understand how [medical] science became [and could again become] implicated in tragedies"[24] of the proportion of the concentration camp experiments. It became implicated, as I have already suggested, because the Nazi research community did not appreciate, as their fellow scientists in the civilized world also did not, that certain subject populations cannot be used for experimental purposes however noble the purpose and however grievous a loss to the advancement of science.[25] Any exception can readily lead to a confusion of means and ends and, thus, invite tragic consequences. A friend of mine, on a recent trip to Israel, overheard a commentary on the repetition of the word justice in Deuteronomy: "Justice, justice, shalt thou pursue."[26] This was the commentary: "Justice can never be adequately pursued only as a goal or an ideal; it is also reflected in the means employed."[27]

Recall that the concentration camp experiments began when German medical science was confronted with an important research question: how better to protect German airmen from the effects of being shot down at

---

24. Mario Biagioli, Science, Modernity and the "Final Solution." In Saul Friedlander, ed.: *Probing the Limits of Representation*. Cambridge, Mass.: Harvard University Press 185, 205 (1992).

25. Hans Jonas: Philosophical Reflections on Experimenting with Human Beings, 98 *Daedalus* 245 (1969)/hereinafter *Philosophical Reflections*.

26. *Deuteronomy* 16:20.

27. Tony Perry, Personal Communication (1994).

higher than expected altitudes due to unexpected advances in British aviation technology. Dr. Sigmund Rascher at first only asked Himmler for permission to conduct simulated, but lethal, high altitude experiments with "two or three *professional criminals.*"[28] Permission was granted and once that fateful step had been taken, both their number and the number of experiments quickly multiplied. And recall that, while incomparable in the eventual number of subjects used or in sadistic suffering, a similar small step was initially taken at Tuskegee. In that instance it was a matter of time: an experiment that was to last for only six months was gradually and inexorably extended to forty years with ever-increasing human cost. And Tuskegee also teaches us that under some circumstances consent should not even be asked for and a contemplated experiment should never be conducted. The USPHS physicians had greater moral obligations than to advance science. Once the money for treatment had run out, they should have packed their bags, gone home and alerted the public and Congress that their efforts at treatment were brought to a halt by economic necessity. This was not a golden opportunity to exploit a so-called experiment in nature, but a moral opportunity to cease and desist.

This brings me to the Nuremberg Code. It is a pity, if not a tragedy, that it has been treated so dismissively, deemed of such little relevance for the conduct of contemporary research. Shortly after its promulgation it was relegated to historical status, considered a document solely responsive to the Nazi misdeeds and intended to insure that research on the scale of Auschwitz and Dachau would never occur again. Such a narrow view constitutes a fateful misreading of the Code. The Nuremberg Tribunal's first principle that "the voluntary consent of the human subjects of research is absolutely essential"[29] emphasizes, without any mention of physical injury, that in the conduct of research, it is obligatory to obtain subjects' voluntary consent. The research community advanced many arguments for finding the entire Nuremberg Code too inhospitable for the conduct of research,[30] but I believe one concern loomed uppermost in their minds: the impediment to scientific progress which fidelity to the first principle would impose.

The Tribunal's consent principle disregarded the tensions between the inviolability of the subjects of research and the claims of science to advance knowledge, tensions which the research community has customarily resolved in favor of the humanitarian pursuit of knowledge, particularly when only subjects' dignitary interests are at stake. Instead, the Tribunal's principle was grounded in fundamental jurisprudential, philosophi-

---

28. *Trials of War Criminals, supra* note 1, Vol. I at 142.

29. *Ibid.* Vol. II at 181.

30. Henry K. Beecher, *Research and the Individual,* Boston: Little, Brown and Company 227-234 (1970).

cal, and bioethical assumptions that spoke only to the place of autonomy and self-determination in interactions between physician-scientists and subjects, including patient-subjects. The judges realized this when, immediately after setting forth their ten principles, they wrote:

> Our judicial concern, of course, is with those requirements which are purely legal in nature—or which at least are so clearly related to matters legal that they assist us in determining criminal culpability and punishment. To go beyond that point would lead us into a field that would be beyond our sphere of competence.[31]

Thus, the majestic first principle resolved the tensions between core concepts inherent in modern Anglo-American jurisprudence and core beliefs inherent in the pursuit of science by making it clear that autonomy and self-determination come first. As the commentary section to Principle One stated in most uncompromising language, "the person involved should . . . be able to exercise free power of choice, without the intervention of any element of force, fraud, deceit, duress, overreaching, or other ulterior form of constraint or coercion . . . "[32] To be sure a tall order but one that deserved careful exegesis.

The task which confronted the world medical community in the wake of Nuremberg was to explore, justify and delimit necessary exceptions to this basic principle, but only as *exceptions*. This did not happen. Instead, soon after Nuremberg, the Code was replaced by the World Medical Association's Helsinki Code.[33] In its first version, it did not even mention consent among the basic principles, emphasizing in the Preamble instead the importance of scientific research. In its 1975 and 1983 and 1989 versions, informed consent was elevated to a basic principle, yet way down on the list as principles 9 to 11.[34] The first principle of the Nuremberg Code eschewed the balancing of the inviolability of research subjects against the claims of science; it did not speak of risk-benefits ratios; instead, it commanded physician-investigators to be absolutely clear about the research dimension of their invitation which, of course, would include disclosure of the fact that in many research projects one can never be sure about unknown consequences of participation. The latter disclosures, in particular, are all too frequently glossed over, out of concern that patient-subjects will then not volunteer.

---

31. *Trials of War Criminals, supra* note 1, Vol. I at 182-183.

32. *Ibid.* at 181.

33. World Medical Association: Declaration of Helsinki, 2 *British Debit Journal* 177-80 (1964).

34. For an extended discussion, see Jay Katz, The Consent Principle of the Nuremberg Code—Its Significance Then and Now, in George J. Annas and Michael A. Grodin: *The Nazi Doctors and the Nuremberg Code*, New York: Oxford University Press 227-39 (1992).

Consider, for example, the recent informed consent agreement for the hepatitis B study during which several patient-subjects died. After mentioning the known risks, it merely went on to say that "FIAU (fialuridine) is a new medication and its side effects have not been completely described."[35] It was not a new "medication." It was an "experimental drug" with unknown potential hazards, and both these facts should have been highlighted in bold print. When the principal investigator was asked why patient-subjects were not warned that FIAU might worsen the disease, he responded, "we did not imagine that would happen."[36] George Annas commented on such blindspots perceptively: "Researchers tend to think that they do good, that they don't do bad . . . they tend to minimize or totally downplay the risks."[37]

When human beings are marked for extinction, holocausts are of course inevitable. The cruelty and torture inflicted during the concentration camp experiments were a by-product of the political ideology of the State that declared certain ethnic and racial groups to be "lives not worth living." That part of the story was amply documented at Nuremberg and understandably created the impression that the concentration camp experiments were a total aberration in the history of medical research. From the perspectives of torture and indiscriminate use, as I have already suggested, this is a correct assessment. Yet, the focus on torture and physical injury, so pervasive in the concentration camp experiments, invites overlooking the violations of human beings' dignitary interests, the transgressions of respect for persons, which remain problems for contemporary research. For even today the primacy of respect for subjects' autonomous decision-making is honored more in form than substance.

If one puts aside the unnecessary suffering with which these experiments were conducted, then the contributions which the ideology of science, of medical science, made to what happened comes into sharp focus. Ever since the mid-nineteenth century, the beginnings of the age of medical science, human experimentation has become increasingly part of the practice of medicine. And medicine throughout the ages has been a mix of Hippocratic altruism—"I will follow that system of regimen which . . . I consider for the benefit of my patients"[38]—and Hippocratic authoritarianism—"[conceal] most things from the patient while you are attending to him."[39] Until the age of medical science, both trends were at least patient

35. Jay H. Hoofnagle: Six-Month Course of FIAU for Chronic Hepatitis B, *Clinical Research Protocol* (Feb. 10, 1993).

36. Jay H. Hoofnagle, quoted in Lawrence L. Altman, Fatal Drug Trial Raises Questions about Informed Consent, *The New York Times* B7 (Oct. 5, 1993).

37. George J. Annas, quoted in *ibid.*

38. Oath of Hippocrates (5th Century B.C.), in *Hippocrates* Vol. I (W.H.S. Jones translation) Cambridge, Mass.: Harvard University Press 299-301 (1972).

39. *Decorum, Ibid.* Vol. II at 297.

centered, but from then onward medical interventions with patients also began to serve the interests of future patients, as well as the interests of science and scientists to advance the frontiers of knowledge. This radical change in the practice of medicine has not been fully appreciated.[40] Otherwise, with the vast expansion of research, accompanied by the inevitable objectification of patients whenever they also serve as research subjects, the boundaries between research and practice would have been more sharply delineated. In the United States, the Federal Regulations for the conduct of research have begun to make such distinctions, but the regulations need to be drafted more rigorously, so that it becomes clear that the moral dimension of medical research is different from that of medical practice. The authority that physicians can perhaps be allowed to exercise in clinical practice cannot be readily transposed into medical research.

From all that I have set forth, it should come as no surprise that the vision of better protecting the dignitary interests of subjects of research, not using them as means for our ends without their free consent, a vision inherent in the judgment at Nuremberg, still eludes us. Such a commitment might, at least for a while, impede research by braking the ideology of science's inexorable march toward progress. Yet, how significant an impediment it may turn out to be is hard to predict because scientists will then be forced to develop new methodologies for the conduct of research that are not predicated on both the ready availability of patient-subjects and the easy manipulation of the disclosure process such that consent becomes meaningless. And should progress be impeded, so be it; progress, as Hans Jonas reminded us, "is an optional goal, not an uncompromising commitment."[41] If we are willing to learn from the past, we must realize that other moral values are perhaps of greater significance.

Medicine can learn from the Holocaust that the objectifying proclivities inherent in scientific research invite the dehumanization of patient-subjects and this constitutes an ever-present danger. Respect for person based on full disclosure and then also on consent can evade this danger. Therefore, the Tribunal's first principle must be restored to its pre-eminence and any exceptions rigorously justified. Doing so will, of course, not prevent future politically inspired Holocausts. But before this happens again, medical science can learn a great deal from its past collaboration with the Nazis by confronting the fact that its ideology, unless the greatest care is taken, readily invites abuse of research subjects.

The question remains before us: can a commitment to human dignity, even in civilized societies, prevail against the inexorable march of

---

40. For an extended discussion, see *Human Experimentation, supra* Note 12 at 12-18.

41. *Philosophical Reflections, supra* note 23 at 245.

scientists' and the public's longings for medical progress, or must it remain an unattainable dream? This question takes me back to the beginning of time. Faced with the first act of moral blindness, leading to murder, the book of *Genesis* asked another question: "Am I my brother's keeper?"[42] The question was left unanswered, perhaps because each generation must find its own answer, not to murder of which Cain and the Nazi physicians were guilty, but to the many other acts of moral blindness which we all too readily tolerate. *Genesis'* question still awaits an affirmative answer for many human pursuits, including the conduct of human experimentation in which humanitarian concerns for future well-being can obliterate concerns for present lives.

If this question were answered affirmatively, then the angels who now bar our entry to paradise with flaming swords might lay down their arms, and we could return to paradise. This will not happen, and we shall have to be content with less, but I hope with more than we now have. Some will surely chide me for asking for so much more. Perhaps; I only wanted to alert us to the need to be careful in our scientific pursuit and to heed Albert Camus' warning, "the plague bacillus never dies or disappears for good; it can lie dormant for years and years"[43] until it once again exacts its price. Perhaps, in the shadow of the Holocaust, I wanted to dream and at the same time chart a road on which we might travel, at least for some distance, toward paradise.

---

42. *Genesis* 4:9.

43. Albert Camus, *The Plague,* Stuart Gilbert translation, New York: Alfred A. Knopf 278 (1957).

11

Nazi Science—The Dachau Hypothermia Experiments*

Robert L. Berger

It is widely recognized that the experiments performed on prisoners in German concentration camps during the Second World War were in fact brutal crimes committed under the guise of medical research. There is controversy, however, about the use of the results obtained from those studies. Among the approximately 30 known projects, the controversy has focused most intensely on the experiments involving hypothermia in humans that were performed at the Dachau concentration camp.[1] The debate among scientists and ethicists has spread to the public through the print and broadcast media.[2-6] Positions range from a total ban to advocacy of the uninhibited use of the material. At one pole, Arnold Relman, editor-in-chief of the *Journal,* has noted that the Nazi experiments "are such a gross violation of human standards that they are not to be trusted at all" and said that the *Journal* would not allow citations of the Nazi work.[1] In contrast, Robert Pozos, a physiologist specializing in hypothermia, has advocated the free use of the results, believing that they can advance contemporary research on hypothermia and save lives.[2,7] By 1984 more than 45 publications had made reference to Dachau experiments.[1] A much larger body of literature on hypothermia, however, has not referred to these controversial studies.

In the immediate postwar period, Andrew Ivy, a physician-scientist and American Medical Association representative at the Nuremberg war-crimes trials, declared that the Nazi experiments on humans were of no medical value.[8] Leo Alexander, a psychiatrist and consultant to the American Chief of Counsel for War Crimes, reported at first that the Dachau study had produced credible data, but he subsequently reversed his position and concluded that the results were not dependable.[9,10] More recently, several investigators have endorsed the data from the Dachau experiments

* From the Departments of Cardiothoracic Surgery, New England Deaconess Hospital and Harvard Medical School. Address reprint requests to Dr. Berger at 135 Francis St., Boston, MA 02215.
Supported in part by the Thoracic Foundation.

either explicitly or implicitly by citing the results.[2,7,11-13] According to these sources, the study generated data unavailable elsewhere about the response of unanesthetized persons to immersion hypothermia, providing particularly important information on lethal temperatures, specific reactions to cooling, and methods of rewarming. These endorsements contributed to an impression that the Dachau hypothermia project represents good science despite its offensive ethics. There are doubts, however, about the scientific integrity of the work.[1] An evaluation of its scientific rigor is needed to shed light on the reliability of the results and on the need to pursue the ethical debate about their use. This paper presents a critical analysis of the experimental protocol and the results reported, and an examination of the credentials and reliability of the investigators.

The Dachau Human Hypothermia Study

The immersion-hypothermia project was conducted at the Dachau concentration camp between August 1942 and May 1943. Its purpose was to establish the most effective treatment for victims of immersion hypothermia, particularly crew members of the German air force who had been shot down into the cold waters of the North Sea.[14] The subjects in the experiment were male civilian prisoners belonging to various religions and nationalities, as well as Russian prisoners of war. Their participation was usually forced, but occasionally it was "voluntary" in response to promises, rarely fulfilled, of release from the camp or commutation of the death sentence.[14]

During the experiments, the subjects were immersed in a tank of ice water. Some were anesthetized, others conscious; many were naked, but others were dressed. Several different methods of rewarming the subjects were also tested. Responses of body temperatures, clinical manifestations, and selected biochemical and physiologic measurements were purportedly monitored, and autopsies were performed. (Rectal measurements of temperature are given throughout this paper.)

In an attempt to conceal the atrocities, the original, incriminating records of most of the concentration camp studies of humans were destroyed before the camps were captured by the Allied forces. A large body of information was later recovered, however, pertaining to the extensive communications between the investigators and Heinrich Himmler, the Reichsführer of the SS (Nazi special police). Immediately after the war, Leo Alexander investigated the Dachau hypothermia experiments and prepared a 228-page report that included 68 pages of personal commentary about the background and substance of the study and a reproduction of a 56-page comprehensive report to Himmler on the Dachau experiments, signed by Drs. Holzloehner, Rascher, and Finke and dated October 21, 1942.[9] A separate communication notes that the report, referred to in this paper as the Dachau Comprehensive Report, had been prepared by Rascher for presentation at a medical conference for military personnel on hypothermia.[15]

Although the Dachau Comprehensive Report does not report on all the immersion experiments performed at Dachau, it is the only original account available about the project, and it includes sufficient information to evaluate the work. Indeed, the Alexander report containing the Dachau Comprehensive Report is essentially the only primary reference cited in the literature on the Dachau study. It also served as the main source of material for the present analysis, in addition to relevant information from other documents and sources. This discussion highlights representative data from the Dachau Comprehensive Report. I will have more to say later about Dr. Rascher, Reichsführer Himmler, and the others involved in directing the experiments.

Because the Dachau hypothermia experiments were performed almost 50 years ago, I have exercised care in this analysis to avoid judging them by contemporary standards. It is noteworthy, however, that despite the explosive growth of medical science during the second half of the century, the basic principles of scientific investigation have not changed appreciably.

Experimental Design

The descriptions in the Dachau Comprehensive Report of the design, materials, and methods of the experiments are incomplete and reflect a disorganized approach. Only an impression of the scope of the study can be formed from the fragmentary information provided. The size of the experimental population and the number of experiments performed are not disclosed. Only from postwar testimony do we learn of 360 to 400 experiments conducted on 280 to 300 victims—an indication that some persons underwent more than a single exposure.[16,17] Such basic variables as the age and level of nutrition of the experimental subjects are not provided, and the various study subgroups are not segregated. The numbers of subjects who underwent immersion while naked, clothed, conscious, or anesthetized are not specified. The bath temperatures are given as ranging between 2 and 12°C, but there is no breakdown into subgroups, making it impossible to determine the effect of the different temperatures. The end points of the experiment— time spent in the bath, specific body temperature, subject's clinical condition, death, and the like—are not stated .

At least seven different methods of rewarming the subjects after immersion were tested. No information is available about the physical characteristics of each heat source, the initial body temperature of the victims, or the elapsed time between the cessation of cooling and the start of rewarming. For one method tested, the temperature of the warm bath was specified for only two experiments. One assistant later testified that some victims were thrown into boiling water for rewarming.[18]

The frequency and timing of data collection are not stipulated in the report. Postwar testimony revealed that whenever possible, some assistants and victims altered the temperature readings and changed the timing of blood sampling in the attempt to save lives. The frequency of such laudable alteration of the data is unknown.[19]

Blood pressure was not measured. Cardiologic monitoring was limited to heart sounds and electrocardiography, but in the shivering victims no tracings were obtained during immersion or after removal from the bath. Therefore, dangerous or even fatal cardiac arrhythmias escaped detection during the unmonitored periods.

In summary, the basic information essential for documenting an orderly experimental protocol and evaluating the results is not provided. We know enough, however, to conclude that the methods of study were clearly defective.

Analysis of Reported Results

According to the Dachau Comprehensive Report, anesthesia and bath temperatures ranging from 2 to 12°C had no demonstrable effect on the rate of cooling. These surprising observations are at variance with generally accepted concepts and raise strong doubts about the experimental approach. For example, Keatinge noted that immersion in water at 5°C is tolerated by clothed men for 40 to 60 minutes, whereas raising the water temperature to 15°C increases the period of tolerance to four to five hours.[20] Moreover, the report contains no specific information about the effects of age, clothed as compared with unclothed immersion, or nutritional state on the rate of body cooling.

Cardiac arrhythmias are described in the Dachau Comprehensive Report as being slow, fast, or irregular, without reference to standard nomenclature. Ventricular fibrillation, known to be a common cause of death from hypothermia, and atrial fibrillation, the most frequent cardiac irregularity from hypothermia, are not even mentioned. The term atrial flutter, the only conventional designation mentioned, is used to label a tracing of atrial fibrillation. The unusual characterization of common cardiac arrhythmias and their misinterpretation suggest a lack of expertise in cardiac physiology.

According to the Dachau Comprehensive Report, the subjects' body temperatures continued to fall after they were removed from the cold bath, and it was postulated that this "after drop" might be responsible for death after rescue from cold water. The temperature curves in the Dachau Comprehensive Report, however, show the presence of the "after drop" to be variable.

The data for one of the more crucial aspects of the project, the assessment of the lethal temperature level, are incomplete and inconsistent. An assistant testified that the victims were cooled to 25°C.[4] In a short Intermediate Report, Rascher noted that all those whose temperatures reached 28°C (an undisclosed number) died.[21] However, the postscript to the Dachau Comprehensive Report maintains that "with few exceptions" the lethal temperature was 26 to 27°C. In a further inconsistency, the Dachau Comprehensive Report notes that in six fatal experiments the terminal temperature ranged between 24.2 and 25.7°C. Even more puzzling is the claim in the table cited to support this point that in these victims death was observed to occur between 25.7 and 29.2°C. The mortality rate for this fatal range of hypothermia is not supplied, so the lethality of the lethal temperature remains undefined. The temperatures reached in the majority of the 80 to 90 victims who died are not reported. Moreover, because the demographic characteristics, nutritional state, and general health of this cohort are not described, it is impossible to determine whether the results apply to populations outside a concentration camp.

The Dachau Comprehensive Report states that in seven experiments the victims died 53 to 106 minutes after the start of cooling. Alexander reports, however, that a review of Rascher's experimental records and statements by his close associates disclosed that it took between 80 minutes and six hours of immersion to kill the naked victims, whereas the clothed men died after six to seven hours of cooling.[10]

The information on the lethality of the experiments is also inconsistent. In the Dachau Comprehensive Report, Rascher writes in one place that the hypothermia study was not designed to produce fatalities, and in another presents data on seven lethal experiments, and he refers to 13 deaths. In fact, two assistants testified that at least 80 to 90 victims died during the experiments, and only two were known to have survived the war, both of whom became "mental cases."[16,17] The sequence is reminiscent of Rascher's disclosures on mortality in another study, on high altitude, which contained a similar chain of discrepancies.[9]

Firm conclusions about the efficacy of several techniques of rewarming are offered, despite a paucity of supporting data. Detailed results presented in the form of time-based temperature curves are reported for only three groups of experiments. The graphs reveal that body-temperature recovery was fastest with immersion in warm water, but that rewarming and presumably survival were achieved with the other methods, too. The description of one set of experiments and the accompanying temperature curve in the Dachau Comprehensive Report show the quality of the reporting (Figure 1, cf. p. 92). The text states that a method of rewarming with a combination of a warm bath and a body massage was tested, but in the supporting figure, treatment with a light box is added at the end of the study. The number of experiments and the demographic characteristics of the victims in this subgroup are not specified. Nor are the temperature of the bath and the intensity of the electric heat source, or the frequency and timing of the measurements of temperature. Although no warming was instituted for approximately 12 minutes after the victims were removed from the ice-water bath, the temperature curve shows no "after drop" such as that previously described as being regularly observed. The duration of resuscitation in a warm bath is 10 minutes, according to the text, but it lasts 20 minutes in the figure.

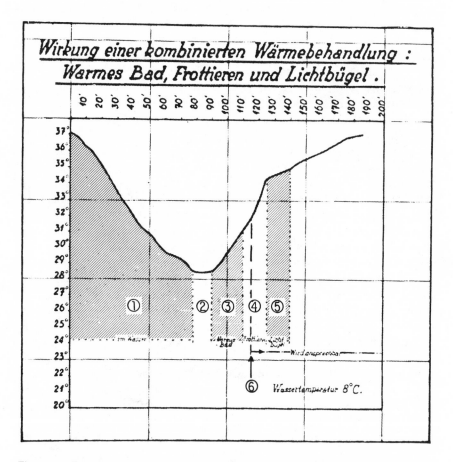

Figure 1. Reproduction of Figure 10 from the Dachau Comprehensive Report. The horizontal axis shows minutes, and the vertical axis temperature (°C). The German title may be translated as "Effect of combined rewarming treatment: warm bath, massage and light box." The water temperature was 8°C. The arrows and numbers (1 to 6) were superimposed by the present author. Translations of the corresponding notations from the German are: 1. in water; 2. period out of bath (no German notation); 3. warm bath; 4. massage; 5. light box; and 6. response to speech (regaining of consciousness).

The conclusion is drawn that immersion in a warm bath for rewarming is the best method of treatment, and preferential use of this technique is recommended. However, since survival rates—the ultimate criterion of the effectiveness of a rewarming technique—are not given in the Dachau Comprehensive Report, no judgment about the merits of the various resuscitative techniques is warranted, and the recommendation that a warm bath is the best therapy cannot be justified on the basis of the data. The credibility of the results has been compromised further by the postwar disclosure that most victims who were thrown into a tub of boiling water for rewarming died, making it probable that in fact rewarming in a warm bath had the highest mortality.[18] Incidentally, the role of immersion resuscitation remains controversial to this day.[22]

The Dachau Comprehensive Report maintains, without any supporting data, that warm-bath rewarming had no undesirable side effects. With the grossly inadequate techniques of hemodynamic and electrocardiographic monitoring used at Dachau, circulatory failure and cardiac arrhythmias, the two most likely untoward reactions, could not be evaluated accurately. Therefore, the statement about the lack of harm is not justified.

According to the Dachau Comprehensive Report, death from cooling was caused by heart failure due to peripheral vasoconstriction and cold-induced structural myocardial injury. However, there is no mention of clinical signs of cardiac failure or evidence of myocardial damage at autopsy. Extensive experimental and clinical experience has clearly shown that contrary to the claim from Dachau, death from hypothermia is usually due to ventricular fibrillation, and cold does not injure the heart but instead protects it. Indeed, selective myocardial cooling is routinely used to preserve the myocardium during cardiac surgery. Appropriate electrocardiographic monitoring and histologic examination of myocardial tissue in the Dachau victims could have identified the true mechanism of death.

To support the concept that death invariably resulted from cardiac and not respiratory failure, the report advances the claim that breathing continued for as long as 20 minutes after "clinical standstill of the ventricle." This sequence of events is at variance with the time-honored observation that spontaneous respiration does not continue for long after the cessation of cardiac function, and it suggests that the investigators lacked the means or competence to recognize cardiac arrest. Another possibility is that the phenomenon of persistent breathing after cardiac arrest was fabricated.

The concept that local application of cold to the occiput and dorsal neck accelerates cooling was advanced by Himmler and is demonstrated convincingly in the Dachau Comprehensive Report with temperature curves from one set of experiments. Rascher also maintained that death and cerebral bleeding occurred only when the occiput and neck were submerged in the ice water, implying that immersion hypothermia does not result in death if the structures above the neck are kept out of the water. Although the scalp is an efficient heat-exchanging surface,[23] I could find no evidence in the rich literature on induced or accidental immersion hypothermia that this relatively small area has such a pivotal role in the cooling response. The observation was probably fabricated; Gagge and Herrington remarked that the Dachau results may have been "exaggerated" to support Himmler's theory.[24]

The statement in the Dachau Comprehensive Report that cooling was complicated by cerebral edema and hemorrhage is at variance with the vast experimental and clinical experience on record. In animals, hypothermia shrinks rather than swells the brain.[25] Cerebral edema has not been observed in cases of accidental hypothermia or surface or core-induced hypothermia for cardiac surgery.[26] The last of these techniques is used in more than 250,000 operations annually in the United States alone without concern about the development of cerebral edema from hypothermia. Similarly, cerebral hemorrhage has not been observed as a result of experimental or clinical hypothermia. Thus, this report from Dachau probably represents a fabrication of data. It is also possible that brain injuries were inflicted by beatings or were sustained during the desperate struggles of the victims in the ice tank.

Background and Organization

The hypothermia project was proposed by Air Force Field Marshal Erhard Milch and approved by Himmler.[14] Because Rascher's qualifications as an investigator were limited, two presumed experts, Drs. Holzloehner and Finke, were recruited to help with the experiments.[9,14,27] However, Rascher took charge of the project despite his lack of qualifications, whereas the two experienced investigators functioned essentially as part-time consultants, apparently without the power to ensure acceptable scientific standards.[9,14] Two months after the start of the project, Holzloehner and Finke thought that the work had been completed and withdrew. Rascher continued alone, directing another 350 experiments with the explanation that he needed additional material to complete a thesis required to support his application for a university appointment.[16]

Reichsführer Himmler, the other principal behind the project, had absolute authority over the concentration camps. Although educated in agriculture, the Reichsführer fancied himself a medical scientist and was intimately involved in the administrative and scientific aspects of the studies of humans. All human experimentation within the concentration-camp system required Himmler's approval.[9] He outlined the objectives of the projects and at times even the experimental approach.[19] When his scientific suggestions were not pursued, Himmler pressured the investigators into carrying out his proposals.[9,14,28,29] The Reichsführer expressed special interest in the hypothermia project and traveled to Dachau several times to witness experiments.[9,18] Thus, the study represents a private venture by two unqualified ideologues, conducted in a prison setting quite alien to the standards of an academic environment. With Himmler's aid, Rascher thwarted repeated attempts by the medical establishment of the military to influence, participate in, or wrest control of the project.[14]

The Principal Investigator

Sigmund Rascher was born in 1909. He started his medical studies in 1930 and joined both the Nazi party and the storm troopers (the SA) three years later. After a volunteer internship, Rascher served for three years as an unpaid surgical assistant. He was barred temporarily from the University of Munich for suspected Communist sympathies.[9,19] In 1939, the young doctor denounced his physician father, joined the SS, and was inducted into the *Luftwaffe*.[19,29] A liaison with and eventual marriage to Nini Diehl, a widow 15 years his senior who was a one-time cabaret singer but also the former secretary and possibly mistress of the Reichsführer, gained Rascher direct access to Himmler. A strange partnership evolved between the junior medical officer and one of the highest officials of the Third Reich. One week after their first meeting, Rascher presented a "Report on the Development and Solution to Some of the Reichsführer's Assigned Tasks During a Discussion Held on April 24, 1939."[19] The title of this paper foretold the character of the ensuing relationship between the two men. Because of Rascher's servile and ingratiating approach to Himmler, his "connections were so strong that practically every superior trembled in fear of the intriguing Rascher who consequently held a position of enormous power."[14]

Rascher's short investigative career included a leading role in the infamous high-altitude experiments on humans at Dachau, which resulted in 70 to 80 deaths.[8,9] He was also involved in testing a plant extract as a cure for cancer. The genesis of this project illustrates Rascher's style and influence. Professor Blome, the deputy health minister and plenipotentiary for cancer research, favored testing the extract in mice. Rascher insisted on experiments in humans. Himmler sided with Rascher. A Human Cancer Testing Station was set up at Dachau. The deputy health minister collaborated on the project, held approximately 20 meetings with Rascher, and visited the junior officer at Dachau several times.[30]

Another of Rascher's major research efforts focused on the introduction of a pectin-based preparation, Polygal, to promote blood clotting. He predicted that the prophylactic use of Polygal tablets would reduce bleeding from wounds sustained in combat or during surgical procedures. The agent was also recommended for the control of spontaneous gastrointestinal and pulmonary hemorrhages. Combat wounds were simulated by the amputation of the viable extremities of camp prisoners without anesthesia or by shooting the prisoners through the neck and chest.[18]

Rascher also claimed that oral premedication with Polygal minimized bleeding during major surgical procedures, rendering hemostatic clips or ligatures unnecessary and shortening operating times.[31] He published an enthusiastic article about his clinical experience with Polygal, without specifying the nature of some of the trials in humans. The paper concluded, "The tests of this medicine 'Polygal 10' showed no failures under the most varied circumstances."[32] Rascher also formed a company to manufacture Polygal and used prisoners to work in the factory.[33] A prisoner who was later liberated testified that Rascher's enthusiasm for Polygal's anti-infectious properties was probably sparked by news of the introduction of penicillin by the Allies and by his eagerness to reap fame and receive the award established for inventing a German equivalent. He initiated experiments in humans apparently without any preliminary laboratory testing. In one experiment, pus was injected into the legs of prisoners. The experimental group was given Polygal. The controls received no treatment. Information filtered to Dr. Kurt Plotner, Rascher's physician rival, that the controls were given large, deep subcutaneous inoculations, whereas the victims in the experiments received smaller volumes of pus injected intracutaneously. Plotner reportedly investigated the matter and discovered that the Polygal used was saline colored with a fluorescent dye.[9]

The frequent references to Rascher in top-level documents indicate that this junior medical officer attracted extraordinary attention from Germany's highest officials.[9,14] His work was reported even to Hitler, who was pleased with the accounts.[34] Rascher was not well regarded in professional circles,[14,19] however, and his superiors repeatedly expressed reservations about his performance.[14,19] In one encounter, Professor Karl Gebhardt, a general in the SS and Himmler's personal physician, told Rascher in connection with his experiments on hypothermia through exposure to cold air that "the report was unscientific; if a student of the second term dared submit a treatise of the kind [Gebhardt] would throw him out."[35] Despite Himmler's strong support, Rascher was rejected for faculty positions at several universities. A book by German scientists on the accomplishments of German aviation medicine during the war devoted an entire chapter to hypothermia but failed to mention Rascher's name or his work.[36]

Rascher collected human skin for making saddles, riding breeches, ladies' handbags, and other personal items. He sold the finished products to colleagues. Although Rascher's private ventures rivaled his scientific exploits in grotesqueness, the story that emerges as the most fateful deception of his life involved his claim to have had three children, who were not in fact his own. In an attempt to please Himmler by proving that the growth of the Aryan population could be accelerated through an extension of the childbearing age, Rascher made it known that his wife had given birth to three children in quick succession after turning 48 years old. During her fourth "pregnancy," Mrs. Rascher was arrested for attempting to kidnap an infant. The ensuing investigation disclosed that the other three Rascher children had not been born to Mrs. Rascher but had been bought or abducted.[34] Himmler felt betrayed, and in April 1944 his protégé was arrested. Besides complicity in the kidnapping, Dr. Rascher was accused of financial irregularities, the murder of a German assistant, and scientific fraud.[19] Dr. and Mrs. Rascher were subsequently executed, presumably on Himmler's orders.

Discussion

This review of the Dachau hypothermia experiments reveals critical shortcomings in scientific content and credibility. The project was conducted without an orderly experimental protocol, with inadequate methods and an erratic execution. The report is riddled with inconsistencies. There is also evidence of data falsification and suggestions of fabrication. Many conclusions are not supported by the facts presented. The flawed science is compounded by evidence that the director of the project showed a consistent pattern of dishonesty and deception in his professional as well as his personal life, thereby stripping the study of the last vestige of credibility. On analysis, the Dachau hypothermia study has all the ingredients of a scientific fraud, and rejection of the data on purely scientific grounds is inevitable. They cannot advance science or save human lives.

In the light of these findings, attempts to use the data from the Dachau experiments have been puzzling. The persistence of the claim that the work offers usable or valuable information is difficult to understand. One probable reason is the extremely limited availability of the Alexander report and the tendency of investigators to use secondary citations without consulting the primary source. Wider circulation of the Alexander report would thoroughly expose the true nature of the work and put an end to the myth of good science at Dachau. Future citations are inappropriate on scientific grounds.

Inferior science does not generally come to the attention of the ethicist because it is usually discarded by scientists. Ethical dialogues deal with work of sound scientific but controversial moral content, and the mere fact that a debate is conducted implies that the subject under consideration has scientific merit. If the shortcomings of the Dachau hypothermia study had been fully appreciated, the ethical dialogue probably would never have begun. Continuing it runs the risk of implying that these grotesque Nazi medical exercises yielded results worthy of consideration and possibly of benefit to humanity. The present analysis clearly shows that nothing could be further from the truth. Although the Dachau experiments opened the dialogue about an important ethical issue, the discontinuation of debate about these experiments should not bring an end to exploration of the larger subject—the implications of the use of ethically tainted data. But the Dachau study is an inappropriate example for that purpose.

I am indebted to Mr. Heinz Wartski for his help with translation of the German material.

Endnotes

1. Moe K. Should the Nazi research data be cited? Hastings Cent Rep 1984; 14(6):5-7.

2. MacNeil-Lehrer Report. New York and Washington: PBS, August 1. 1988.

3. "Newswatch." New York: CBS, June 19, 1988.

4. Doctor to use Nazi data on human freezing. Associated Press. May 1988.

5. Wilkerson I. Nazi scientists and ethics of today. New York Times. May 21, 1989:34.

6. Siegel B. Nazi data: a dilemma for science. Los Angeles Times. October 30 1988:1 .

7. Pozos R. Can scientists use information derived from concentration camps? In: Conference on the Meaning of the Holocaust for Bioethics, Minneapolis. May 17-19, 1989. Transcription of official recording. Minneapolis: Center for Biomedical Ethics, University of Minnesota, 1989:1-17.

8. Mitscherlich A., Mielke F. Doctors of infamy: the story of the Nazi medical crimes. Norden H. trans. New York: Henry Schuman, 1949.

9. Alexander L. The treatment of shock from prolonged exposure to cold especially in water. Combined Intelligence Objectives Subcommittee. Target no. 24. Report no. 250. Washington, D.C.: Office of the Publication Board, Department of Commerce, 1946.

10. *Idem.* Medical science under dictatorship. N Engl J Med 1949; 241:39-47.

11. Burton AC, Edholm OG. Man in a cold environment: physiological and pathological effects of exposure to low temperatures. London: Edward Arnold, 1955:205.

12. Golden FStC. Rewarming. In: Pozos RS, Wittmers LE Jr, eds. The nature and treatment of hypothermia. Minneapolis: University of Minnesota Press, 1983: 194-208.

13. Hegnauer AH. Lethal hypothermic temperatures for dog and man. Ann N Y Acad Sci 1959; 80:315-9.

14. Freezing experiments. In: Trials of war criminals before the Nuremberg Military Tribunals. Vol. I. Washington, D.C.: Government Printing Office 1946-49: 186-217.

15. Letter from Rascher S to Brandt R. In: Trials of war criminals before the Nuremberg Military Tribunals. Vol. I. Washington, D.C.: Government Printing Office, 1946-49:221-2.

16. Testimony of Neff W. In: Trials of war criminals before the Nuremberg Military Tribunals. Vol . I. Washington, D.C.: Government Printing Office 1946-49:260-5.

17. Affidavit by Blaha F. In: Trial of the major war criminals before the International Military Tribunal. Vol. 5. Nuremberg, Germany: Secretariat of the Tribunal, 1948:168-72.

18. Testimony of Pacholegg A. In: Nazi conspiracy and aggression. International Military Tribunal. Suppl A. Washington, D.C.: Government Printing Office, 1947:414-22.

19. Benz W. Dr med Sigmund Rascher Eine Karriere. Medizine in NS-Staat: In Dachauer Hefte. 4 Jahrgang, 1988 Heft 4:190-214.

20. Keatinge WR. Survival in cold water: the physiology and treatment of immersion, hypothermia, and drowning. Oxford: Blackwell Scientific Publications, 1969.

21. Rascher S. Intermediate report. In: Trials of war criminals before the Nuremberg Military Tribunals. Vol. I. Washington, D.C.: Government Printing Office, 1946-49:220-1.

22. Danzl DF, Pozos RS, Hamlet MP. Accidental hypothermia. In: Auerbach PS, Geehr EJ, eds. Management of wilderness and environmental emergencies. St. Louis: C.V. Mosby, 1989.

23. Froese G, Burton AC. Heat losses from the human head. J Appl Physiol 1957; 10:235-41.

24. Gagge AP, Herrington LP. Physiological effects of heat and cold. Annu Rev Physiol 1947; 9:409-28.

25. Rosomoff HL. Protective effects of hypothermia against pathological processes of the nervous system. Ann N Y Acad Sci 1959; 80:475-80.

26. Blair E. Clinical hypothermia. New York: McGraw-Hill, 1964:208-9.

27. Affidavit by Sievers W. In: Trials of war criminals before the Nuremberg Military Tribunals. Vol. I. Washington, D.C.: Government Printing Office, 1946-49:274-8.

28. Letter from Himmler H to Rascher S. In: Trials of war criminals before the Nuremberg Military Tribunals. Vol. I. Washington, D.C.: Government Printing Office, 1946-49:244-5.

29. Berben P. Dachau 1933-1945: the official history. London: Norfolk Press, 1975: 123-37.

30. Affidavit by Sievers W. Document No. 473. The Alexander papers. Special collections. Boston: Mugar Memorial Library, Boston University.

31. Polygal experiments. In: Trials of war criminals before the Nuremberg Military Tribunals. Vol. I. Washington, D.C.: Government Printing Office, 1946-49:669-83.

32. Rascher S., Haferkamp H. "Polygal" a hemostat to be administered orally. Document No. 438. The Alexander papers. Special collections. Boston: Mugar Memorial Library, Boston University, 1943.

33. Deposition of Walter Neff on 12/13/1946. The Alexander papers. Special collections. Boston: Mugar Memorial Library, Boston University.

34. Statement by Gen. Wolff K. Report No. WClU/LDC/1436a-APS/HC. In: The Alexander papers. Special collections. Boston: Mugar Memorial Library, Boston University.

35. Letter from Rascher S. to Sievers. In: Trials of war criminals before the Nuremberg Military Tribunals. Vol. I. Washington, D.C.: Government Printing Office, 1946-49:255-7.

36. Grosse-Brockhoff F. Pathologic physiology and therapy of hypothermia. In: German aviation medicine during World War II. Washington, D.C.: Department of Air Force, Surgeon General, 1946:828-42.

12

The Personal, Public, and Political Dimensions of Being a Mengele Guinea Pig

Eva Kor

Thank you very much for asking me to speak at this distinguished forum and many thanks for working so hard to organize this important event. I would like to explore the personal, public and political dimensions of being a Mengele guinea pig and an Auschwitz survivor.

My hope is that my story, my struggle, my search in trying to understand who I am, why these terrible things happened to me, and how I fit into this big world, will convey some important messages and lessons which I will point out later.

I would first like to share with you some humorous experiences. In 1979, when I began my college education at Indiana State University, I took a class in Holocaust 101. I said to my professor, Dr. Pierard, "I hope I pass your class. It would be very embarrassing to flunk it when I survived Auschwitz." Did you ever feel that you were born in the wrong place, at the wrong time? Well, I was born in the wrong place, at the wrong time, with the wrong religion, and the wrong sex. My parents had two older daughters and very much wanted a boy. When the midwife was delivering my twin sister, Miriam, my father asked, "Nu, what do we have?" "A girl, but don't despair, another one is coming!," said the midwife. So, when I was born, I was the last vanishing hope for my parents to have a boy. My father often said, "Eva, you should have been a boy!"

It is a sad fact, but my destiny was sealed at birth. Being born Jewish in Europe in the thirties was politically wrong, and I was destined to end up in Auschwitz. My only luck was that I was born a twin, and that Dr. Josef Mengele was fascinated with research on twins.

I was only six years old, and we were in first grade in a Hungarian school. There was a disturbance in the classroom. Miriam and I—the TWO DIRTY JEWS—were automatically blamed and punished for it, even though we were completely innocent. Our books were filled with hatred against Jews. One of the math problems, for example, went something like this, "If you have 5 Jews and you kill 3, how many are left?" Harassing and killing Jews was the law of the land. It was not only permitted, but encouraged. Many people were eager to hurt and harass us. At times we couldn't get out of the house. I asked my parents to stand up to these Nazi hoodlums, but they said that there was nothing they could do, and that I would be better off if I learned to take it.

Four years of Nazi occupation in Hungary did not prepare me for a place like Auschwitz-Birkenau. Nothing in this universe could prepare anyone for a place like that. There I became one of the 3,000 twins who were used in Mengele's experiments. We were subjected to a lot of blood taking, and were injected with a variety of germs and chemicals. Every part of my body was poked, measured, photographed, painted and compared with charts. At times, we had to sit naked for six to eight hours a day. It hurts me even today that they tried to reduce me to the lowest form of existence—a mass of living, breathing cells.

During all the experiments I felt like a little soldier who had to obey orders in order to survive. I desperately wanted to survive this nightmare; it was my only way to fight back. The first day in camp I made a silent pledge that I would do everything in my power to help us to survive.

It was a very lonely battle. I don't think that Miriam and I ever talked very much about anything except that we were hungry and tried to figure out a way to "organize," that is steal, in camp language, more food. I guess children who face life and death become quiet and introverted.

Nothing was ever explained to us, nor was there any effort made to minimize the risk to our well-being. On the contrary, we were injected with many chemicals and deadly germs. In June or July of 1944, I was injected with a deadly germ that made me very ill with an extremely high fever, trembling and swelling in my legs and arms. I was taken to the hospital and put into the barrack of the living dead. Next day, Dr. Mengele came in with four other doctors. He looked at my fever chart, then said sarcastically, "Too bad, she is so young, but she has only two weeks to live." I made a second silent pledge then that I would do everything in my power to prove him wrong, to survive and to be reunited with Miriam.

For two weeks I was between life and death. I received no food, no water, no medication. I remember waking up on the barracks floor as I was crawling, trying to reach the end of the barracks where there was a faucet with water. I would fade in and out of consciousness, and even in this state I kept telling myself, "I must survive." And I did.

In 1985, I finally compared notes with Miriam. She told me that for the first two weeks she was under SS surveillance. She was not taken to the lab. They were waiting for something to happen, but they didn't tell her what. Were I to die, Miriam would have been killed with a phenol shot in the heart, and then Mengele would have done the comparative autopsy. But I didn't die. After two weeks, Miriam was taken back to the lab and was injected with something that destroyed her kidneys. In 1987, after Miriam's kidney failed completely, I donated my left kidney. Miriam died on June 6, 1993, from complications related to the kidney problems.

On January 27, 1945, on a cold snowy day, Auschwitz was liberated. It was a glorious day. We were free, and we were alive. We beat the odds! In 1946, at a memorial service, the Rabbi said that if we had any soap from camp to bring it the next day to the burial ceremony because it was made out of human fat. I was eleven years old. I had two bars of soap from Auschwitz. After that I could not wash with soap for years and developed severe nightmares that the soap I used was made out of my own parents. I had no psychologist, no doctor, no help of any kind. I never told anyone about it, and somehow I grew up, but I was always alone with my problems and my pain.

In October 1967, when kids in our neighborhood played tricks and Halloween pranks, something snapped inside me. Emotionally it threw me back to the Nazi harassment. My strong reaction to the pranks made me very popular with the pranksters. They painted swastikas and threw bricks at my home. This nightmare lasted for twelve years. It ended when NBC aired the Holocaust show. The pranksters saw it and understood my reaction. In those days I was a nervous wreck. No one understood me. Even my son was ashamed of me, but somehow I survived this, too.

I never talked to Miriam about anything related to our Auschwitz experience until 1979. Many so called experts say that we felt guilty or ashamed that we survived. In my case this is 100% false. I was always proud that I survived. I believe that I kept quiet because I could not deal with the pain.

In the late seventies, I was trying to find out more information about our experiments. I read many books but could find no details of Mengele's experiments. So I set out to locate the other Mengele Twins to piece together our eyewitness accounts, but we didn't know what he injected into us. In 1984, I founded an organization called C.A.N.D.L.E.S. an acronym for Children of Auschwitz Nazi Deadly Lab Experiment Survivors. As Irene Hizme, a twin, says, it's a very exclusive club to belong to; you have to be a Mengele twin. In 1980, I began to lecture. I was pleased and surprised that people were supportive, caring and interested in my story. For more than 100 lectures, I was cool, calm, and collected, but I ended every one with a very strange statement: "I know it happened to me, but I always feel like I am standing up here looking down at this little girl and telling her story." One day I broke down and cried during my lecture. Suddenly I could feel all the pain and fear I felt in camp.

The little girl and I became one. Lecturing in public became my greatest therapy.

In 1985, I initiated and organized the memorial return of the Twins to Auschwitz and a mock trial of Josef Mengele in Jerusalem. The world press followed us around. Politicians sent us greetings and wanted to appear with us. I thought that our long struggle was over, and we would finally get the help and support we needed to find our files and finally learn what was injected into our bodies in Mengele's lab.

On January 23, 1985, one day before my departure for Auschwitz, Rod Prince, NBC bureau chief from Chicago came with Andy Franklin and a camera crew to Terre Haute, to follow me around for a special NBC report. Our press coverage in Auschwitz and Jerusalem was fantastic and overwhelming, but two weeks later when I was back in Terre Haute, I called Mr. Rod Prince. I could not reach him. My repeated calls were not returned. I had enough of these cat and mouse games. I demanded to talk to him. I asked for a copy of the footage he shot in Terre Haute. He said he didn't know what I was talking about, that he never filmed me, nor had he ever been in Terre Haute. So much for the free press. I felt then that something was very, very wrong, and it was not my fault, but I became politically incorrect again. Four months later, a bunch of dry, broken bones were unearthed in Embu, Brazil. The U.S. government told us these bones were Mengele's. I wanted to learn the truth, so I organized an inquest in Terre Haute. My sister was harassed by the Israeli government not to come, and I was threatened by the Justice Department. They tried to intimidate me. When I started working on telling our story, it never entered my mind that I was doing something politically wrong, and I couldn't understand why. In 1985, I made a third silent pledge that I would do everything in my power to learn the truth about Mengele and find our files. I am still working on that one.

In summary, my personal experiences of being a Mengele guinea pig have been filed with physical and emotional pain, and it has been a very lonely battle. The political dimension is the most difficult top understand, and the most dangerous. I don't want Mengele in jail. I don't want to blame the U.S. or Israel for any mistakes. I don't want to punish anybody. I just want the information on our experiments. My most rewarding experience has been with you, the public, and I want to thank you for it.

Thank you so very much for listening to my story. I would like to point out what we can learn from it: 1) Never ever give up, no matter how difficult the problem; even if it looks hopeless, don't give up. 2) You the doctors, have chosen a wonderful but very difficult profession: I am sure that this is not news to you. Wonderful because you can do so much good, for you can ease pain and suffering, discover new medical treatments and save lives. Difficult because you are walking a very thin line. On one hand, you have to be cool and use the best logic and scientific judgment in treating your patients and doing your research; but you must remember, however, that you are dealing with human beings, and you should treat your patients the way you would want to be treated if you were in their place. I applaud your hard work in scientific research. Thanks to it, my son Alex is a survivor of an advanced stage of testicular cancer. I am aware of the great importance of medical and scientific research, but I, the human guinea pig, ask you to please remember that you are doing your research for the sake of human beings, and not for the sake of science alone. The moment you forget, you have crossed that thin line, and you are going in the direction of and with the arrogance of the Nazi doctors. 3) The problems of our world seem to be so overwhelming that we might think that the effort of one person could be meaningless, but I am here to tell you that every one of us can make a difference. Imagine the world all dark; suddenly a CANDLE is lit, "THE LIGHT OF ONE LITTLE CANDLE CAN ILLUMINATE THE DARKNESS OF THE ENTIRE UNIVERSE." I challenge you to light your CANDLES to illuminate some dark corner in the universe. I would like to note that there are many brightly lit CANDLES at this conference. We are sending a powerful beam of light to illuminate the dark corners of human experimentation in the world.

13

The Changing Landscape of Human Experimentation: Nuremberg, Helsinki, and Beyond

George J. Annas

Since World War II there have been persistent efforts at both the national and international level to develop rules to protect the rights and welfare of subjects of human experimentation.[1] These efforts have focused primarily on codifying the rights of subjects, and protecting their welfare by prior peer review of research protocols. In recent years research regulations have been under attack by politicians, drug companies, researchers, and advocacy groups. In less than half a century, human experimentation has been transformed from a suspect activity into a presumptively beneficial activity. With this transformation, traditional distinctions between experimentation and therapy, subject and patient, and researcher and physician have become discouragingly blurred. Issues of power, money, control, and fear of death have often been more central than protection of the rights and welfare of research subjects.

Special problems regarding rights and welfare of subjects have been recognized in research involving vulnerable populations, including pregnant women and fetuses, children, prisoners, and mentally-impaired

---

1. See generally *The Nazi Doctors and the Nuremberg Code: Human Rights in Human Experimentation* (George J. Annas & Michael A. Grodin eds., 1992), [hereinafter *Nazi Doctors*]; Bernard M. Dickens, et al., "Editor's Introduction to Research on Human Populations: National and International Ethical Guidelines," 19 *Law Med. & Health Care* 157 (1991).

people. But as premature death becomes a rarity in developed countries, and death itself becomes more alien and feared, the most vulnerable research subject, the one most consistently transformed into an object (a mere means to an end), has become the terminally ill patient. How did terminally ill patients come to be so sought-after as research subjects? Can current international research guidelines protect their rights and welfare in research trials? And if not, what additional steps are required to protect the rights and welfare of this uniquely vulnerable population?

A careful examination of the international research guidelines set forth during the past fifty years leads to the conclusion that a project that began as one to protect both the rights and welfare of human research subjects is now concentrated on rights protection in the developed nations, and on welfare protection in the developing nations. In both settings the basic rationale for these two diverging models is the same: desperation fueled by fear of death.[2]

The Nuremberg Code

The Nuremberg Code was formulated by United States judges sitting in judgment of Nazi physician-experimenters following World War II. The Nazi experiments involved systematic and barbarous interventions in which death was the planned endpoint. The subjects of these experiments were concentration camp prisoners, mostly Jews, Gypsies and Slavs.[3] The judges at Nuremberg viewed human experimentation as suspect, and the Nuremberg Code itself resulted from horrendous non-therapeutic, nonconsensual prison research.

---

2. The most quoted words in experimental medicine are not from any legal or ethical canon, but from *Hamlet:* "Diseases desperate grown By desperate appliance are relieved, Or not at all." William Shakespeare, *Hamlet,* act 4, sc. 2 (Edward Hubler ed., Signet Classic 1963). As with terminal illnesses such as cancer and AIDS the best strategy regarding the protection of research subjects is prevention. The King's "desperate diseases" speech begins with his musings on Hamlet, as he says,

> How dangerous is it that this man goes loose!
> Yet must not we put the strong law on him:
> He's loved of the distracted multitude,
> Who like not in their judgment, but their eyes.

Id.

The same thing may be said about human experimentation. It is loved by the public, but primarily because it is little understood, and its promise of "miracle" cures seems real. Nonetheless, the dangers to human rights and welfare of research subjects are such that we must "put the strong law on him" and develop and enforce reasonable research regulations.

3. *Nazi Doctors, supra* note 1.

The Nuremberg Code, despite its inherent limitations, remains the most authoritative legal and ethical document governing international research standards, and one of the premier human rights documents in world history. The judges based the Nuremberg Code on a natural law theory, deriving it from universal moral, ethical, and legal concepts. The Code protects individual subjects first by protecting their rights. Voluntary, informed, competent, and understanding consent is required by the first principle of the Code, and principle 9 gives the subject the right to withdraw from the experiment. The consent of the subject is necessary under the Nuremberg Code, although consent alone is not sufficient. The other eight provisions of the Code are related to the welfare of subjects, and must be satisfied *before* consent is even sought from the subject. The subject cannot waive these provisions. The requirements of the provisions include a valid research design to procure information important for the good of society that cannot be obtained in other ways; the avoidance of unnecessary physical and mental suffering and injury; the absence of any *a priori* reason to believe that death or disabling injury will occur; risks that never exceed benefits; and the presence of a qualified researcher who is prepared to terminate the experiment if it "is likely to result in the injury, disability, or death of the experimental subject."[4]

---

4. The Nuremberg Code:
1. The voluntary consent of the human subject is absolutely essential.

This means that the person involved should have legal capacity to give consent, should be so situated as to be able to exercise free power of choice, without the intervention of any element of force, fraud, deceit, duress, overreaching, or other ulterior form of constraint or coercion; and should have sufficient knowledge and comprehension of the elements of the subject matter involved as to enable him to make an understanding and enlightened decision. This latter element requires that before the acceptance of an affirmative decision by the experimental subject there should be made known to him the nature, duration, and purpose of the experiment; the method and means by which it is to be conducted; all inconveniences and hazards reasonably to be expected; and the effects upon his health or person which may possibly come from his participation in the experiment.

The duty and responsibility for ascertaining the quality of the consent rests upon each individual who initiates, directs or engages in the experiment. It is a personal duty and responsibility which may not be delegated to another with impunity.

2. The experiment should be such as to yield fruitful results for the good of society, unprocurable by other methods or means of study, and not random and unnecessary in nature.

3. The experiment should be so designed and based on the results of animal experimentation and a knowledge of natural history of the disease or other problem under study that the anticipated results will justify the performance of the experiment.

4. The experiment should be so conducted as to avoid all unnecessary physical and mental suffering and injury.

5. No experiment should be conducted where there is an *a priori* reason to believe that death or disabling injury will occur; except, perhaps, in those experiments where the experimental physicians also serve as subjects.

The Declaration(s) of Helsinki

Physician-researchers viewed the Nuremberg Code as confining and inapplicable to their practices, because it was promulgated as a human rights document by judges at a criminal trial, and because the judges made no attempt to deal with clinical research on children, patients, or mentally-impaired people. The World Medical Association has consistently tried to marginalize the Code by devising The Declaration of Helsinki, a more permissive alternative document, first promulgated in 1964, and amended three times since. This document is subtitled "recommendations guiding doctors in clinical research" and is just that, recommendations by physicians to physicians. The Declaration's goal is to replace the human rights-based agenda of the Nuremberg Code with a more lenient medical ethics model that permits paternalism. U.S. researcher Henry Beecher probably best expressed medicine's delight with the Declaration of Helsinki's ascendancy when he said in 1970: "The Nuremberg Code presents a rigid act of legalistic demands. . . . The Declaration of Helsinki, on the other hand, presents a set of guides. It is an ethical as opposed to a legalistic document and is thus more broadly useful than the one formulated at Nuremberg. . . ."[5]

The core of the Declaration of Helsinki divides research into therapeutic ("Medical Research Combined with Professional Care") and non-therapeutic, eliminating the necessity for subject consent in some cases.[6]

----

6. The degree of risk to be taken should never exceed that determined by the humanitarian importance of the problem to be solved by the experiment.

7. Proper preparations should be made and adequate facilities provided to protect the experimental subject against even remote possibilities of injury, disability, or death.

8. The experiment should be conducted only by scientifically qualified persons. The highest degree of skill and care should be required through all stages of the experiment of those who conduct or engage in the experiment.

9. During the course of the experiment the human subject should be at liberty to bring the experiment to an end if he has reached the physical or mental state where continuation of the experiment seems to hlm to be impossible.

10. During the course of the experiment the scientist in charge must be prepared to terminate the experiment at any stage, if he has probable cause to believe, in the exercise of the good faith, superior skill, and careful judgment required of him, that a continuation of the experiment is likely to result in injury, disability, or death to the experimental subject.

Nazi Doctors, *supra* note 1, at 2.

5. Quoted in W. Refshauge, "The Place for International Standards in Conducting Research for Humans," 55 *Bull. World Health Org.* 133-35 (Supp. 1977). See also the comparison made by the world's leading liver transplant experimenter, Thomas Starzl: "The Helsinki Declaration was shorter [sic] and easier to read." Thomas Starzl, *The Puzzle People: Memoirs of a Transplant Surgeon*, 146 (1992).

6. *Nazi Doctors*, *supra* note 1, at 335-36.

The major addition to the 1975 version (mirroring developments in the United States and elsewhere) was the encouragement of formal peer review of research protocols. For example, a new "basic principle" provided that: "The design and performance of each experimental procedure involving human subjects should be clearly formulated in an experimental protocol which should be transmitted to a specially appointed independent committee for consideration, comment and guidance."[7]

The movement to displace the consent requirement of the Nuremberg Code with prior peer review by a medical committee found its greatest success in the 1975 Declaration. For example, the physician need not obtain the subject's informed consent to medical research combined with professional care if he submits his reasons for not obtaining consent to the independent review committee.[8]

Council for International Organizations of Medical Sciences and the World Health Organization

Scientific organizations were even more hostile to the Nuremberg Code than were the world's physicians. In 1967 the president of the Council for International Organizations of Medical Sciences (CIOMS), for example, said that, "On the whole [the 1964 Declaration of Helsinki] corrects what in the Nuremberg Rules was circumstantial, related to Nazi crimes, and places these Rules more correctly in the context of generally accepted medical traditions."[9] Shortly thereafter, officials in the World Health Organization (WHO) were informed by officials at the National Institutes of Health that WHO grant proposals would not be considered unless they were approved by a WHO ethical review committee. WHO had no such peer review committee, and set about to form one. This was followed by a 1978 agreement between WHO and CIOMS to "develop guidelines to assist developing countries in evolving mechanisms that would ensure the observance of principles of medical ethics in biomedical research."[10] The result was an 1982 document (currently under revision) designed to provide guidance to developing countries.

---

7. *Nazi Doctors*, *supra* note 1, at 334.
Principle I.2 of the 1989 revision of the Declaration (Helsinki IV) provides that the experimental protocol "should be transmitted for consideration, comment and guidance to a specifically appointed committee independent of the investigator and the sponsor, provided that this independent committee is in conformity with the laws and regulations of the country in which the research experiment is performed.

8. Sharon Perley, et al., "The Nuremberg Code: An International Overview," in *Nazi Doctors*, *supra* note 1, at 159.

9. Refshauge, *supra* note 5, at 137.

10. Michael Grodin, "Historical Origins of the Nuremberg Code," in *Nazi Doctors*.

Remarkably, the 1982 Guidelines contain the statement: "Both the Nuremberg Code and the original Declaration of Helsinki of 1964 have been superseded by Helsinki II [1975]."[11] Helsinki II did supersede Helsinki I, but it could not, of course, supersede the judgment at Nuremberg. The Nuremberg Code is based on international natural law and ethics that even the prior positive law to the contrary in Nazi Germany could not supersede. Thus the Nuremberg Code is *the* basis for international law and ethics in the area of human experimentation, and lowering its standards can be accomplished neither by a vote of a group of researchers, nor by legal rule in any individual country. In this regard, individual countries can only legitimately *add* protections to the Nuremberg Code.

Nonetheless, the heart of the WHO/CIOMS project seems to compromise the Nuremberg Code's requirement for consent of the research subject as an integral part of international law and ethics. Instead, the 1982 Guidelines rely heavily on "an independent impartial prospective review of all protocols."[12] For the first time in an international document, special attention is given to children, pregnant and nursing women, and mentally ill and mentally-impaired people. However, adults in developing countries, perhaps unintentionally, are given the same uncomprehending status as children and the mentally ill.[13] For example, the rights of subjects are subordinated to the view that researchers and community leaders have of their welfare. Thus in developing countries it is suggested:

> [W]here individual members of a community often do not have the necessary awareness of the implications of participation in an experiment so as to adequately give informed consent, the Guidelines suggest that the decision on whether or not to participate should be elicited through the intermediary of a trusted community leader. . . . [T]he intermediary should make it clear . . . that participation is entirely voluntary and that he may abstain or withdraw from the experiment at any time.[14]

On the other hand, the standards for "externally sponsored research" done in developing countries are appropriately strict. Such research must meet not only the ethical standards of the host country, but also the ethical standards of the initiating country.[15] If this standard (No. 28) is taken

---

11. WHO/CIOMS, "Proposed International Guidelines for Biomedical Research Involving Human Subjects," CIOMS, Geneva (1982) at 23 [hereinafter "Proposed Guidelines"]. This language was deleted from the August 1992 redraft of the revisions.

12. *Id.* at 15.

13. Carel B. IJsselmuiden & Ruth R. Faden, "Research and Informed Consent in Africa: Another Look," 326 *New Eng. J. Med.* 830, 832 (1992).

14. *Id.* at 26-27. See also Perley et al, *supra* note 8, at 163; substantially similar language remains in the August 1992 redraft.

15. "Proposed Guidelines," *supra* note 11 at 31-32.

seriously, following the rights and welfare requirements of the Nuremberg Code would be required in most instances of United States and European-sponsored research in developing countries. Nonetheless, CIOMS greatly confuses the very concept of international law and ethics, seemingly encouraging countries to find their lowest common denominator in subject protection.

A 1992 draft revision of the 1982 Guidelines opens with a recharacterization of human research project in developing countries. It states that there is a "positive duty to do good," and that "Research is being seen as a good in itself, and as the discharge of an ethical responsibility."[16] This is, to my knowledge, the first time research has been privileged over treatment, and virtually no explanation is presented in the document for this radical assertion. If the developed countries have ethical responsibilities to the developing countries (and I believe they do), then the responsibilities of providing food, clothing, housing, education, and basic medical care must all have a much higher priority than providing research protocols. Thus, what seems at the center of this reconceptualization of research is not the "discharge" of an "ethical obligation," but gaining access to a population of research subjects for research that will primarily benefit citizens in the developed world.[17]

In summary, although the concept of vulnerable populations has been recognized, there are no international research guidelines that provide special rules or protections for the terminally ill, and there are no specific rules for research on terminal illnesses such as cancer and AIDS. We have witnessed a general trend away from the Nuremberg Code toward considering the protection of *either* rights (consent) or welfare (prior peer review) sufficient for human subject protection. With regard to research on terminal illnesses such as AIDS and cancer in the developed countries, this usually means that the research will be seen as therapy, and patients (subjects) who have the disease will be expected to protect themselves through the mechanism of informed consent. In developing countries, on the other hand, research on AIDS may be characterized as "community-based," and prior ethical review seen as sufficient protection for the rights and welfare of community members. In both cases the primary justification for research on terminal illnesses is the same: desperation in the face of death.

---

16. This April 1992 draft language was dropped in the August 1992 redraft, and hopefully will not be resurrected in the final document.

17. See *e.g.* Lawrence K. Altman, "AIDS Vaccine to be Tested on Human Volunteers Bypassing Animal Trials," *New York Times*, Nov. 11, 1991 at A7.

Research on Dying Patients: AIDS and Cancer

Perhaps the primary reason that existing national and international research guidelines have little practical relevance for individuals with terminal illnesses is that the terminal diagnosis itself determines both what researchers and physicians deem "reasonable," and what the subjects (patients) themselves find acceptable—even desirable. Many researchers themselves fear death, and believe that terminally ill patients really can't be hurt (they are "going to die anyway") and therefore have "nothing to lose." Prior peer review of protocols under such circumstances becomes pro forma and provides no meaningful protections for subjects. Likewise, terminally ill patients who are told that medicine has "nothing to offer" them have come to view experimental protocols as treatment. Therefore, instead of being suspicious of experimentation, patients may *demand* access to experimental interventions as their right. Under such circumstances informed consent alone provides no meaningful protection.

Psychiatrist Jay Katz has noted that when medicine seems impotent to fight the claims of nature, "all kinds of senseless interventions are tried in an unconscious effort to cure the incurable magically through a 'wonder drug,' a novel surgical procedure, or a penetrating psychological interpretation."[18] Although physicians often justify such interventions as simply being responsive to patient needs, "they may turn out to be a projection of their own needs onto patients."[19] Similarly, transplant surgeon Francis Moore has observed of transplant experiments based on the "desperate remedies" rationale: "There must be some likelihood of success before the desperate remedy becomes more than a desperate search for an opportunity to try a new procedure awaiting trial."[20] AIDS activist Rebecca Pringle Smith put it similarly, "Even if you have a supply of compliant martyrs, trials must have some ethical validity."[21]

Susan Sontag has noted that cancer and AIDS have become linked as perhaps the two most feared ways to die in the developed world. In her words, "AIDS, like cancer, leads to a hard death . . . The most terrifying illnesses are those perceived not just as lethal but as dehumanizing, literally so."[22] And although philosopher Michel Foucault was not speaking of the medicalization of death by cancer and AIDS, he could have been when he chronicled how the power of government over life and death has shifted in the past two centuries. "Now it is over life, throughout its un-

---

18. Jay Katz, *The Silent World of Doctor and Patient,* 151 (1984).

19. *Id.*

20. Francis D Moore, "The Desperate Case: CARE (Costs, Applicability, Research, Ethics)," 261 JAMA 1483, 1484 (1989).

21. Quoted in Joseph Palca, "AIDS Drug Trials Enter New Age," 246 SCI. 19, 20 (1989).

22. Susan Sontag, *Illness As Metaphor*; and, *AIDS and Its Metaphors,* 126 (1989).

folding, that power establishes its domination; death is power's limit, the moment that escapes it. . . ."[23] In human experimentation on the terminally ill we have Foucault's vision of public power played out in private: researchers take charge of the bodies of the dying in an attempt to take charge of the patient's lives and prevent their own personal deaths, and death itself.[24]

The Nazi doctors' chief defense at Nuremberg was that experimentation was necessary to support the war effort. Now combating disease has itself become a "war," as we speak of a "war on cancer" and a "war on AIDS." And in that war, patients, especially terminally ill patients, are conscripted as soldiers. As former editor of the *New England Journal of Medicine,* Franz Ingelfinger, put it: "[T]he thumb screws of coercion are most relentlessly applied" to "the most used and useful of all experimental subjects, the patient with disease."[25] But as Sontag reminds us, war metaphors are dangerous in disease because they encourage authoritarianism, overmobilization, and stigmatization. In her words:

> No, it is not desirable for medicine, any more than for war, to be "total." Neither is the crisis created by AIDS a "total" anything. We are not being invaded. The body is not a battlefield. The ill are neither unavoidable casualties nor the enemy. We—medicine, society—are not authorized to fight back by any means whatever. . . .[26]

Cancer

In the early 1980s the President's Commission for the Study of Ethical Problems in Medicine and Behavioral Research attempted to get agreement on categorizing Phase 1 drug studies with anticancer agents. Are they research or therapy? Federal Food and Drug Administration (FDA) regulations state that Phase I studies are intended to have no therapeutic content, but are to determine "toxicity, metabolism, absorption, elimination, and other pharmacological action, preferred route of administration, and safe dosage range."[27] Nonetheless, National Cancer Institute (NCI) researchers insisted that Phase 1 cancer studies, using cancer patients as subjects, should be described as therapeutic. The Assistant Secretary of

---

23. Michel Foucault, *The History of Sexuality,* 138 (Robert Hurley trans., 1990).

24. *Id.* at 143.

25. F. J. Ingelfinger, "Informed (But Uneducated) Consent," 287 *New Eng. J. Med.* 465, 466 (1972).

26. Sontag, *supra* note 22, at 182-183.

27. *President's Commission for the Study of Ethical Problems in Medicine and Biomedical and Behaviorial Research, Protecting Human Subjects,* 65 (1981) [hereinafter *President's Commission*].

List of Illustrations

Ziel und Weg

Zeitschrift des Nationalsozialistischen Deutschen Ärzte-Bundes, e.V.

3. Jahrgang   1933   Heft 9

Wir übernehmen die Führung

Presseempfang beim Aufklärungsamt für Bevölkerungspolitik und Rassenpflege im Hotel „Kaiserhof" zu Berlin, bei dem Dr. Groß und Prof. Staemmler über die Notwendigkeit zielbewußter Mitarbeit der Presse sprachen.
Das Bild zeigt links Pg. Med.-Rat Dr. Gütt vom Reichsinnenministerium, der dort die rassenhygienischen Fragen bearbeitet. Am Rednerpult Pg. Prof. Staemmler, rechts am Tisch u. A. Dr. Groß und Dr. Wagner, München.

phot. Scherl

"We Are Taking Over Control"
Press meeting with "Racial Purity" officials
(Staatsbibliothek zu Berlin—Preussicher Kulturbesitz)

Nicht länger So!

Links: 4 Jahre altes Mädchen, ererbt syphilitisch. Mutter Prostituierte und trotz dieser Krankheit verheiratet. Das Kind ist unehelich.

Rechts: Dreijähriger Junge, taub, verkrüppelt, vollständig verblödet, schielt und kann kaum sehen. Kostet der Stadt Berlin täglich 5 Mark. Eine 5 köpfige Familie mit arbeitslosem Ernährer erhält wöchentlich etwa 24 Mark Unterstützung und muß davon noch die Miete bezahlen.

Hält man sich alle diese Tatsachen vor Augen und bedenkt man weiter, wie an dem gesunden Rassegefüge des deutschen Volkes ständig der Einbruch fremder Rassen nagt, man denke doch nur an den Einbruch jüdischen Blutes in den letzten 100 Jahren in das deutsche Volk, dann wird man erst die kulturschöpferische Tat zu würdigen wissen, die in der Gesetzgebung der Sterilisation Erbminderwertiger liegt.

Was verstehen wir überhaupt unter Sterilisation? Unter Sterilisation auf operativem Wege verstehen wir die Unfruchtbarmachung der Ausführungsgänge der Keimdrüsen, d. h. die Durchschneidung des Samenleiters beim Manne und der Eileiter bei der Frau. Die operative Sterilisierung beim Mann ist ein harmloser Eingriff und bei der Frau dank der heutigen Technik ein Eingriff ohne weiteres Risiko.

Man hat früher häufig Kastration und Sterilisation verwechselt. Stellenweise geschieht es anscheinend auch noch heute. Die Erbpflege hat mit der Kastration nichts zu tun.

Die Sterilisierung ist eine rasse-hygienische Maßnahme, die Kastration eine medizinische Angelegenheit. Die Kastration, die ebenfalls die Fortpflanzung verhindert, aber gleichzeitig damit auch die sexuelle Persönlichkeit verändert (Eunuche), spielt eine wichtige Rolle bei der Heilung von sexual Abnormen und Sexualverbrechern. Diese verbrecherischen Kranken fallen auch nicht unter das Sterilisationsgesetz, sondern die Regierung hat sich vorbehalten, gerade um dem Sterilisationsgesetz das Odium des Strafvollzuges zu nehmen, diese Menschen in einem besonderen Gesetz zu erfassen.

Das Sterilisationsgesetz, das am 1. Januar 1934 in Kraft tritt, und das bisher nur als Rahmengesetz bekannt ist, die näheren Ausführungen werden noch dazu erlassen, bestimmt:

Nur noch So!

Die Bilder bedürfen keiner Erklärung

"No Longer Like This, But Only Like This"
Sterilization program promoted in July 1933
(Staatsbibliothek zu Berlin, Preussischer Kulturbesitz)

Bekanntmachung

Das Sondergericht Hohensalza hat zum Tode verurteilt am 5. März 1943

Ludwika Wawrzyniak, geb. Brzurska, aus Golina, Kreis Konin,

wegen gewerbsmäßiger Abtreibung.

Das Urteil ist heute vollstreckt worden.

(Übersetzung)

Przez Sondergericht w Hohensalza skazana została na śmierć dnia 5. marca 1943 Ludwika Wawrzyniak, ur. Brzurska, z Golina, Kreis Konin, za zawodowe spedzanie płodu.

Wyrok został dzisiai wykonany

Hohensalza, den 31. März 1943.

Der Oberstaatsanwalt

T 6079 — 67315

"Announcement: Ludwika Wawrzyniak,
Sentenced to Death for Performing Abortions" 1943
(Archiwum Pan'stowa, Bydgoszcz, Poland)

Eine Schwangerschaft darf nicht unterbrochen werden!

Hüte Dich vor Ratschlägen und Eingriffen Unberufener!

"Pregnancy Should Not Be Terminated:
Protect yourself from advice and intervention of outsiders"
From "A Healthy Woman, A Healthy People" Exhibit
(German Hygiene Museum, Dresden)

"Girls Today,
Mothers
Tomorrow,"
May 1935

(Staatsbibliothek
zu Berlin,
Preussische
Kulturbesitz)

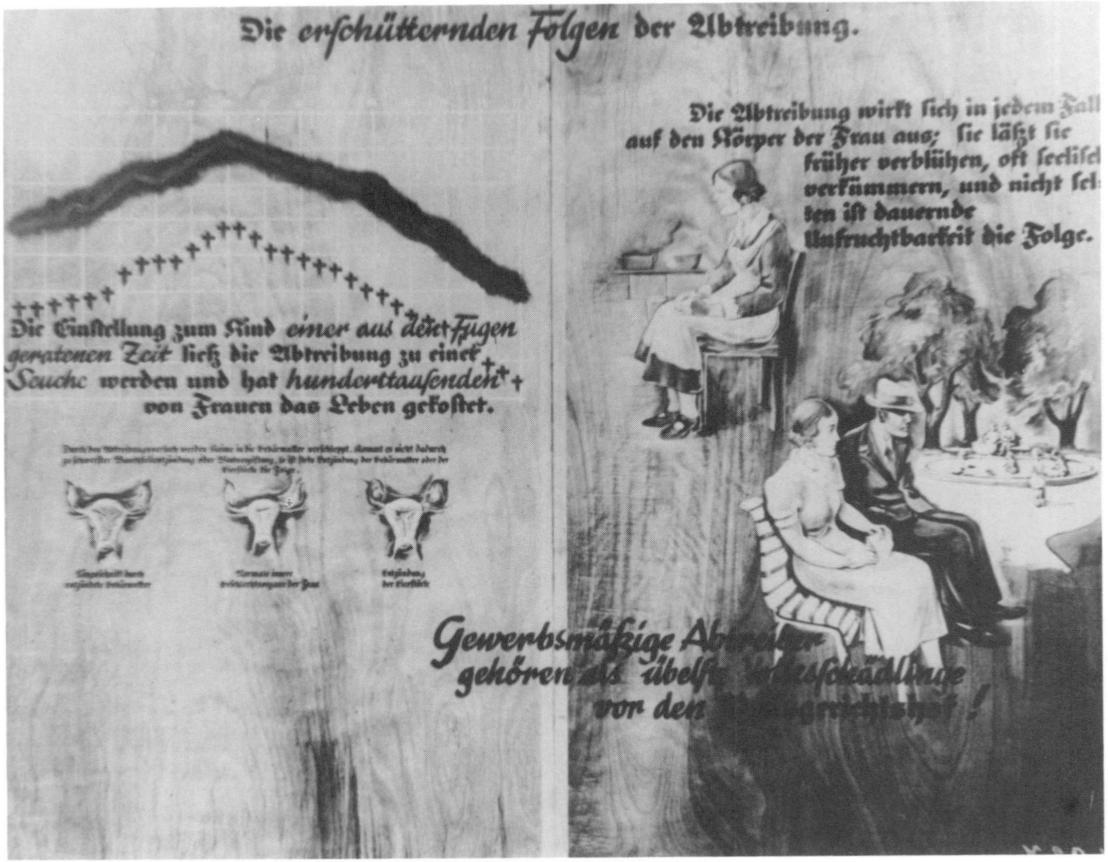

"The Disturbing
Consequences
of Abortion"

From the Exhibit
"Ewiges Volk"
(Eternal People,
1938)

(German Hygiene
Museum,
Dresden)

"Die Frau"
From the Exhibit "Die Frau" (The Woman: 18 March-23 April 1933)
(German Hygiene Museum, Dresden)

"The Body—
A National Entity
in Microcosm"

(German Hygiene
Museum,
Dresden)

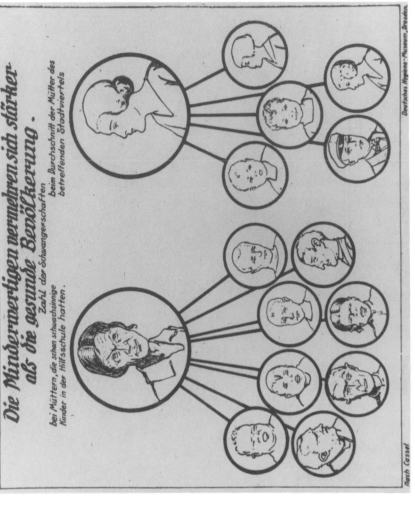

Die Minderwertigen vermehren sich stärker als die gesunde Bevölkerung.

bei Müttern, die schon schwachsinnige Kinder in der Hilfsschule hatten.

Zahl der Schwangerschaften beim Durchschnitt der Mütter des betreffenden Stadtviertels

Nach Cassel.

Deutsches Hygiene-Museum, Dresden.

"Inferior Races Multiply
Faster than the Healthy
Population"

Left: Mothers with
        retarded children
Right: Mothers with
        healthy children

(German Hygiene
Museum, Dresden)

EVA
Miriam
Eva Mozes Kor-only survivor
The Mozes Family last picture Fall 1943, Portz - Hungary

Eva and Miriam Mozes, experimented upon
by Dr. Josef Mengele at Auschwitz,
with her family prior to the Nazi Occupation of Hungary
(Eva Mozes Kor collection)

Eva and Miriam Mozes
liberated at Auschwitz,
27 January 1945

(Eva Mozes Kor
collection)

Eva Mozes Kor and Miriam Mozes Zeiger in December 1991,
on the site of their 1945 liberation
during a documentary film production on Josef Mengele.
(Eva Mozes Kor collection)

Dr. Karl Brandt, Hitler's "escort physician" since 1934,
at the Nuremburg Doctors Trial.
Sentenced to death by hanging on 20 August 1947.
(U.S. Army, Ray D'Addario, photographer)
Courtesy of Dr. Michael Grodin.

the Department of Health and Human Services (HHS) wrote to Congress in 1981:

> Notwithstanding the fact that some individuals within HHS may not concur, the official position of the Department, including NCI, NIH, and FDA, is to regard Phase 1 trials of anti-cancer drugs as *potentially* therapeutic. The often small, but real possibility of benefit must be weighed against the nearly 100 percent probability of death if experimental therapy is not attempted for the advanced cancer patients who participate in Phase 1 studies.[28]

The President's Commission never received a better answer to its inquiry, and this answer is not helpful. In a sick person, virtually any intervention, even a placebo, can be described as "potentially therapeutic," and once this misleading label is applied, the nonbeneficial Phase 1 study is de facto eliminated and transformed into "experimental therapy." Any distinction between experimentation and therapy is lost. Under these circumstances the President's Commission could only bow weakly to informed consent: "It is important that patients who are asked to participate in tests of new anti-cancer drugs not be misled about the likelihood (or remoteness) of any therapeutic benefit they might derive from such participation."[29]

American oncologists use so many approved drugs for unapproved uses that it seems fair to conclude that for most cancers there are no standard treatments, and sound scientific studies are needed. A 1990 survey, for example, found that fully one-third of all the drugs used on cancer patients are of unproven safety and efficacy for the purpose for which they are given; and unapproved use is even more prevalent for malignancies that have metastasized than for earlier cancers.[30] Unapproved chemotherapy for patients being treated with palliative intent is twice the rate for curative intent, indicating an appropriately higher degree of risk-taking for quality of life enhancement. Oncologist Charles Moertel, commenting on the study, noted that the major beneficiaries of such an approach to cancer treatment are the "appointment book of the oncologist" and "the pharmaceutical companies and their stockholders."[31] In short, business ethics seem to be supplanting medical ethics. As to the argument that oncologists are just responding to the demand of dying patients, Moertel responded: "This argument abandons the scientific basis for medical prac-

---

28. *Id.* (quoting letter from Edward N. Brandt, Jr., Assistant Sec. for Health Dept. of Health and Human Services, to the Hon. Henry A. Waxman, Chairman, Subcomm. on Health & Environment (Nov. 20, 1981, at 3-4)).

29. *President's Commission, supra* note 27, at 43.

30. Thomas Laetz and George Silberman, "Reimbursement Policies Constrain the Practice of Oncology," 266 JAMA 2996, 2997 (1991).

31. Charles G. Moertel, "Off-Label Drug Use for Cancer Therapy and National Health Care Priorities," 266 JAMA 3031 (1991).

tice and could just as well be used to justify quackery. Also, one wonders how many patients with advanced pancreatic cancer, for example, would really demand cytotoxic drugs if the sheer futility of such therapy was honestly explained."[32]

If we accept patient demand as sufficient justification to mistreat them, it is a short step to say that the patient should have the right to demand to be killed by his physician. In fact, this very argument was made in early 1992 in the *New England Journal of Medicine,* where another oncologist noted that cancer chemotherapy, while it can prolong life, often makes the patient's dying "unbearable."[33] He went on to argue that, "since we physicians brought the patient [subject] to the state she is in, we cannot abandon her by saying that euthanasia violates the purpose of our profession."[34] The use of killing as "damage control" for a physician-created harm to patients is chilling. It is far better to avoid the harm than to use it to justify killing. The quest to master terminal illness may, however, make killing by physicians seem reasonable.[35]

The "desperate remedies" rationale used to justify experimentation on the terminally ill is seriously flawed. There are fates worse than death, and many Americans have written living wills and health care proxies to *prevent* their lives from being prolonged under certain circumstances.[36] Likewise, the horrible and prolonged deaths of Barney Clark and William Schroder on the permanent artificial heart insured the end of all further experiments with the Jarvik 7.[37] Although the device can obviously prolong life, it cannot do so at an acceptable level of quality. The conclusion is clear: dying patients are real people, not objects, who value quality over quantity of life, and cannot be legally or ethically used simply as a means to an end. Individuals do have a right to refuse *any* treatment or experiment. But respecting patient autonomy does *not* require that we accept demands for mistreatment, experimentation, torture, or whatever the dying might want, anymore than we must accede to demands for illegal

---

32. *Id.* See also Cornelius 0. Granai, "Ovarian Cancer—Unrealistic Expectations," 327 *New Eng. J. Med.* 197 (1992).

33. Guy I. Benrubi, "Euthanasia: The Need for Procedural Safeguards," 326 *New Eng. J. Med.* 197 (1992).

34. *Id.* at 198.

35. See, *e.g.,* Physician-philosopher Leon Kass, who has argued "We do not yet understand that the project for the mastery of nature and the conquest of death leads only to dehumanization; that any attempt to gain the tree of life by means of the tree of knowledge leads inevitably also to the hemlock. . . ." Leon R. Kass, "Suicide Made Easy: The Evil of 'Rational' Humaneness," *Commentary,* Dec. 1991, at 19, 24.

36. See Nancy M.P. King, *Making Sense of Advance Directives* (1991).

37. George J. Annas, "Death and the Magic Machine: Informed Consent to the Artificial Heart," 9W. *New Eng. L. Rev.* 89 (1987).

(but effective) drugs like heroin and LSD, unlicensed practitioners, or a physician-induced death.

Closely related to the difficulty of distinguishing research from treatment is distinguishing the role of the researcher from the role of the physician when these two conflicting roles are merged in one person. For example, in a 1992 article on cancer and AIDS research two prominent commentators seem to assume that "cancer researchers" are properly seen as doctors providing "treatment" to "patients."[38] Little attention has been paid to the researcher's inherent conflict of interest. It is unlikely that patients can ever draw the distinction between physician and researcher, because most simply do not believe that their physician would either knowingly do something harmful to them, or would knowingly use them simply as a means for their own ends. Cancer researchers, however, know better. James F. Holland, for example, has said simply, "Patients have to be subsidiaries of the trial . . . I'm not interested in holding patients' hands. I'm interested in curing cancer . . . Every patient becomes a piece of scientific data."[39] As candid as Holland is, it seems almost certain that his patients come to him for a cure, and look upon him as their physician—not as simply a researcher. In such a circumstance, the Helsinki Declaration's theoretical division between therapeutic and non-therapeutic research is meaningless.

Finally, we should emphasize that which has generally been marginalized: most studies on the terminally ill, including cancer and AIDS clinical trials, are funded by private drug companies that have tremendous financial stakes in their success. Clinical investigators may even "own equity interest in the company that produces the product or may serve as paid consultants and scientific advisers," roles that at least call their objectivity into question.[40] Medical ethics is being eroded by a new commercialism in medicine. This fact has led most leading medical journals in the United States to require financial disclosure prior to publication of research results. However, neither Institutional Review Boards (IRBs) nor individual subjects are routinely informed of the financial aspects of proposed clinical trials, even though the finances often create major potential conflicts of interest among the sponsor, the researcher, and the patient-subject.

One need not search far for examples. In early February 1992, the stock of U.S. Bioscience lost $550 million in value in one day after the

---

38. David J. Rothman and Harold Edgar, "Scientific Rigor and Medical Realities Placebo Trials in Cancer and AIDS Research," in *AIDS: The Making of a Chronic Disease,* 194-206 (E. Fee & D. Fox eds., 1992).

39. Dena Kleiman, "In Search for Cancer Cure, Patients Come Second," *New York Times,* Feb. 18, 1986, at Bl, B7.

40. Arnold Relman, "What Market Values are Doing to Medicine," *The Atlantic Monthly* 99, 103 (Mar. 1992).

FDA review panel refused to recommend approval of its drug, Ethyl (a drug said to protect healthy cells from the toxic effects of cancer chemotherapy).[41] One week later another United States biotechnology company lost half of its value in one day when a clinical trial of one of its cancer drugs was halted because of adverse effects on the subjects.[42] Financing may be *the* major change in clinical trials over the past two decades, and this change has not been mirrored in research regulations. New research findings are often reported first on the financial pages of newspapers, and only later in the medical literature. It thus came as little surprise in March 1992, when Dow Corning openly declared that its decision to discontinue the manufacture of silicone breast implants was made strictly on "the basis of business."[43]

AIDS

AIDS has always been perceived as the disease in which there literally is *no* distinction between treatment and experimentation. This is because there is no cure for AIDS. The disease primarily strikes the young, leading to a death that is premature by virtually any calculation, and existing treatments that can prolong life are far from satisfactory. In addition, many people with the disease have no access to health care, so the only way they can obtain medical care is to enroll in an experimental drug trial. Thus, although theoretically wrong, ACT-UP's (AIDS Coalition to Unleash Power) political slogan, "A Drug Trial is Health Care Too," tragically is factually correct in many U.S. settings. However, the slogan serves to wrongly conflate experimentation with therapy, and to encourage people with AIDS to seek out experimentation as treatment, and physician-researchers to see AIDS patients as potential subjects who have "nothing to lose."

As the *Wall Street Journal* editorialized in 1988, supporting a loosening of FDA testing procedures for people with cancer, Alzheimer's disease, and AIDS: "AIDS patients have driven home to the U.S. medical and political establishment what enormous risks human beings in death's grip will take to gain relief or respite."[44] This editorial identified the

---

41. Michael Waldholz, "U.S. Bioscience Holders Are Latest to Get Costly Lesson," *Wall St. J.*, Feb. 4, 1992, at B6.

42. Floyd Norris, "Drug's Test Pains MGI Investors," *New York Times*, Feb. 11, 1992, at Cl; James P. Miller, "MGI Pharma Suffers 52% Fall in Stockprice," *Wall St. J.* Feb. 11, 1992, at B3

43. Philip J. Hilts, "As It Quits Implant Business." See also "Maker Says Product is Safe," *New York Times*, March 20, 1992, at A12. Michael Waldholz, "An Unapproved Drug for Alzheimer's Gets a Big Marketing Push," *Wall St. J.*, Aug. 25, 1992, at Al.

44. "New Ideas for New Drugs," *Wall St. J.*, Dec. 28, 1988, at A16. See also

problem and illustrated why regulation is necessary. The FDA is not in the business of regulating "hope" for "relief or respite" but of determining whether "relief or respite" from particular drugs and devices is likely. Deregulation of human experimentation cannot produce new drugs or treatments. Money can, however, be made by pharmaceutical companies by exploiting our fear of death and desperation. It seems fair to conclude that virtually all of the drugs that have been developed for AIDS treatment have been over-priced, and financially exploitative of those with AIDS.[45] Again, business ethics seem to be supplanting medical ethics.

Although the cover story is compassion, the movement to loosen FDA's research rules should be seen for what it is: a political strategy by a free market administration bent not on helping people with AIDS, but on exploiting the AIDS epidemic to loosen drug regulations and maximize profits for the pharmaceutical industry.[46] For example, Jay Plager, counselor to the former Undersecretary of the Department of Health and Human Services, asserted that one purpose of early drug release regulations is to give "desperately ill patients the opportunity to decide for themselves whether they would rather take an experimental drug or die of the disease untreated."[47] And former FDA Commissioner Frank Young said of AIDS that "there is such a degree of desperation, and people are going to die, that I'm not going to be the Commissioner that robs them of hope."[48] The FDA must concentrate on using science to identify beneficial treatments, not on using faith healing to promote hope that an unproven drug might be beneficial. There is some evidence that AIDS activists now recognize this. At the July 1992 International AIDS conference in Amsterdam, for example, ACT-UP member Mark Harrington said he believed that regulatory reforms often "go for naught." In his words, "What is the point of streamlining access and approval when the result is merely to replace AZT

Andrew Pollack, Gene "Therapy Gets the Go-Ahead," *New York Times* Feb. 14, 1992 at Dl; Mireya Navarro, "Into the Unknown: AIDS Patients Test Drugs," *New York Times*, Feb. 29, 1992, at 1, 29. See also Rothman and Edgar, *supra* note 38 at 205.

45. See, *e.g.*, "Forcing Poverty on AIDS Patients," *New York Times,* Aug. 30, 1988 at A18 (editorial); Maher, "Pitiless Scourge: Separating Out the Hype from the Hope on AIDS, Barron's," March 13, 1989, at 6, 22; Eric Savitz, "No Magic Cure: The War on AIDS Produces Few Gains, Except on Wall Street," *Barron's,* Dec. 16, 1991, at 10.

46. See generally George J. Annas, "Faith (Healing), Hope and Charity at the FDA: The Politics of AIDS Drug Trials," 34 *Vill. L. Rev.* 771 (1989).

47. Robert Pear, "U.S. to Allow Use of Trial Drugs for AIDS and other Terminal Ills," *New York Times*, May 21, 1987, at Al.

48. Phillip M. Boffey, "FDA Will Allow AIDS Patients to Import Unapproved Medicines," *New York Times,* July 24, 1988, at Al, Al9.

[with] mediocre, toxic, expensive" drugs.[49] Harrington urged others to follow his example and volunteer for experiments involving basic science.[50]

Of course, it remains unethical to conduct a clinical trial in a manner in which no reliable data can be generated. As Anthony Fauci, director of the National Institute of Allergy and Infectious Diseases, has properly noted, the primary goal of clinical trials is "not to deliver therapy. It's to answer a scientific question so that the drug can be available for everybody once you've established safety and efficacy."[51] On the other hand, community activists have made some important points regarding AIDS, and some rules for AIDS research in the United States are appropriately changing. Three are of note: (1) Representatives of the gay rights and AIDS communities are being asked to join governmental scientific advisory panels which set research priorities; (2) people with AIDS are being placed on local IRBs to evaluate community-based AIDS research protocols; and (3) end points involving quality of life instead of death are being explored in evaluating the results of AIDS drug trials.[52] Emphasis on quality of life measures seems especially relevant in diseases like AIDS and cancer where brief increases in longevity may be possible only at the cost of severe suffering.[53]

Strategies such as promoting unproven AIDS drugs by press conference and press release, and changing research rules for political gain, foster false hope and financial exploitation. Terminally ill AIDS and cancer patients can be harmed, misused, and exploited. It has even been persuasively argued that we as a society have developed a "cure or kill" attitude that permits us to use the terminally ill as "volunteers" for our experiments designed to banish death:

> Our quest for a formula that will banish death seems to make it acceptable to try questionable regimens on the aged and terminally ill. . . . Those who insist on using the dying as experimental subjects . . . see death as abnormal and dying patients as subhuman. We cast the terminally ill in modern rites of sacrifice, putting patients

---

49. Quoted in Lawrence K. Altman, "At AIDS Talks, Reality Weighs Down Hope," *New York Times*, July 26, 1992, at A1.

50. *Id.*

51. Joseph Palca, "AIDS Drug Trials Enter New Age," *246 SCI.* 19 (1989).

52. Carol Levine et al., "Building a New Consensus: Ethical Principles and Policies for Clinical Research on HIV/AIDS," IRB, 1-22 (report which indicates an emerging consensus of the formation and conduct of clinical trials for AIDS research) (Jan.-Apr., 1991), and *see* Vanessa Merton, "Community-Based AIDS Research," 14 *Evaluation Rev.* 502 (1990) (discusses the development and design of the Community Research Initiative of New York City, an IRB that reviews community-based AIDS research).

53. Office of Technology Assessment, Congress of the United States, *Unconventional Cancer Treatments,* 228 (1990).

of experiments . . . through what one might see as torture in the hope of postponing the inevitable.[54]

Of course, consent is no justification for the torture or inhumane treatment of human beings. We must stop treating terminally ill cancer and AIDS patients as subhuman by offering them questionable experiments in the guise of treatment. We cannot justify this behavior on the basis of either their demand for it or our belief that the ultimate good of mankind will be served by it. Researchers who believe their subjects cannot be hurt by experimental interventions *should be disqualified* from doing research on human subjects on the basis that they cannot appropriately protect their subjects' welfare with such a view. Likewise, subjects who believe they have "nothing to lose" and are desperate because of their terminal illness should also be disqualified as potential research subjects because they are unable to provide voluntary, competent, informed or understanding consent to the experimental intervention with such a view. It should be emphasized that these are proposed *research* rules that would not necessarily apply to treatment in a doctor-patient relationship untainted by conflicts of interest.

What Should be Done Generally?

Action to protect research subjects in our new age of cancer and AIDS seems reasonable on both the international and national levels. On the international level we have already seen that the Nuremberg Code, the Helsinki Declaration, and WHO/CIOMS guidelines are almost universally seen as advisory and ethical only. They have no legal status in most individual countries, and they provide no mechanism for accountability or sanction of researchers who disregard their precepts. Moreover, the content and structure of medical research has changed radically in the past decade, as we have moved away from medical ethics, towards commerce and business ethics. It would therefore seem reasonable at this time to seek more definitive action or international research rules from the United Nations. Although the United Nations never formally adopted the Nuremberg Code, its consent principle did become an important part of the United Nations International Covenant on Civil and Political Rights, which was promulgated in 1966 and adopted by the United Nations General Assembly in 1974.[55] Article 7 of this covenant states: "No one shall be subjected to torture or to cruel, inhuman or degrading treatment or

---

54. Ralph Brauer, "The Promise that Failed," *New York Times*, Aug. 28, 1988 sec. 6 (magazine) at 34, 76.

55. Perley et al., *supra* note 8, at 153.

punishment. In particular, no one shall be subjected without his free consent to medical or scientific experimentation."[56]

Most physicians would, of course, be shocked at having anything they do to patients considered "torture or cruel, inhuman or degrading treatment." They would thus view the Covenant's provisions much the same way they view the Nuremberg Code: as a criminal law document not applicable to anything done in the doctor-patient relationship. It should be noted, however, that in Nazi Germany no distinction between torture and experimentation was possible and many contemporary experiments produce "unbearable" suffering.

Because none of the existing conventions of the United Nations deal in a detailed manner with human experimentation, M. Cheriff Bassiouni has proposed that the United Nations adopt a specific criminal Covenant on Human Experimentation:

Section 1. Acts of Unlawful Medical Experimentation

1.0 The crime of unlawful medical experimentation consists of any physical and/or psychological alterations by means of surgical operations or injections, ingestion or inhalation of substances inflicted by or at the instigation of a public official, or for which a public official is responsible and to which the person subject to such experiment does not grant consent as described in Section 2.

Section 2. Defense of Consent

2.1 For the purpose of this Article a person shall not be deemed to have consented to medical experimentation unless he or she has the capacity to consent and does so freely after being fully informed of the nature of the experiment and its possible consequences.

2.2 A person may withdraw his or her consent at any time and shall be deemed to have done so if he or she is not kept fully informed within a reasonable time of the progress of the experiment and any development concerning its possible consequences.[57]

Professor Bassiouni believes this draft Code was rejected because some member countries thought it might impinge upon the practices of their pharmaceuticals industry.[58] If true, this is a serious condemnation of the drug companies involved. It also makes clear the need to include privately funded research in the Code as well. The Code's purpose is to articulate *human* rights that *all* members of the human community share by virtue of being human.[59] Human rights are more important than either

---

56. G.A. Res. 2200 A, U.N. GAOR, 21st Sess., Supp. No. 16, at 49, U.N. Doc. A/0316 (1966).

57. M. Cheriff Bassiouni, et al., "An Appraisal of Human Experimentation in International Law and Practice," 72 *J. Crim. Law & Criminology* 1597-1666 (1981).

58. Perley, *supra* note 8 at 166.

medical or business ethics, and are *not* a matter of "internal affairs." Because the United Nations is the only credible international body capable of articulating an international code of conduct for human experimentation, an international Covenant on Human Experimentation based on the Nuremberg Code, covering all non-therapeutic research and all therapeutic research on competent individuals, should be adopted. Additional provisions regarding children, the mentally impaired, and the terminally ill [see *infra.*] should be included.

An international tribunal for human experimentation should also be established. Such a tribunal could be established to enforce a United Nations-adopted Code, initially limited to civil sanctions and financed with a small percentage of the human research budget of member states. Without an international tribunal with the authority to judge and punish violators of international norms of human experimentation, we are left where we began: international norms of human experimentation are relegated to the domain of ethics, and are ignored or subverted in that domain. This is because without the possibility of judgment and punishment, there is no international law worthy of the name, only international ethics.

An international tribunal will not be established overnight; therefore, we should agree to voluntarily take some steps immediately. With regard to human rights, we should insist on informed consent from all potential subjects capable of giving it. With regard to human welfare, we must be much more insistent that nonresearchers and nonphysicians make up a significant proportion (at least half) of all ethical review committees. This step will not solve the power problems inherent in expertise, but will help expose the extent to which the agenda of the researcher/scientist diverges from that of the nonexpert citizen. In addition, all research protocols should be made public, and the financial arrangements and sources must be made available to both review committees and subjects to expose (and hopefully curtail) conflicts of interest. All meetings of such review committees should be open to the public, because openness helps to dilute the power of expertise and democratically enfranchise the public.

The Special Problems of Terminally Ill Research Subjects

Because the voluntary and understanding nature of consent of the terminally ill subject is compromised, and because this population is especially subject to exploitation by researchers who are often unrealistically optimistic in their expectations and believe their subjects cannot be harmed, adoption of the following additional safeguards is suggested. The primary goals of these safeguards should be to protect the quality of life

---

59. Ruth Macklin, "Universality of the Nuremberg Code," in *Nazi Doctors, supra* note 1, at 240-257.

of conscious patients and to protect the unconscious from being used simply as objects for the ends of others.

Proposed Regulations Governing Research on Terminally Ill Patients

1. For the purpose of these regulations a "terminally ill patient" is one whose death is reasonably expected to occur within six months even if currently accepted and available medical treatment is used.

2. In addition to all other legal and ethical requirements for the approval of a research protocol by national and local scientific and ethical review boards (including IRBs), research in which terminally ill patients participate as research subjects shall be approved only if the review board specifically finds that:

   (a) The research, if it carries any risk, has the intent and *reasonable probability* (based on scientific data) of improving the health or well-being of the subject, or of significantly increasing the subject's length of life without significantly decreasing its quality;

   (b) There is no *a priori* reason to believe that the research intervention will significantly decrease the subject's quality of life because of suffering, pain, or indignity attributable to the research, and,

   (c) Written informed consent will be required of all research participants over the age of sixteen in research involving any risk, and such consent may be solicited only by a physician acting as a *patient rights advocate* who is appointed by the review committee, is independent of the researcher, and whose duty it is to fully and objectively inform the potential subject of all reasonably foreseeable risks and benefits inherent in the research protocol. The patient rights advocate will also be empowered to monitor the actual research itself.

3. The vote on and basis for each of the findings in subpart (2) shall be set forth in writing by the review board, and be available to all potential subjects and the public.

4. All research protocols (including the financial arrangements between the sponsor and the researcher) involving terminally ill subject shall be available to the public, and the meetings of the scientific and ethical review boards on these protocols shall be open to the public.

The major features of this proposal are worth emphasizing. The first is that so-called non-therapeutic research may not be performed on terminally ill patients at all unless there is no risk to the patient. Nor may "potentially," or "hopefully," or "possibly" therapeutic research be performed—the research must have "the intent and *reasonable probability* (based on scientific data) of improving the health or well-being of the subject. . . ." The fact that there is no treatment for the condition does *not* make any intervention "therapeutic" or even "probably" therapeutic. Phase

1 cancer drug research, for example, may not be performed on terminally ill subjects under these guidelines because there is no reasonable probability that it will benefit the subjects. Second, for subjects over the age of sixteen, only the subjects themselves are permitted to give consent for any research that involves any risk. Unless the condition is unique to children, no experimentation should be done on children until it has been demonstrated to meet the "reasonable probability" standard in adults. Proxy consent is acceptable only for *no* risk research (such as observation and monitoring studies, blood sampling, and research involving comatose patients). Third, the researcher is disqualified from obtaining the subject's consent. This task must be performed by an independent physician acting as a patient rights advocate, and whose primary obligation is to protect the rights and welfare of the potential research subject. Finally, the protocols, their financing, votes on them, and meetings concerning them, shall be open to the public.

These steps should help to protect both the rights and welfare of the terminally ill. Changes in codes and procedures alone, however, will not be sufficient to clarify societal goals for research and the practice of medicine, to define the meaning of progress, or to delineate the appropriate content of the practice of medicine. Resolving these central questions requires a recognition on the part of both society and medical practitioners that immortality is not a reasonable goal for medicine or humanity,[60] that there are fates worse than death, and that quality of life is more important than quantity of life.[61]

We can harm the terminally ill by treating them as objects with nothing to lose. They are our most vulnerable population, and need much more protection than they are currently afforded. It will take reality-based care for the dying, rather than fantasy-based experiments on the dying, to reclaim medicine's commitment in The Declaration of Geneva: "The health of my patient will be my first consideration."[62]

[This article is based on a lecture Professor Annas gave as the Schroeder Scholar-in-Residence at Case Western Reserve University School of Law. The Schroeder Scholar-in-Residence program honors the founder of the Case Western Reserve University Law-Medicine Center, Professor Emeritus Oliver C. Schroeder, Jr., by bringing to the law school each year a distinguished scholar who conducts faculty workshops, meets with students, and delivers a formal public address, known as the Schroeder Lecture. Copyright 1992 by George J. Annas.]

---

60. See, *e.g* Hans Jonas, "The Burden and Blessing of Mortality," *Hastings Center Rep.* Jan.-Feb. 1992 at 34, 39.
61. See, *e.g.,* Daniel Callahan, *What Kind of Life: The Limits of Medical Progress* (1990).
62. World Medical Association, Declaration at Geneva, 1948.

IV.

Women and the Reich

14

The Stations of the Cross

Vera Laska, Ed.
Dagmar Hájková and Hana Housková

Vera Laska:
Crude and at times phantasmagoric punishments, hard labor, constant hunger, the absence of legitimate medical attention, degenerate medical experiments including vivisection, executions by shooting or injections and mass murders by gas were the stations of the cross that the women had to walk once they passed over the threshold of Ravensbrück.

Mass gassing was "farmed out" because Ravensbrück did not boast permanent gas chambers. The management tried to rectify this deficiency in January 1945 by transforming part of a warehouse into a gas chamber, but capacity was a mere 150 or so a day, and the approaching front line made the SS abandon it in early April. Still, hundreds of women were liquidated this way. Among the last ones was a group of Czechs, singing their national anthem to the last minute of their lives, and an older German woman, who kept screaming at the SS that her three sons were fighting in the German army.

Hunger was a matter of course all the time, but toward the end of the war it reached such proportions that it was suspected that the corpses chewed up in some blocks were mutilated not by the rats but by humans. One woman was seen eating what another had thrown up. Yet after liberation the warehouses were found full of beans and other food.

Epidemics were frequent and took a horrendous toll. Without hygiene, baths or medicine, the women died like flies of tuberculosis, typhoid fever, spotted typhus, diarrhoea, scabies or simply of malnutrition. Rats and lice were rampant. A second crematorium had to be erected in

NOTE: "The Stations of the Cross" is by Dagmar Hájková and Hana Housková in Dagmar Hájková, et al, *Ravensbrück* (Prague: Naše vojsko, 1961), pp. 95-112. Translation copyright by Vera Laska. Reprinted with the kind permission of the publisher and the authors. [This text appears in *Women in the Resistance and in the Holocaust* (1983)].

1944, and a new "corpse detail" (Leichenträgerkolone) was established to gather the dead.

The constant cross that the women had to bear was incessant labor, in long, mostly twelve-hour shifts, often at night. It kept draining the life juices of all. The women built roads and a railroad extension, the camp headquarters and homes for the SS guards; they moved bricks in a human chain, hands over hands, until they were bloody shreds; they carted cement, sand, also garbage and manure, on the run; they felled trees and labored in the fields.

A few "lucky" ones worked in the camp offices, kitchens and warehouses, with a chance to swallow a few extra scraps of food. Others were employed in the furrier workshops, transforming tons of fur coats taken from victims of transports to various concentration camps into army gloves, pilots' boots and uniform linings. By the spring of 1944, 4,500 women labored at the Ravensbrück branch of the Dachau Enterprises, making prisoners' striped uniforms and reconstructing army uniforms full of gunshot holes, blood and lice.

By far the largest number of women were employed at slave labor in various industries. Siemens had one of its factories directly at the camp (others at Buchenwald and Gross-Rosen, among others). Here 2,500 women manufactured munitions, electrical parts of submarines, field phones and parts of the V-2 rockets. Water was so scarce that they were not allowed to flush the single latrine; the German Kommandant had the exclusive right to do that!

Hundreds were working at branch camps at Neubrandenburg, Ganthin, Wansbeck and others. They were shipped out to over two dozen factories and estates as slave labor. They worked for companies like Patin, Grahl, Luftmuna, Heinckel, Junkers, AEG, Hermann Göring Werke, even for the V-Waffen Erprobungsstelle at Peenemünde, and, of course, for I. G. Farben which among others supplied their delousing powder that did not work, and the Zyklon B gas for the gas chambers that did. The slightest slackening of the tempo was considered sabotage and could mean return to the punitive block in camp, the Bunker, or to the insane asylum, where gassing was on daily order. For stealing rubber bands to hold up their pants that were issued without elastic, twelve women were almost shot. For bringing garlic to the Siemens factory, thus endangering metal, two Ukrainian women were put into the Bunker and never seen again.

Interestingly, the SS collected daily wages for their charges, but the laborers never saw a penny of the two to four Marks they earned per day.

Such was the work situation of the Ravensbrück women. To round out the picture of their lives and deaths, read the following excerpts from eyewitnesses' testimonies about the medical practices in Ravensbrück. They included the sterilization of women who through the institutionalized barbarity of Nazi philosophy were considered "unworthy of reproduction" *(fortpflanzungsunwürdig), and the vivisection of those most pitiful of all pitiful victims, the human guinea pigs nicknamed the "rabbits."*

* * * * *

Dagmar Hájková and Hana Housková:

Until February 1942 we had seen all kinds of horrors. But then we came face to face with something that could have been conceived only in the pervert[ed] minds of fascists. For the first time we became witnesses to mass murder.

Preparations had been under way already during January and at the beginning of February. Lists of incurable and seriously ill women had to be prepared. . . At the same time the management of the camp launched a propaganda campaign that the selected women would go to some kind of an institution where they would not have to work. Many women believed that and volunteered.

One cold February morning trucks arrived with a commando of SS men. Their way with the sick was not exactly considerate. They grabbed the stragglers and were throwing them on the trucks helter-skelter. The unfortunate women were tripping over their crutches and over each other on the floor of the truck strewn thinly with straw.

Thus the first one hundred and fifty left. The rest were awaiting their turn, hoping for some news about the place where they were supposed to go.

The news arrived before we knew it. It was on the third day after the transport had left. In the morning we went to work. In our warehouse a surprise was awaiting us: on the floor the clogs, underwear and dresses of the departed ones, with their numbers on them. But not only that; there were also the canes, crutches, artificial limbs, false teeth—all the things that sick people needed as long as they remained alive.

The trucks that had brought back this gruesome legacy carried off the next group of the sick, and on the third day the whole process was repeated. Altogether they removed 1,600 women; they were gassed in the sanitarium for the mentally ill in Bernburg near Dessau . . .

In March 1942 a transport of 1,000 women left to "found" [the women's camp in] Auschwitz. It consisted of the entire punitive block and a few additional prisoners selected by the SS women transferred to Auschwitz.

In August 1942 it was the turn of the Jewesses. The whole Jewish block was sent to Auschwitz. By that time we knew quite well why the huge chimneys there were puffing smoke day and night. . . .

In February 1944 again lists were prepared of all women who were weak, old, sick or unable to work. . . . In two days Chief Nurse Marschall and Doctor Treite,[1] sitting on top of the examining table at the Revier,

---

1. Chief Nurse Elisabeth Marschall was a no nonsense German always "doing her duty" and "following orders." Percy Treite, the director of the Revier, was

selected over 800 women. Some of them were young; these were the daughters of the older women who did not want to be separated from them . . . They were taken to Lublin and from there to Auschwitz. At the time Auschwitz was being evacuated in January of 1945, a handful of them returned to Ravensbrück. All the others had perished.

There were also smaller transports. For these they selected mostly sick, old, weakened, mentally ill and tubercular women. They were taken to other "liquidation centers." There were many of these. For instance I recall a transport of women with tuberculosis, which left in early 1944 for Barth, and a transport of French women from Paris, taken to be gassed in June of 1943.

In early 1945 transports were shifted back and forth under terrible circumstances. One transport from Ravensbrück to Reichow remained for four weeks without food, water and air, locked in cattle cars, often just standing on the railroad tracks. All the women died.

In February 1945 a transport of 250 older women left Ravensbrück. By then all Germany was in incredible chaos; not even the perfect SS and Gestapo organizations were functioning any longer. The women were carted all over Germany in closed cattle cars. Seventy-two of them returned; they were so eaten up by lice that the flesh was falling off their bones; their bodies were full of deep wounds, under which we could see the bones and tendons. In spite of the ministrations of a Soviet doctor, a prisoner who did all she could to save them, thirty more died.

It was not only the civilians who were being evacuated before the advancing Soviet army. Concentration camps were also being emptied. The horror filled "death transports" were criss-crossing all Germany.

In January of 1945 Auschwitz was being evacuated. Around 6,000 women embarked on a horrible march on foot to Ravensbrück. It was one of the worst marches. Along the way 2,000 perished or were shot. The sick were evacuated in closed cattle wagons. From among the several hundred, about 150 still survived the insane trip. Then in Ravensbrück they were gassed.

* * * * *

Dr. Treite, who had been a surgeon in a Berlin clinic, whence he came to Ravensbrück, started operating in the Revier, the camp hospital.

He had his periods. For instance he wanted to learn goiter operations. The Revier messengers were dispatched all over the camp to all blocks to report women with a swollen neck. . . . He then selected twenty

---

a talented organizer: he was less sadistic than most of his colleagues, but still performed sterilizations, selections and ordered poisonings. His mother was English.

or a few more, and for the following few days, every afternoon at two o'clock, there were goiter operations.

Once he felt he gained the needed routine and expertise in these operations, he turned to appendices. . . . Then came varicose veins, hernias, and gynecological cases. . . .

He trained prisoners as his nurses. First there was Isa Sicinska, a Polish medical student, a beautiful and intelligent girl, later the young Belgian Annette, and shortly before the end, the Czech Hana Housková.

After he became handy with easier operations, he launched into large "scientific" ones on adrenal glands. This was a daring operation, transplanting a human organ, and he made careful preparations. He picked a woman suffering from asthma and another one who was healthy. Both were Russian. He removed the healthy woman's adrenal glands and implanted them into the woman with asthma. The operation was successful, but then both women died. Then Treite rushed into gynecological surgery, and after that into kidney, urinary tract and stomach operations. The "stomachs" all died.

Encouraged by this example, and also fired by their own ambitions, other doctors, like Richter and Orendi,[2] started operating. Richter was also learning. He was not a surgeon, he did not understand surgery, yet he operated unprofessionally but obstinately. He operated in the examining room.

The results of such operations? Just as it could be expected. Richter lost one of his first patients under the knife, the next one soon after surgery. The third one, a Pole, remained at the Revier for a long time, with a draining tube in her back, discharging a constant drip of thin yellow pus into a receptacle under her bed, before she died. The same was the case with a Belgian girl, who suffered for almost ten months before she died.

Orendi also discovered that he had great surgical talents. Perhaps he was just terribly bored because he ran out of money for his drinking bouts in the SS canteen, or because he lost out with the female SS supervisors, for competition was big. He killed a number of prisoners with his operations.

Dr. Orendi inscribed his name into the annals of Ravensbrück with still another "medical" exploit. In the early part of May 1944 the cubicle of the women in charge of Block 10 had to be cleared. The window was boarded up, and straw was spread on the floor. A new inmate supervisor was appointed in the person of Carmen Mory, a malicious pervert.[3] Then into this space of 9 x 9 feet Orendi placed mentally ill women. . . .

---

2. Bruno Orendi was Dr. Treite's assistant; he had two years of medical school.

3. Carmen Mory was a professional spy, possibly a double agent; she was sentenced to death for murder at the Ravensbrück trial in Hamburg after the war.

First there were only ten of them. Then more were brought in, and even with their high mortality rate, their number in this den of doom reached the fantastic number of fifty and finally eighty.

Here at this den, at a safe distance of course, often stood the spoiled brat Orendi and [he] had a ball. This was his project! His "Orendi Express," or his "Shanghai Express," as he referred to it roaring with laughter.

In front of his eyes lay these unfortunate women; later on they only stood, pressed one against the other, their naked, emaciated, bloody, dirty bodies covered with feces, urine and rotten straw swaying in some insane waves or like stumps left after a forest fire. . . .

It was devastating. The terrible stench, the yelling, the inhuman screams like those of tortured animals, spread all over the camp day and night. The SS woman Binz, who after a successful career at the Bunker became chief supervisor, liked to bring the SS men here for some fun.

Nobody except Carmen Mory had the courage to enter this crazed whirl. They were scared of her; even in their confused minds they sensed her bestiality. The German prisoner nurse Paula also dared to go in among them; she was strong as a man. She was the one who bound the violent ones with leather belts.

The worst of it was that the doctors at times locked even normal women among these demented and raging creatures as a form of punishment, justifying it as "need for observation."

By the end of November they were all sent on a transport to Minsk, where they met their deaths. . . .

*   *   *   *   *

The harvest of death in Ravensbrück was growing with each month, each day. But that was not enough for the Nazis. Death had to be prodded on. Again the doctors took the stage. The first one to start the killings by injections was Dr. Rosenthal[4] in the spring of 1942.

One day at the Revier he stopped by a little Gypsy girl who had galloping consumption. He ordered her to a small room at the end of the corridor where the corpses were gathered until their number would justify a trip

---

4. Dr. Rolf Rosenthal was a practical man. At one time there were two German prisoners with similar names in the Revier; one died, but the death certificate was sent by mistake to the family of the other. Rosenthal calmly ordered his nurse to administer a deadly injection to the other one—and the problem was solved. He had an affair with his prisoner nurse Gerda Quernheim (the one who drowned newborn babies in pails of water), even performed an abortion on her; but when the affair was discovered, they were both sent to the Bunker. Milena Jesenská, who died in Ravensbrück in 1944 after four years of unspeakable misery, discovered that the couple, while trysting nights at the Revier, also killed women inmates and removed their gold teeth or fillings. (Buber-Neumann, *Kafkova přítelkyně Milena*, p. 212.)

to the crematorium. The little girl, as if by premonition, resisted. . . . The nurse Gerda, who was an informer and secretly Rosenthal's mistress, carried her to the small room, followed by Rosenthal with the injecting needle in his hand. The little Gypsy girl was his first victim.

The deadly substance was evipan, used as an anesthetic in minor surgery. Administered slowly it prevented vomiting. But injected all at once, it caused instant death.

After the first successful experiment this method of killing became standard procedure. Besides Rosenthal and Gerda, who killed this way also an old German political [individual], these injections were administered by nurse Margarete Hoffman who killed seven Jewesses in one session.

Of course this insidious manner of killing could not be kept secret for long, and the prisoners were scared stiff of all injections. When some resisted and cried, they were first given a sedative and then were killed in their sleep.

But even that was not sufficient. Injections were too slow, and perhaps too expensive. So then they started killing with poison powder. . . .[5]

It started in Block 10 where there were 500 tubercular women. One evening Gerda distributed the "sleeping powder." With a nice smile she inquired who could not sleep at night. That first night about twenty "fell asleep" . . . the next day another five, towards the evening seven, and the following day about a dozen. The rest remained unconscious for two or three days, then came to. Since this whole affair caused quite a panic in Block 10, this "noble" procedure was moved to the Gypsy block.

The powder was administered also by Treite during his visits in the Revier blocks, his later denials in court notwithstanding. They were handed out also by Carmen Mory and Vera Salveguart, prisoners in the service of the Nazis. This method of murder was used most often especially toward the end of the war.

* * * * *

Sterilization was another "medical" activity in the camp, still another "contribution to science." . . . It was started in the spring of 1942 when Dr. Clauberg had requested permission for his sterilization experiments with a special substance. Himmler granted his permission for these experiments in Ravensbrück in a letter dated July 10, 1942 and marked "Reich secret,"[6] addressed to Clauberg:[7]

---

5. In those years in Europe many medicines, including aspirin, were marketed in powdered rather than pill form, each dose packaged in a folded piece of paper the size of a bandaid.

6. Letter written on Himmler's office stationery by Obersturmführer (Lieutenant) Brandt, transmitting the wishes of Reichsführer (Head of SS) Heinrich Himmler.

7. Much has been written about the "angel of death" of Auschwitz, former physician Josef Mengele, who specialized in experiments on twins, dwarfs and

". . . According to your judgment, go to Ravensbrück and there carry out the sterilization of Jewish women... How much time is needed to sterilize 1,000 Jewish women? They should not know anything about it. You may use an injection during a general check up. The effect of the sterilization must be thoroughly tested . . . by locking up together a Jewish woman with a Jewish man, and then we shall see the result after a while."

Thus one day an inconspicuous, polite and taciturn gentleman appeared at camp. He and Dr. Oberhauser[8] remained every evening in the examining room. They saw Gypsies, asocials, Jewesses and young Germans, imprisoned for illegal fraternization with the enemy, whose file from the Gestapo had been already marked with an order for sterilization. Even though they were strictly forbidden to talk, rumors started that they

---

Gypsies, and who was the person most instrumental in the selections at Auschwitz. Less is known about this professor Karl Clauberg, M.D. from Königshütte, who later pursued his experiments on live specimens in Auschwitz, where he had a much wider range of victims. Here he was one of the mainstays of the infamous Block 10, the only female block in the male camp of Auschwitz I, the mysterious block with boarded windows; from the slots the captive women could see the twice daily executions of both men and women in the equally infamous Block 11.

All kinds of experiments were carried out by different doctors here, among them castrations and sterilizations. The doctors made no bones about it that their purpose was to prepare for the sterilization of certain groups and nationalities, most likely Slavs, after the war.

Clauberg's sterilization project started with about 350 or 400 mostly Greek and Dutch women on December 18, 1942. He injected into their uterus consecutively iodiprin, F 12a, which was diluted novocain, and citobarium. He also subjected the women to x-rays. The process resulted in peritonitis, inflammation of the ovaries, and high fever. The ovaries were then removed, usually in two separate operations, and then sent to Berlin for further analysis. Most women who survived these experiments ended in the gas chambers.

By July 1943, Clauberg could proudly report to Himmler that under proper conditions he could sterilize, without an operation, as many as a thousand women a day. At the end of 1944 a new block was being built for experiments with artificial insemination, for the greater glory—and population—of Germany; but the evacuation of Auschwitz put an end to that. Clauberg left Auschwitz with over 5,000 scientific photographs in his briefcase.

Ota Kraus and Erich Kulka in their *Továrna na smrt* [*Factory for Death*] (Prague: Naše vojsko, 1957) quote testimonies of Sylva Friedmannová from Prešov, Czechoslovakia, Dora Klein, M.D., from France and several others about this gruesome subject. See also Miklos Nyiszli, *Auschwitz* (Greenwich, Conn.: Fawcett, 1961).

8. Dr. Herta Oberhauser was a "well bred" woman with a cultured background. Yet she killed prisoners with oil and evipan injections, removed their limbs and vital organs, rubbed ground glass and sawdust into wounds. She drew a twenty-year sentence as a war criminal, but was released in 1952 and became a family doctor at Stocksee in Germany. Her license to practice medicine was revoked in 1960.

were sterilized. Then one day, almost a year later, the inconspicuous gentleman inconspicuously left.[9]

At the war crime trials in Hamburg and Nuremberg[10] it was disclosed that he had fulfilled his task well; he reported personally to Himmler that he was capable of sterilizing 1,000 women per day "as required. . . ."

At the beginning of January, 1945 another gentleman arrived at Ravensbrück. It was the x-ray specialist from Auschwitz, Professor Schumann.[11] Now Gypsies between the ages of eight and eighteen were asked to report to the Revier, as well as Jewish women from last year's transport. These Gypsy children's mothers had to sign, mostly by three x-es, that they voluntarily agreed to the operations on their children. Then the Gypsies and the Jewish women were taken in groups to the x-ray room, and soon the block resounded with the terrifying screams of the tortured girls. When they emerged, they were deathly yellow and white like ghosts. They were holding their tummies and wailing without end. The mothers had been waiting in front of the Revier, but the SS women were chasing them away with blows and kicks.

Some special substance and a solution of silver nitrate were introduced into the oviducts of each victim. This was sterilization by the so-called Clauberg method that had been tested by its inventor almost three years ago. The solution soon caused a violent inflammation, which in turn closed the oviducts, thus leading to permanent sterility.

It was unspeakable. Not only could these girls never become mothers but there was a great danger that the foreign substance would get into the gastric cavity and evoke inflammation there. This was exactly what happened with the first cases, and four girls died of peritonitis. Treite operated on two, but could not save either one. One died right after the operation, the other remained in the Revier. Pus was drained from her stomach constantly through an inserted tube into a basin under her bed. How could a poor little girl produce so much pus? Finally after three weeks of suffering she also died.

---

9. He [Clauberg] surfaced in Auschwitz (see footnote [7] above).

10. The Hamburg war crime trials dealt with crimes committed at Ravensbrück, those of Nuremberg (referred to here) with those of the physicians.

11. Dr. Horst Schumann was a graduate of Auschwitz, where in 1942, in the woman's camp Bla, he had set up an x-ray station. Here men and women were forcibly sterilized by being positioned repeatedly for several minutes between two x-ray machines, the rays aiming at their sexual organs. Most subjects died after great suffering. The frequently following ovariotomies were performed also by the Polish prisoner, Dr. Wladyslav Dering. Dering once bet with an SS man that he could perform ten ovariotomies in an afternoon, and won his bet. Some of his victims survived. Dering was declared a war criminal but eluded justice and for a time practiced medicine in British Somaliland.

They called it also salpingography. After the war the committee that prepared the documentation for the Ravensbrück museum established that just between the 4th and the 7th of January 1945 over 100 children were sterilized by this method.

Aside from children, adult women were also sterilized, mostly Gypsies. Dr. Treite carried out these sterilizations surgically, by tieing up the oviducts. The subjects of these operations were young German women who arrived to (sic) the camp already with this order for sterilization in their dossiers, Gypsies, Jews, and a few unfortunate creatures who were simply pulled out of the line at the time of office hours for this gynecological operation. Two of the first operated [on] this way were Gypsy children on whom the previous method (by flooding the oviducts) did not succeed. They were kept in the Revier, and after the second x-ray check they were prepped for an operation. The doctors were so insensitive that they discussed the whole matter in front of the two children. . . .

*   *   *   *   *

In June 1942, two men arrived in Ravensbrück. One was elderly, with graying hair and the noble visage of a scientist, the other one younger. Dr. Oberhauser ran out to meet them, and so did doctors Schidlauski and Rosenthal. There was much polite welcoming. . . . Ten women from among the numbers 7700 and 7900 of the Lublin transport were called in for a special check-up.

Meanwhile we found out that these two men were not members of any commission, as we had first thought, but doctors from the SS hospital in Hohenlychen near Ravensbrück. Oberhauser boasted to us that it was Professor Gebhardt,[12] the great scientific celebrity, Himmler's friend, who came to us to carry out scientific experiments. What an honor that of all places he had picked Ravensbrück. The other one, she said, was his assistant and right hand, Dr. Ernst Fischer.

The ten Polish women were brought in, and behind closed doors they were examined. It took a long time, and nobody was allowed to be even in the corridor. The next morning we found out that five of the Poles had been admitted to the Revier. Their room was under lock and key, and the SS nurse Erica Milleville was in charge.

Office hours were canceled, everything was being disinfected, and all prisoners working at the Revier had to leave. But they forgot the of-

---

12. Dr. Karl Gebhardt, Himmler's childhood friend, had a green light from him for his vivisection of women at both Ravensbrück and Auschwitz. In the former camp, he admittedly operated on 60, but survivors of Ravensbrück put the number closer to 100, mostly Poles between the ages of fourteen and twenty-five. He was an SS Brigadeführer (Major General) and stated in May 1943: "I carry the full human, surgical and political responsibility for these experiments." He was shot as a war criminal in 1948.

fice which was way at the end of the hall, or they had thought that nothing would be heard that far. Thus the girls in the office heard a terrible scream and then quiet, the kind of quiet that is always the foreboding of the greatest horrors. The quiet of a new, cunning death.

The first day they operated on two. Two days later on the three others. The screams never ceased from that chamber of torture. The Revier was full of them. The girls were not given any pain-killers, so that the course of the experiment would not be impaired in any way. Dogs that had undergone the same experiments received strong doses of morphine for five days.

After a few days the first Pole, a girl of seventeen, died. Her leg was huge, swollen, monstrous, blue with red wounds, and the stench emanating from them was nauseating. The Poles from the Revier told that Gebhardt cut the leg off and took it with him.

Oberhauser was telling us that these were great scientific experiments that should solve a number of important questions in the treatment of shot wounds and other war injuries, and especially of gangrene and bone transplants. She also let it slip that for the first experiment in our camp they had used a man.

Live human guinea pigs! As a matter of fact, we never called those who were operated on anything but "rabbits."[13] The first five were followed by another five in a few days. Gradually there were more and more of them. The moment that the Revier messenger came to the block with her list that so and so should report to the Revier, we knew what it was all about. . . .

There were two kinds of experiments. In the first type gangrene, tetanus or staphylococcic bacteria were implanted or injected into artificially cut wounds of healthy extremities. This happened in the case of the first five, who were desperately and hysterically screaming and who all died, one of tetanus, two of gangrene, one of blood poisoning, and one bled to death.

The other operations were called by the "scientists" bone, muscle and nerve surgery. In such cases, for instance, parts as large as two inches (5 cm.) were removed from the shin bone and replaced with metal supports or not replaced at all; in this case the doctors were waiting [to see] "how the organism will help itself." Muscles and nerves were removed and replaced by others, taken from another healthy woman.

The bone transplants were supposed to prove that without the periosteum[14] bones could not grow; muscle and nerve operations served [as]

---

13. Derived from the German *"Versuch Kaninchen,"* meaning experimental rabbit or guinea pig. Of all the women martyred by the Nazis, perhaps the "rabbits" suffered the most excruciating tortures, although there were countless close seconds, incubated in the demonic minds of the prisoners' captors.

14. Membrane of connective tissue that invests all bones except joints.

research on regeneration of tissue. Such operations took two to three hours. They repeatedly removed from some women's hips and calfs larger and larger parts of muscles; naturally this resulted in the ever increasing weakening and deformation of the extremities. In order to carry out better and more detailed "research," they removed some women's entire hips, shoulder joints or the whole upper extremity together with the shoulder blade. Then the professor, or his assistants, also physicians from Hohenly-chen, like Grawitz, Kogel and Schulz, wrapped these in sheets and carried them to their car. Naturally, the women thus operated on were immediately after the surgery killed by an injection. Allegedly the doctors attempted to transplant these healthy limbs onto crippled soldiers whose crushed limbs had been amputated at the SS hospital in Hohenlychen.

According to the Hamburg trial with the Ravensbrück war criminals, it was Dr. Grawitz[15] who issued the orders for certain operations, for instance those that were to determine the healing effects of sulphonamids.

Why test new compounds on guinea pigs or dogs, when they could be tested on humans safely and without any legal repercussions?

All the while that the vivisections on the "rabbits" were going on, the whole camp was buzzing with talk. Everybody wanted to help them. The agricultural details smuggled in pieces of fresh vegetables, or a crushed little bouquet of wild strawberries. . . . From the kitchen the girls were sending a little marmalade, a sliver of bread and even margarine. . . . If they could not "organize"[16] anything or were unable to smuggle it in, they sent at least a note, with primitive drawings of cities and villages, parks, streets and river banks, along which life was going on, or little poems about the sun in the sky, gardens in bloom, songs of rivers and meadows.

Later on the "rabbits" were no longer in one locked room but in several unlocked ones, and secretly we brought them pain-killers; we were scared to death that the SS doctors would find us out; then they would take revenge not only on us but also on the poor "rabbits."

Clearly all these operations had terrible consequences, especially when the experiments were repeated on the same "rabbit" twice, three times, even six times, by both methods. If a wound caused by gangrene or some other suppurating infection healed, it was opened again and re-infected, or the limb opened at another, still healthy spot. New sections of

---

15. Dr. Ernst Grawitz, SS and Police Gruppenführer (Lieutenant General), was the top doctor in the SS. He was the one who suggested to Himmler in the summer of 1941 gas chambers as means to the "Final Solution," *i.e.*, the mass extermination of Jews. He knew of and kept an executive's eye on numerous other experiments with human guinea pigs at various concentration camps, for instance, body resistance to freezing, jaundice, typhus (research done for I. G. Farben), and the drinkability of sea water. He committed suicide in 1945.

16. "To organize" in concentration camp parlance meant to steal or to get by hook or crook; similar to the G.I.'s "to liberate," except under more dangerous circumstances.

bones were cut out, or other parts of nerves from the calf removed. As a result of putrefaction and excised muscle tissues, the poor women's legs became several centimeters shorter and of course weaker. Healthy, beautiful people were artificially transformed into cripples; healthy, beautiful legs became grotesquely twisted limbs of skin and bone. It was the more ghastly because in the majority of cases the victims were young girls.

This was how Professor Gebhardt was earning his stripes. At first he had performed these operations with the assistance of Dr. Fischer, and with the cooperation of Doctors Oberhauser, a female, Rosenthal, Schidlauski and their helpers. Who helped them a lot was nurse Erica Milleville, their chief nurse, whom they evidently fully trusted.

And they earned their keep! Professor Gebhardt was rewarded by Hitler with the Gold Cross, Dr. Oberhauser with the Iron Cross.

Who were all these females serving "science" as guinea pigs? First of all the Poles who arrived with transports already marked by the Gestapo for the death penalty. They hung on to the hope that if they would undergo these operations "voluntarily," they would receive a reprieve and their lives would be spared. But the executions did not stop, and behind the camp the "rabbits" were also dropping under the salvos of their executioners. As we followed their cases, three of them were shot.

Altogether, according to the investigation commission, 74 Poles were subjected to the operations. . . . 13 either died or were shot. Thus of 74 Polish "rabbits" in Ravensbrück, 61 remained to give testimony after liberation about the incredible bestialities of the Nazis.

Besides the Poles there were other "rabbits," some mentally ill or incurable women; they were Ukrainians, one Czech and one Yugoslav, who was sent to Mauthausen and there went insane in the Bunker, one German professional criminal and a Russian, who had had polio...

The operations continued until August of 1943. During this time the Polish women revolted twice. Once, when the first ten were supposed to be crippled for the second time, they refused. The procedure that followed was simple. The whole Polish block was locked, the windows boarded, and all the 400 women left there three days and three nights without food, drink or air. Naturally, after this treatment, the ten "volunteered."

The second revolt had worse consequences. That was in the summer of 1943. The Poles knew by then that not even the operations would save them from being shot. To be killed and before that be tortured and tormented? Ordered to report to the Revier, they simply did not show up. There were about twenty of them. Some remained in their block, others spread out and hid in other blocks.

They were caught by the SS women with dogs and forcefully dragged to the Bunker. Ten were jailed in the Bunker, and six were operated on in the cells, by force, dressed as they were, without any sterilization on the ground, where the SS men were holding them down.

That is how the last "rabbits" underwent bone operations . . .

Of course their tormentors wanted to send them to the gas in the last moment. They did not want to allow such witnesses to remain alive. But the girls were well hidden. They were in different blocks, under other numbers and names (of deceased prisoners), in the Revier, even in the punitive block; they were handed from place to place, depending where the greatest danger was threatening. The entire camp supported them.

15

Nursing Issues during the Third Reich

Susanne Hahn

When the National Socialists came to power on January 30, 1933, the nursing profession in Germany was split up between many different professional organizations, with different levels of training, characterized by subordination, discipline, social insecurity due to mass unemployment, and not very much interested in politics.

Nearly three quarters of all nurses belonged to the great Christian welfare organizations, *i.e.* the Lutheran Organization and the Catholic— Diacon Caritas.

Some time ago, a nurse, looking back to the year 1933, came to the following conclusion when remembering what happened in her hospital after Hitler had come to power:

> "Well, actually, everything went by so quietly, there was nothing special, I cannot remember that we reacted in any particular way, we just continued to do our work, only different people were coming . . . no, really, I have to tell you honestly, it was not the case that we were in any way concerned by these events, it was simply a transition."[1]

In reality, however, the reorganization and ideological brainwashing of German nurses started immediately after 1933:

> "The requirements which German nurses in social and medical service have to meet in the new state are completely different from the previous period in many respects. The new state does not only want to look after the sick and weak; it also wants to secure a healthy development of all national comrades, and also to improve their health, if their inherited biological predisposition allows for it. Above all, the new state wants to secure and promote a genetically sound, valuable race and, in contrast to the past, not to expend an exaggerated effort on the care for genetically or racially inferior people. Of course, such people must be looked after, but no longer be supported and promoted at the cost of the more valuable peo-

---

1. Ernst Albers: Interview der Krankenschwester Amelie Meyn am 4. November 1988. Persönliche Mitteilung.

ple,"[2] said Dr. Friedrich Bartels, who was a senior civil servant in the Ministry of the Interior and Deputy Leader of the Reich's medical profession.

A predominant role in this process of ideological reorientation of nursing was played by the National Socialist Nurses' Organization, which had emerged from the "Red Swastika Nurses" in 1934. Its influence, however, remained relatively small—by 1939 only 9.2% of German nurses had joined the organization. The free nurses, a high proportion of whom had been organized in the health section of the trade unions during the Weimar Republic, were forced to join the German Labour Front, where the national socialist nurses and the nurses of the German Red Cross were also members. The nurses of the Red Cross were retrained on the basis of military principles after 1934, and they were above all trained for the recruitment and training of laymen.

The Christian welfare organizations also verbally proclaimed their support for the new state.[3] However, it is well known that, contrary to such declarations of loyalty, there was also resistance towards the national socialist health policy, for instance on the issue of sterilization and later euthanasia.[4] The Christian hospitals also refused to organize their staff on the basis of the leader/followers principle, and they did not join the German Labour Front. And they refused to meet the requirements of the national socialist state which urged them to train increasing numbers of nurses, because they were still aware of the problems they had had during the mass unemployment of the great depression, which had threatened their very existence.

Although the Ministry of the Interior tried as early as 1933 to unite the five great nursing associations within the Reich's Nursing Alliance of German Nurses and Ward Attendants, and thus to gain more ideological influence, the unruly denominational nurses still formed an overwhelming majority.

When preparations for a new war started in 1935, it became necessary to exert influence on the nursing profession which was expected to provide the necessary medical support in a forth-coming aggression.

---

2. Friedrich Bartels: Der neuen Zeitschrift zum Geleit. Dienst am Volk 1 (1933), 1.

3. P.M. Fischer: Der Neuaufbau und wir. Krankendienst 14 (1933), 143-144; Siebert: Die Organisation des Kaiserswerther Verbandes. In: 1836-1936. Hundert Jahre Mutterhausdiakonie. Eine Handreichung für evangelische Pfarrer und Religionslehrer. Hrsg. vom Kaiserswerther Verband deutscher Diakonissen-Mutterhäuser. Kaiserswerth 1936, S. 20-22.

4. Kurt Nowak: "Euthanasie" und Sterilisierung im "Dritten Reich." Die Konfrontation der evangelischen und katholischen Kirche mit dem Gesetz zur Verhütung erbkranken Nachwuchses und der "Euthanasie"-Aktion. Hermann Böhlaus Nachfolger, Weimar 1980.

This task was tackled at four different levels:

1. Increasing the number of nurses

2. Strict and unified organization of the nursing profession's associations

3. Development of special medical skills

4. Ideological brainwashing

The *increase in the number of nurses* was part of the four-year plan started in 1936 and oriented towards the preparation of war. Erich Hilgenfeldt, Chairman of the National Socialist People's Welfare and main office leader of the NSDAP party for popular welfare, demanded an annual increase of 15,000 to 20,000 nurses; in fact, however, only 4,000 nurses were trained per year in the first years of the Third Reich. The failure to increase numbers was above all due to a lack in training places, as the Christian associations, as mentioned above, refused for economic and political reasons. The National Socialist People's Welfare and the National Socialist Association of Nurses did not yet have the necessary facilities, and the towns and villages gave financial reasons for not being able to set up nursing schools.[5] Therefore, the state strived to gain access to hospitals by preparing a "Law for the furtherance of nursing" as early as 1936. The bill, however, failed in the proposed form, obviously due to disputes between the Ministry of the Interior and the NSDAP leadership over areas of responsibility.[6]

The issue of training nurses and the problems of lacking training places were eventually resolved by the "Law on the regulation of nursing," which was passed in 1938. Section 2, paragraph 2 of this law ruled:

The Minister of the Interior shall "take measures to recruit and maintain sufficient numbers of young people for the nursing profession to ensure the health care for the whole population, and for this purpose shall be able to set conditions for those in charge of public hospitals. The Reich will provide funds to set up and equip nursing schools . . ."[7] The associated "Nursing Regulations" obliged those responsible for public hospitals and clinics to maintain nursing schools.[8]

---

5. Akten der Parteikanzlei der NSDAP: Rekonstruktion eines verlorengegangenen Bestandes. R. Oldenbourg Verlag, München/New York/London/Paris 1983, Microfiche 102 00667-69/3.

6. Ebenda, Microfiche 103 13612-620.

7. Gesetz zur Ordnung der Krankenpflege vom 28. September 1938. Reichsgesetzblatt, Teil I, Nr. 154/1938, S. 1309-1310, § 2(2).

8. Erste Verordnung über die berufsmäßige Ausübung der Krankenpflege und die Errichtung von Krankenpflegeschulen (Krankenpflegeverordnung) vom 28 September 1938. Ebd., S. 1310-1313.

To the extent that the available incomplete and sometimes contradictory statistics can be taken as an indicator of the real situation, one can say that these measures resulted in a considerable increase in the number of nurses, so that altogether about three quarters of a million medical people, among them 300,000 nurses, worked during World War II. The Red Cross Organization was reinforced by many laymen thus and became the strongest organization within the nursing profession, minimizing the influence of the denominational institutions.[9] During the war, nursing legislation was amended to ensure an even faster training of young nurses.

The *tight and unified organization of the nursing profession* was continued in 1935 with the transformation of the "Reich's Association of German Nurses and Ward Attendants" into the "Expert Committee for Nursing within the Association of Free Welfare Work," which was under the strict control of the NSDAP. The Association was led by the Reich's Women Leader Scholtz-Klink, who in her turn, was under the control of Hilgenfeldt and the party's main office, and also represented Hilgenfeldt in public. The Expert Committee comprised the five great nursing associations:

- the National Socialist Nursing Alliance

- the Reich's Alliance of Free Nurses and Ward Attendants

- the Nurses of the Red Cross Organization

- the Nurses of the Lutheran Diaconic Alliance and

- the Nurses of the Catholic organization Caritas.

Each of these was represented by two matrons who were appointed by the Reich's Women's Leader. In 1942 the National Socialist Nursing Alliance and the Reich's Alliance of Free Nurses and Ward Attendants united and became the National Socialist Nurses' Alliance, which now accounted for 14% of all nurses and was responsible for 476 hospitals, 4450 district nurse stations and 300 nursing schools. This National Socialist Alliance, whose members were organized in the German Labour Front in the same way as the Red Cross Nurses, further restricted the influence of the denominational associations.[10]

After 1938, the *medical training* of the nursing staff for the preparation of military assignments was carried out on the basis of the "Law for the Regulation of Nursing" and all stipulations related to it. This law stipulated that the training for professional nurses was allowed only in nursing schools recognized by the state. Whoever wanted to attend such a school had to go

---

9. Hildegard Steppe (Hrsg.): Krankenpflege im Nationalsozialismus. Dr. med. Mabuse Verlag e.V., Frankfurt/M. 1989 (5. Auflage).

10. Susanne Hahn: Krankenpflege in der Zeit der faschistischen Diktatur in Deutschland (1933-1945). Z. Klin. Med. 43 (1988), 2161-2163.

through a one-year practicum in home economics, had to be "politically reliable" and had to prove "1. that he or she was of German or related blood. . ., 2. had completed 18 years of age, 3. had a good reputation which was proved by a certificate of good conduct, 4. had completed normal schooling, and 5. met the health requirements for this profession . . ."[11]

The students received an 18 months training, and apart from "medical and technical training they were introduced into the ethical bases of the profession and received regular physical education."[12] In this period of time the student nurse, irrespective of the hospital in which she received her training, and irrespective of the nursing association to which the hospital belonged, had to enroll in 200 theoretical classes, 100 of which were to be held by doctors. The classes comprised the following subjects:

  I. Professional honour and vocational studies,

  II. Ideological training, hereditary and racial studies, eugenics, population policy,

  III. Structure and functioning of the human body, health studies, general and personal hygiene,

  IV. Study of diseases,

  V. Nutrition . . .,

  VI. Nursing (Looking after the sick and helping with medical examinations, carrying out the doctor's instructions, first aid in accidents, looking after patients with contagious diseases, including venereal diseases, knowledge of official disinfection instructions, looking after the mentally ill and care for dying persons),

  VII. National health care (obstetric care, babycare, prophylactic and aftercare measures),

  VIII. Laws and regulations,

  IX. National insurance and regulations for the prevention of accidents[13]

At the end of their training the student nurses had to pass a state examination in nursing. Then they were allowed to bear the professional title "nurse" or "ward attendant." The law stipulated the following fields of activities for nurses:

  a) Looking after persons suffering from contagious diseases, both in hospitals and at home,

  b) Looking after the sick in general, as long as they were under continuous medical control, and as long as this care was not restricted to general personal hygiene,

  c) helping in anesthetics, operations and other medical procedures

11. Siehe Anmerkung 8, § 7 (3).
12. Siehe Anmerkung 8, § 8 (2).
13. Siehe Anmerkung 8, § 8 (4).

d) helping with the application of electric and other rays and the carrying out of bacteriological, serological and histological investigations.[14]

The improvements which resulted from this 1938 law with regard to the quality and unification of training for nurses, were from the very beginning linked with an *ideological orientation* of the young women who wanted to become nurses. The nursing profession's moral standing was greatly enhanced by calling it a "service to the people," and the ideal female image was one of "serving motherliness." Nursing journals, yearbooks and textbooks for nursing provided an underlying ideological basis for passing on medical knowledge by massive language manipulation. The nursing profession took part in the competitive initiatives organized by the German Labour Front in an annual professional contest. Nursing in World War I was glorified. Moral support was provided by giving the nurses high awards, such as the Iron Cross during World War II.[15]

And finally, nurses themselves were to become ideologically active. This, of course, was first of all a duty for the National Socialist nurses, who, for instance as district nurses, were to support the work of the Public Health Offices and set up and consolidate a relationship of confidence between the doctors and the population. The work of district nurses was mainly focused on:

1. Economically depressed areas, *i.e.* densely populated industrial areas with housing shortages and unhygienic living conditions.

2. Areas with shortcomings in health care, such as remote areas where it was difficult to contact doctors, the chemist, the midwife or health worker due to the large distances.

3. Political emergency areas.

4. Border zones[16]

Nurses were obliged to reconcile victims of forced sterilization with the state,[17] and when it became obvious that Germany was unable to win the war, the nurses were to become "helpers not only with regard to the health task," but they were also expected to "communicate optimism and the will to win" and to discharge cured, but also "capable and eager-to-work national comrades"[18] from the hospital.

---

14. Zweite Verordnung über die berufsmäßige Ausübung der Krankenpflege und die Einrichtung von Krankenpflegeschulen (Ausführungsverordnung) vom 28. September 1938. Reichsgesetzblatt, Teil I, Nr. 154/1938, S. 1314-1315, § 1 (1).

15. Susanne Hahn: Faschistische Ideologie und Krankenpflege in Deutschland von 1933 bis 1945. Zschr. ärztl. Fortbild. 83 (1989), 359-361.

16. Karin Böttger: Die NS-Schwesternschaft. Jahrbuch der Krankenpflege 2 (1938), 152-158., zit. S. 156.

17. Maria Cauer: Leitfaden für die Berufserziehung in Krankenpflegeschulen. Verlag Elwin Staude, Berlin/Osterwieck 1940, S. 15.

Despite many disputes within the NSDAP leadership bodies over areas of competence, and despite considerable shortcomings of the nursing laws, which did not succeed in fully meeting the demand for nurses during the war, it can be said that the strategy of the Nazis was successful in ensuring the readiness of nurses to provide the medical backbone for a war of conquest. Even the Christian associations did not oppose the aggressive plans, but declared enthusiastically that we have "all provided our service not least in grateful devotion to our Führer . . . May God bless him so that he will be with our German people for many years to come."[19]

Of course one has to differentiate when talking about what nurses really did during the war. There were a few in direct resistance,[20] but certainly many more who tried to improve the lot of sick or wounded individuals by small refusals, forging of patient records and similar things. On the other hand, there were many nurses who, without the slightest remorse, took part in forced sterilizations and in discharging the patients from Jewish hospitals, psychiatric clinics and old peoples' homes, to be sent to special killing clinics or to concentration camps, where they were eventually killed.[21] And after all, nurses were also directly involved in such killings.[22] But the majority of nurses worked at the front or in the hinterland or at home, and looked after wounded soldiers and the civilian population with great dedication, high professional skills and in human greatness.[23] Many nurses lost their lives in the service of "the Führer and the people."

Apart from a few exceptions, the nurses did not become aware of the dehumanization processes in medicine which took place in the period of national socialist dictatorship, nor did they understand that their skills and devotion, their ability to heal and cure, were used to prolong an antihuman war which was going to claim many more victims. This lack of awareness was perhaps due to the fact that the majority of nurses were

---

18. Leonardo Conti: Aufruf zum Jahresbeginn. Die Deutsche Schwester 12 (1944), 1.

19. Constantin Frick: Geleitwort. Gesundheitsfürsorge 14 (1940), 1-2, zit. S. 1; vgl. Kreutz: Treuegruß an die Caritasjünger der deutschen Ostmark. Krankendienst 19 (1938), Anhang Heft 5.

20. Abschiedsbrief von Gertrud Seele. In: Hildegard Steppe, siehe Anmerkung 9, S. 182-183.

21. Susanne Hahn: Zum Schicksal jüdischer Ärzte nach 1933 in Leipzig. Zschr. ärztl. Fortbild. 85 (1991), 174-176; Susanne Hahn und Georg Lilienthal: Totentanz und Lebensborn. Zur Geschichte des Alters- und Pflegeheims in Kohren-Sahlis bei Leipzig (1939-1945). Med.hist. J. 27 (1992), 340-358.

22. Aussage einer Krankenschwester 1965 vor einem Münchner Gericht. In: Hildegard Steppe, siehe Anmerkung 9, S. 152.

23. "Mutti" im Lazarettzug. Die Deutsche Schwester 11 (1943), 28; EK II für Ilse von Kistowski. Die Deutsche Schwester 12 (1944), 84-85.

used to serving and obedience in a nursing profession which was organized on the basis of the mother house principle, and that most of them were not interested in politics. That the nurses did not recognize that they were systematically misused for war purposes and the anti-human aims of the national socialist health policy, that they did not oppose this policy but became themselves involved in it, can be considered the basic failure of the German nursing profession during National Socialism. Although the national socialist leadership succeeded in ensuring the medical and ideological preparation of nurses for war in spite of all existing problems, neither the increasing number of nurses, nor the devotion and excellent skills of the members of all alliances managed to ensure adequate medical care at the front and in the civilian sphere and to prevent the collapse of the medical system. It is an illusion to believe that a sufficient number of tightly organized, well-trained and ideologically prepared nurses and other medical staff can ensure a sound medical framework for war or make war more humane.

V.

*Jewish Doctors
in the Shadow of the Reich*

16

Creativity in the Face of Disaster: Medicine in the Warsaw Ghetto

Charles G. Roland

General Introduction

I will attempt to discuss briefly three areas relating to the medical history of the Warsaw ghetto. These are: (1) The hospital system within the ghetto; (2) the original research into starvation and its effects on the human body, carried out in 1942; and (3) the operation of a clandestine medical school for 15 months beginning in May 1941.

Medical Structure of the Ghetto[1]

Shortly after the Germans occupied Warsaw at the end of September 1939, they dissolved the *Kehilla* and instructed the Jews to create a new type of governing body called the *Judenrat*. Adam Czerniakow was installed as chairman. The *Judenrat* was given the impossible task of carrying out all internal governance of the Jews, both before and after the establishment of the Warsaw ghetto. Partly, the impossibility of the task derived from the fact that the only source of funds was from taxation of the Jews themselves. But the Jews were not allowed to work outside the Jewish community, with few exceptions.

Hospitals

The strains of setting up a functioning medical system were immense. Czyste Hospital, one of the largest and most modern hospitals in Poland, was a Jewish institution located outside what became the Warsaw ghetto. It was consequently forced to move inside in January 1941, leaving much of its equipment and supplies for German use. Inside the

---

1. See Charles G. Roland, *Courage under Siege: Disease, Starvation, and Death in the Warsaw Ghetto* (New York: Oxford University Press, 1992), esp. Chapter 4, "Structure of the Medical System in the Ghetto," pp. 53-75.

ghetto, the hospital was split into several sections since there was no single building suitable for housing it. The hospital staff performed prodigies but were never able to approach pre-war standards. Sanitation was permanently impeded by the German bombardment of September 1939. Water mains in the ghetto area remained unrepaired. Electrical service was sporadic and unreliable. On at least one occasion, electricity was cut off during a surgical procedure because the bill had not been paid to the German-controlled city of Warsaw.

Conditions in the various hospitals were abhorrent by the summer of 1941. A year later, as the ghetto began to be decimated as its inhabitants were consumed in the gas chambers at Treblinka, the situation was ghastly. Two patients sharing a bed was routine, and often three attempted to divide the meager space. The initial practice of separating infectious patients from those requiring or recovering from surgery began to fail from sheer numbers.

There was a children's hospital within the ghetto, Berson and Bauman. It offered one main advantage over Czyste Hospital. Berson and Bauman was located inside the so-called Jewish Quarter before the war. Therefore it was also inside the ghetto, actually in the Small Ghetto, and did not experience the massive dislocation of moving to inadequate quarters or being forced to leave equipment and supplies behind. This institution did good service, albeit under great strains, until about September 1942. When the Small Ghetto was eliminated, Berson and Bauman ceased to exist as a Jewish hospital. The buildings survived the war and can be seen still in downtown Warsaw.

There were about 700 physicians in the ghetto, many of them first-rate practitioners and scientists of national and even international repute. Others were less notable, but the majority seem to have labored honestly and patiently against impossible odds. A very few behaved badly.

It was in this general situation of chaos, disorganization, uncertainty, and often terror that the *Judenrat* health officers and hospital officials worked to provide adequate medical services to almost half a million persons. Chief among the medical leaders of the Warsaw ghetto were:

> Izrael Milejkowski (1887-1943), head of the department of health that the *Judenrat* was forced to create. Milejkowski played a significant role in encouraging the creation of the underground medical school, but his chief contribution to the medical history of the ghetto was his support of the project to study starvation.

> Ludwig Hirszfeld (1884-1954) was the most scientifically prominent member of the ghetto medical profession. During World War I, Hirszfeld, serving in Serbia, had first described the organism that ultimately was named *Salmonella hirszfeldi*. Among other subjects, he had studied the blood groups and their inheritance, one of the areas of knowledge that Nazi Germany twisted into a "scientific" rationale for what became lethal racial dogma. Hirszfeld's baptism as a Catholic,

years before, was declared irrelevant and he had to enter the ghetto. He escaped to "Aryan" Warsaw sometime in 1943, and he survived the war.

Janusz Korczak (1878-1942) was born Henryk Goldszmidt, in Warsaw. Although a physician he achieved international fame as a writer and educator. Janusz Korczak, his pen-name, became the only name he used. He ran an orphanage along increasingly progressive lines during the 1920s and 1930s.

Juliusz Zweibaum (1887-1959) established the technical courses that were the cover for the clandestine medical school. He was dean of the school. Before the war he had been a *docent* at Warsaw University and a histologist.

Hunger

Arguably, hunger was the most basic problem in the Warsaw ghetto. Essentially every Jew was, sooner or later, desperately hungry. After the ghetto was closed off, the pace of mortality from starvation accelerated profoundly. The Nazi doctor, Wilhelm Hagen, estimated that almost 60,000 Jews died of starvation in Warsaw. By 1941, the official ration provided 2613 calories per day for Germans in Poland (including the *Volkdeutsch*), 699 calories for Poles, and 184 calories daily for Jews in the ghetto.

Some Jews tried to survive by eating coagulated horse blood spiced with salt and pepper and spread on bread. A ghetto physician, Dr. Jakob Penson, mixed bovine blood (from cows illegally slaughtered in the ghetto), with onions and fat, and fed the combination to patients swollen with hunger edema. His plan was to reduce the swelling by raising levels of blood protein. It didn't work.

A painful account that illustrates the sort of fundamental ethical/moral dilemmas faced by the Jews of the Warsaw Ghetto is that of a starving family of four who were given some soup and four rolls. The children and their father ate their rolls; the mother saved hers till the next day. "During the night her husband, driven by uncontrollable hunger, crawled to her bed, stole the roll from under her pillow, and then fell over dead still clutching his shameful prize."[2]

Scientific Study of Hunger and Starvation

Because of these facts, hunger, the universal fact of the ghetto, became the main focus of a major scientific study carried out by many members of the Jewish medical profession; their rationale was that since everyone was starving, that was what it was sensible to study. The pro-

2. Roland, *Courage under Siege*, p. 99.

ject involved several different areas of medical research. Although some were unfinished because Treblinka gobbled up the researchers, and some were written up but the records were lost, nevertheless, a substantial corpus of work was smuggled out of the ghetto and hidden by sympathetic non-Jewish colleagues. After the war, these surviving reports were published in French and in Polish, and more recently in a somewhat condensed version in English.[3]

This clandestine work began in February 1942 and ended five months later. A detailed exposition of the findings is inappropriate, but a summary will hint at what was accomplished.[4]

General Changes

The first signs of hunger disease were constant thirst and a marked increase in the amount of urine passed. These signs were found after even a short period of sustained hunger. As starvation progressed these symptoms were replaced by profound weakness, causing the patients to become unwilling or unable to work. They described feeling chilled and depressed, and were uninterested in anything but food. The typical sufferer from hunger disease lay curled in the fetal position, sleepy and so cold that they covered themselves as heavily as possible, even in summer.

On admission to hospital the patients were pale, bluish-looking, had faint pulses, and were in a state of collapse. Unlike normal persons, they had little change in blood pressure after physical stress. Their lungs did not seem to function normally, and they often had symptoms of bowel inflammation: noisy bowels, swollen bellies, and copious bowel movements.

The hospitalized patients weighed between 60 and 90 lbs., between 20 and 50 percent below normal. One 30-year-old woman, 5' 8" tall, weighed 53 lbs. In the final stages, all patients, especially the women, looked far older than their years.

In children the earliest changes included apathy and disinterest in playing. Quarrelsomeness and irritability were characteristic. Many of the children seemed mentally retarded though they were known to be normal.

---

3. Emil Apfelbaum (edit.), *Maladie de Famine: Recherches Cliniques sur la Famine Exécutées dans la Ghetto de Varsovie en 1942* (Warsaw: American Joint Distribution Committee, 1946), p. 264; Emil Apfelbaum (edit.), *Choroba Glodowa: Badania Kliniczne nad Glodem Wykonane w Getcie Warszawskim z Roku 1942* (Warszawa: American Joint Distribution Committee, 1946), p. 265; Myron Winick (edit.), Martha Osnos (trans.), *Hunger Disease: Studies by the Jewish Physicians in the Warsaw Ghetto* (New York: John Wiley & Sons, 1979).

4. For greater detail, see Roland, *Courage Under Siege*, Chapter 6, pp. 98-119; also, of course, the three editions of the book on the research project themselves, see footnote 3 above.

Many children were swollen with edema. The remainder resembled skeletons covered with skin. They had all the signs just mentioned for adults, especially diarrhea. Often, children developed contractures, so that the arms or the legs became fixed in a drawn-up position and could not be straightened.

A particularly important finding was their atypical reaction to infectious diseases. When severely starved children developed an infectious disease such as measles, diphtheria, tuberculosis, or chicken pox, they did not show the characteristic clinical picture. Where high temperatures were expected, they had little fever. The diagnostic rashes, such as in measles, were less apparent than in non-starved children.

We know now that the immune systems in these children had failed under the stress of starvation. The Jewish physicians in the Warsaw ghetto recognized the existence of an immune deficiency. Ironically, the ghetto children probably would have responded more or less normally to immunization (had vaccines been available) even though they were much more at risk once they became infected.

Pathological Changes in the Body

In the autopsy room, pathologists examined hundreds of bodies. By September 1942, when Czyste Hospital was destroyed, 3,658 autopsies had been done, and 15 percent of these were performed on patients dying of starvation. The difficulties of carrying out research on hunger disease were profound. The Jewish pathologists pointed out that:

> the poor nutrition and poor general living conditions in the ghetto created a very difficult climate for scientific work. The lack of libraries, the lack of instruments and reagents, and the low morale associated with the constant fear of losing one's life were ever present for all. [In September 1942]. . . the hospital, its institutes, laboratories, autopsy rooms, and library were completely destroyed, making any further work impossible. . . . Organs preserved in formalin were completely destroyed.[5]

Nevertheless, much important work was done. The gross examinations revealed that the weight of the brain remained nearly normal, but the heart, liver, and kidneys were abnormally light. Changes were also found in the intestines, although it seemed on the wards that the patients had dysentery, tests showed that this was not the case.

On Tuesday, 6 July 1942, some of the investigators presented their findings at a scientific meeting in Czyste Hospital. *Judenrat* chairman Adam Czerniakow attended, and recorded that the session was chaired by Dr. Milejkowski and papers were read by several of the medical staff.

---

5. Stein and Fenigstein, *Hunger Disease*, Winick (ed.), pp. 209-210.

Two weeks later the deportations to Treblinka began. Scientific work ended in the Warsaw ghetto.

Dr. Milejkowski completed his Introduction to the Hunger Disease manuscript in October 1942. By then, some 300,000 of his fellow Jews had died at Treblinka. Milejkowski observed dryly that he was actually writing ". . . in one of the undestroyed rooms of the cemetery buildings. This is the symbol of our living and working environment."[6] Other survivors labored on, intent on preserving some scientific contribution from their ordeal. The editor of the English translation of this research particularly praised the Jewish physicians and scientists who undertook these studies:

> These were not investigators who came in, did their tests, and went home. These were physicians, dealing with the easiest disease to cure, and helpless to effect that cure. They cared for their patients in whatever manner they had available, and at the same time carefully noted their deterioration. Afflicted with the same disease, knowing that their time was limited, they persevered.[7]

Zweibaum's Underground Medical School

Although most education in Poland was forbidden by the Nazis, there were some exceptions. One of these was the opening of a few technical or trade schools under German authority. One of these was in the ghetto. On 31 August 1940, Hans Frank, Governor General of the Nazi *Généralgouvernement*, issued a decree authorizing the *Judenrat* to provide some elementary and vocational schooling for the Jewish population.

The Germans believed that they had authorized a program of weeks or months that would produce technicians capable of fighting epidemics. But the medical educators in the ghetto used the approved courses as a front for clandestine medical education, and from May 1941 until July 1942 they operated a full-scale medical school designed to educate young men and women to become physicians. The organizer was *Docent* Zweibaum, formerly of the Warsaw University medical school. He planned a school to provide the early years of basic medical education; later, when Hirszfeld became active in the ghetto, he organized the Superior Course, which consisted of the final four, clinical, years of the Polish medical educational system. Teaching took place in the ghetto hospitals and clinics.

---

6. Cited in Roland, *Courage Under Siege*, p. 118.

7. Myron Winick (edit.), Martha Osnos (trans.), *Hunger Disease: Studies by the Jewish Physicians in the Warsaw Ghetto* (New York: John Wiley & Sons, 1979), p. 43.

The faculty of the ghetto school considered it a division of Warsaw University. For a short time, before the sealing-off of the Jews became total, there was both consultative and administrative cooperation with the outside university, which also functioned clandestinely. But these arrangements could not be sustained.

Just outside the western edge of the ghetto, at the corner of Leszno and Zelazna streets, was a former secondary school that had been taken over as the *Arbeitsamt* or Department of Labor. The upper floors of this building were utilized for medical teaching.[8] The students actually had to leave the ghetto to get to the school, though the distance was only a few yards.

In May 1941, Dr. Josef Stein gave the introductory lecture. He spoke on the ultimate ghetto topic, "Life and Death." The creators of the clandestine medical school had one unanticipated advantage in dealing with the Nazis. Many Germans were terrified of epidemic diseases. They claimed, falsely, that the Jews were especially susceptible to typhus, and then used this premise as an excuse for quarantining them in the ghetto. Nevertheless, many Germans seem to have believed their own paranoid propaganda. This fear may have played a role in obtaining approval for the courses "to combat epidemics" when little other education was permitted.

Ironically, anatomical specimens were difficult to obtain. Bodies were all too readily available but formaldehyde to preserve them was not. Consequently, the students learned their anatomy in hospital morgues, dissecting fresh bodies as part of the autopsy process.

On winter evenings, electricity being expensive and, often, unavailable, the lecture rooms were lit by ill-smelling carbide lamps. The rooms were heated inadequately. Studying at home carried its own risks; if you wanted to work with another student, the visitor had to sleep over because of the curfew.

In September 1942, Marek Balin served in the hospital at the *Umschlagplatz* where, briefly until he ran away, he was forced by the Nazis to select, from among the patients—*his* patients—those for transportation (the euphemism for extermination at Treblinka). Millie Eisen, late in the existence of the ghetto, in the very last hospital, on Gesia Street, saw many of her patients throw themselves off the roof of the building to their deaths, when the German lorries arrived to take them to the *Umschlagplatz*.

Yet in many ways, the experiences of these students were entirely normal. They endured examinations regularly, and the results apparently were recorded and communicated to the gentile school outside the ghetto

---

8. For more detail see Charles G. Roland, "An Underground Medical School in the Warsaw Ghetto," *Medical History* 33:399-419, 1989; also Roland, *Courage Under Siege*, Chapter 10, "Education in the Ghetto," pp. 186-198.

as long as this remained possible. Oral exams were the norm, several examiners often participating. Academic year-end examinations for the first-year class were held 20 January 1942 and the senior-level exams took place two weeks later.

There are no records of the names of the students in the underground school. It has been estimated that up to 500 persons may have been students during some portion of the 14 months the school existed. Few of these men and women survived "relocation in the east." After the war, perhaps 50 students were certified as having been in attendance.

In broad terms, the underground medical school in the Warsaw ghetto was created for two reasons: to carry on normal life, and to flout German regulations. Similarly, students studied in the school for two reasons: to further their education, and to defy the Germans. The survivors had the satisfaction of having succeeded.

17

An Historical and Contemporary View of Jewish Doctors in Germany

Michael H. Kater

In Nazi Germany, the fate of Jewish physicians and patients became a function of a racial doctrine that medicalized German society. Nazi leaders regarded the German people biologistically, as a racial-national body whose health had to be guaranteed. Only pure "Aryans" could sustain this health, while non-"Aryan" Jews would corrupt it. Hence the physical elimination of Jews living among Germans was called for, logically to the "Final Solution of the Jewish Question." It became incumbent on German-"Aryan" physicians to maintain the eugenic, racial health of the German people. These physicians helped in designing and implementing all pieces of Nazi race legislation, whereas German-Jewish physicians were seen as working against these efforts, because it became their principal task to keep all German Jews healthy and alive.

Therefore Jewish physicians were persecuted in the Third Reich, first, in their role as professionals representing economic competition to comparable "Aryan" colleagues, but also, because they strove to keep alive German Jews, who were in their care as ordinary patients.

At an initial stage, Jewish doctors were expelled from the public-health insurance system, which meant the exclusion of "Aryans" as their patients. By early 1934, the percentage of Jewish physicians had been reduced from 16 to 11 percent of the total in the German medical profession. The resulting vacancies were quickly filled by young "Aryan" doctors previously unemployed. In this process, many Jewish doctors were detained in camps, and others decided to emigrate. The remaining Jewish doctors only had Jewish patients to look after, who could not sustain them economically. By late 1935, moreover, no new Jewish doctors whatsoever could be licensed. In the autumn of 1938, all remaining Jewish physicians were decertified, with the exception of a handful who were permitted to practice in centers of large Jewish concentration, such as Berlin or Frankfurt. Thus by early 1939, merely 285 Jewish doctors were left to practice among their co-believers in the Nazi Reich.

During the notorious pogrom of November 9 and 10, 1938, hundreds of Jewish men were manhandled by Nazi paramilitary troops and put in concentration camps. After their return, the few extant Jewish physicians were needed to look after them, but often these doctors had also been caught in the dragnet and were as badly mangled physically and spiritually as their patients.

Deportation to the eastern death camps, starting in the autumn of 1941, represented the climax of this anti-Jewish persecution. Some healthcare delivery still took place in the, usually city-centered, Israelite hospitals under the watchful eyes of the SS. Eventually these hospitals, too, were dissolved (with the exception of the one in Berlin) and all the remaining doctors and patients evacuated to the east. In the camps, Jewish doctors observed the highest standards of medical ethics, often risking their lives for their charges.

Jewish physicians attempting to emigrate to countries such as the United States, Britain, and Palestine faced special difficulties there, largely because of indigenous anti-Semitism. Between 1933 and 1945, anywhere from forty-five hundred to six thousand Jewish physicians were expelled from Germany—some two-thirds of all the country's non-"Aryan" doctors. Around five percent of the Jewish physicians in Germany probably committed suicide. Very likely, close to two thousand Jewish doctors, or about one-quarter of the entire professional group, perished in the Nazi Holocaust.

The immediate cause of such anti-Semitic behavior on the part of the German medical establishment was economic. Until 1933, Jewish physicians had been doing well financially, and they were often admired by their mostly Gentile clients. But by 1932 the Depression had produced a huge surplus of young physicians, who were waiting to enter the health-insurance system, which alone guaranteed permanent professional success. These young doctors knew that Jewish physicians in Germany were over-represented by a factor of ten to one, and such statistics entered into their anti-Semitic arguments.

Still, there were more fundamental tensions dating back to the last decades of the nineteenth century. Whereas the professionalization of the German physicians had, by the 1880s, been virtually completed, this process had coincided with the gradual emancipation of the German Jews, who now were also benefiting from this professionalization. The Jews' increasing success in the academic professions caused antipathy among their non-Jewish colleagues, who tried to encumber them both in academic training and professional practice. Among various charges, mostly having to do with the alleged greed of the Jews, there were those of a sexual nature, because often Jewish physicians were looked upon as sexual predators against their non-Jewish female patients. These specific charges were premonitory of later Nazi accusations that Jews were bent on poisoning the blood of Gentiles through an infusion of their own.

Even in the three decades before World War I there existed an oversupply of physicians for which the Jews were blamed. Quackery, too, was said to be caused by Jews. Gentile doctors claimed to have uncovered plots by Jewish colleagues to boycott non-Jewish physicians, and yet it was they themselves who were guilty of such conspiracy. Many argued that Jews should even be kept out of the professional organizations. Virulently anti-Semitic deputies of the national parliament were eager to restrict the number of Jewish physicians to be licenced, albeit to no avail.

When war broke out in August 1914, Jewish physicians and students of medicine volunteered for the colors like everyone else. They were hoping that the war would remove the still existing injustices in society engendered by Judeophobia. Indeed, brave Jewish physicians, like members of other bourgeois occupations, were for the first time being appointed to commissions in the field.

Moreover, after the defeat of the German Empire, the establishment of the democratic Weimar Republic buoyed the hopes of progressive citizens that the lot of German Jews would be improved. Jewish physicians expected this to happen within their specific professional situation, for they correctly believed that the new constitution would support them. On the one side, conditions did indeed improve; Jewish medical practitioners prospered and multiplied until their proportion surpassed the ten percent mark. Throughout the Weimar period, German-Jewish physicians made great strides as researchers, teachers, specialists, and general practitioners; in addition, they contributed significantly to the fledgling discipline of social medicine.

Yet the beginning of the republic also saw the rise of reactionary forces, who by 1923 quite decidedly opted for a fascist system. They were heralded by the rabidly militaristic and increasingly illegal freecorps. Their anti-democratic tenets included, first and foremost, the most virulent type of anti-Semitism. Jew-hating physicians played key roles in the formation of the new political right in a number of ways: they were leaders of the freecorps; they helped Adolf Hitler and his National Socialists in the formulation of early party dogma; and, as Nazis at the end of the 1920s, they initiated the National Socialist German Physicians' League, which took over the traditional medico-professional organizations as soon as Hitler had come to power in January 1933.

The situation of Jewish physicians in Germany today is determined by the intersection of two factors: the development of the postwar medical profession and the position of Jews in the country. Whereas doctors in West Germany at least have made great strides, to the point where they have reached the top of the income and social pyramid, they have signally failed to come to terms with a questionable professional past that was epitomized by medical crimes in Nazi concentration camps. Knowledge of these abuses, as well as the circumstance that exactly half of all the male physicians between 1933 and 1945 had been members of the Nazi Party, has been suppressed, and members critical of the profession who wanted to probe these questions as early as the late 1940s, have been silenced.

Also ostracized were physician resisters against Nazi ways who had themselves become victims of a twisted postwar sense of retribution and justice. One German doctor, who during the war had been drafted to perform "euthanasia" killings and then had decided to escape this service through self-starvation, as a result had become permanently ill, so that he was unable to resume his medical practice after 1945. The West German law courts refused him compensation or even a decent pension on the basis that he had brought this misfortune upon himself as a war malingerer, and the professional medical organizations opted not to intervene in his behalf. In remarkable contrast to this case stand the examples of exposed Nazi physicians who, like Berlin surgeon Dr. Wilhelm Heim, have played leading roles in the West German medical establishment to this day. In his halcyon years Heim was a chieftain of the Stormtroopers, working out of a Berlin hospital that denied Communist opponents of the Nazis proper care after they had been injured in street fights. In early 1992, Heim was reported to be the candidate for an honorary doctorate from Humboldt University in Berlin.

As the top professional organization, the West German Federal Physicians' Chamber, led by Dr. Karsten Vilmar for decades after 1945, has been at pains to deny the uncomfortable knowledge of the past and even to censure members who have dared to ask questions. What blinkered professionals like Vilmar stressed instead was the alleged continuity of "good" German medicine from Rudolf Virchow and Robert Koch to the skillful organ transplanters of the present. Those Nazi crimes that were acknowledged were attributed to a few hundred deviants, not to a profession that collectively had gone astray.

With very few exceptions, West German scholars who opposed such denial have not come from the medical establishment itself, but from outside of it, such as Cologne geneticist Benno Müller-Hill. Only recently have some of the younger physicians made conscious attempts to come to grips with the baneful past and have encouraged discussion. One of the most vocal of them has been the chairman of the Physicians' Chamber for West Berlin, Dr. Ellis Huber, who sponsored an exhibition as well as an international symposium on the value of human life in early 1989.

If the medical establishment has been an eminently visible part of German society since 1945, resident Jews have been the very opposite. In the absence of exact figures it is estimated that hardly more than 35,000 Jews are living in the reunited halves of Germany today; that would amount to scarcely more than five percent of Germany's Jewish population of 1932. In terms of the current German populace this would mean that among every ten thousand inhabitants, merely four are Jewish. If there were ten thousand Jews in the German Reich by early summer 1945, most of them were survivors of the Holocaust and not all of them originally from Germany. This group eventually was augmented by remigrants; in May of 1977 there were about twenty-seven thousand Jews in West Germany alone.

These Jews in Germany were very much at pains to maintain a low profile. Since then, anti-Semitism in Germany has flared up intermittently, until the murder of five female Turks in Solingen in May 1993 made it clear that any feelings of hatred against Jews among Germans are deeply imbedded in a general xenophobia gripping the country.

Jewish physicians in the Federal Republic today must be viewed against this background. The problem is a complex one because the exact number of Jewish doctors is unknown. After the war, not more than 5 percent of all of the former German-Jewish physicians are said to have been either able or willing to return to their homeland. Those men and women who did return were exceptions, however; most émigré physicians had forged new careers for themselves in foreign countries and were reluctant to start all over again, in a country that had rejected them.

If throughout the 1960s there were not even a hundred Jewish physicians in Germany, today there are probably no more than three hundred. This must be compared with the huge number of approximately 300,000 non-Jewish doctors in the newly consolidated Federal Republic. The statistics signify a marked change from the situation in 1932: whereas then every seventh physician had been Jewish, or more than one hundred in every thousand, today it is merely one in every thousand.

One would like to believe that presently the Jewish physicians are on the road to overcoming their predicament, with the aid of a younger generation of German Jews. Indeed, there now appear to exist three German-Jewish physician associations, one in Berlin, one in Frankfurt am Main, and the third in Munich. But their members cannot help but recall quite recent reprehensible practices by their Gentile colleagues. For instance, in the early 1980s the West German Federal Chamber of Physicians under the presidency of Dr. Karsten Vilmar, initially refused and then complied only under public pressure, to rename the Cologne street on which its offices are located from "Haedenkamp-Strasse" to "Lewin-Strasse." Whereas Dr. Carl Haedenkamp had been a Nazi medical bureaucrat who in the early years of the Hitler regime had assisted willingly in the liquidation of the Jewish tradition within the German professional association, Dr. Herbert Lewin had been a Jewish physician, who was finally deported to Auschwitz. While Lewin himself had survived, his family was killed in the Holocaust. When the Cologne changeover finally was decreed by the town council in April 1986, the Chamber declared its resolve to maintain the old streetname on its official stationary until all the legal proceedings had been completed.

To this very day the German Physicians' Chamber has proved recalcitrant to any examination of the past. In November of 1992, Michael M. Kochen, a Jewish professor of family medicine at Göttingen University, became suspicious when Dr. Hans Joachim Sewering, Dr. Vilmar's predecessor as president of the Chamber, was voted president-elect of the World Medical Association. After checking my book *Doctors Under Hitler*, the Göttingen scholar discovered that Sewering had been a member of the SS and the Nazi Party, and had sent at least one patient, a fourteen-year-old girl, to her "euthanasia" death in 1943. Kochen launched a protest with the help of the international media, whereupon Sewering denied most of the charges in an interview with the *New York Times* in mid-January of 1993. After surviving nurses, members of a Catholic order whom Sewering had worked with in 1943, had stepped forward to certify that Sewering knew what he was doing with his feeble patients, the doctor resigned his president-elect status on January 23, 1993. But he did so protesting that he was the victim of a Jewish conspiracy, for unless he resigned, the World Jewish Congress would attack the World Medical Association. Through all of this, German Chamber of Physicians' president Dr. Vilmar had supported Sewering, especially in officially sponsoring that doctor's resignation statement, thereby implicitly condoning Sewering's anti-Jewish charges. Immediately after the scandal, younger, enlightened German physicians were demanding that Vilmar himself step down from his exposed Cologne position. But not only did Vilmar prevail, he even entrenched himself as treasurer of the World Medical Association, an office that was confirmed at the meeting of that organization in Budapest in October of 1993.

We must conclude, therefore, that although formally speaking Jewish physicians have been allowed to return to Germany, in order to practice there, their number is very small, and, in the face of possible renewed harassment, if not persecution, they tend to keep their Jewish identity hidden, because they know that they cannot expect special protection from the officially entrenched professional organization. This is a sad judgment at a time when political right-extremism once again appears to threaten democracy. It will be interesting to see what happens after the German national elections in the Fall of 1994, and, in particular, whether Jewish doctors, who once gave so much to Germany and to the world, will again feel compelled to leave the country.

NOTE: For full documentation for this article, see Michael H. Kater, *Doctors Under Hitler* (Chapel Hill and London, 1989); and Kater, "Unresolved Questions of German Medicine and Medical History in the Past and Present," *Central European History*, 25 (1992), 407-23.

VI.

Nuremberg's Legacy

18

Historical Origins
of the Nuremberg Code

Michael A. Grodin

The Nuremberg Code consists of 10 principles enumerated in the final judgment of the Doctors' Trial or Medical Case.[1] These principles were formulated in an attempt to establish the substantive standards and procedural guidelines for permissible medical experimentation with humans. They were not identified as a code of medical ethics but rather appear as part of the final legal judgment, where it is claimed that they are derived from the "natural law" of all people. (George Annas discusses the legal standing of the Nuremberg Code in U.S. Law in Chapter 11 of the *Nazi Doctors and the Nuremberg Code*.)

The 10 principles articulating the acceptable limits of human experimentation must be understood in the context of the criminal trials. Nazi physicians and scientists had carried out extensive human experimentation and murders during the war. (Chapter 5 of *Nazi Doctors* describes the extent of Nazi experimentation as part of the indictments for crimes against humanity. Eva Mozes-Kor presents a personal account of the Mengele twin experiments carried out at the Birkenau concentration camp in Chapter 4 of *Nazi Doctors*.) The appropriate standards for the conduct of human experimentation were a major theme recurring throughout the trial. While the tribunal's focus was on the criminal nature of the Nazi experi-

1. *Trials of War Criminals Before the Nuremberg Military Tribunals Under Control Council Law 10* (Washington, D.C.: Superintendent of Documents, U.S. Government Printing Office, 1950). *Military Tribunal 1*, Case 1, *United States v. Karl Brandt et al.,* October 1946-April 1949, Vol. I, pp. 1-1004; Vol. II, pp. 1-352 (1949).

NOTE: Grodin, M.A. "Historical Origins of the Nuremberg Code" in Annas, G.J. and Grodin M.A. Eds. *The Nazi Doctors and the Nuremberg Code: Human Rights in Human Experiments*. Oxford University Press, 1992 pp. 121-144. Reprinted with permission.

ments, the judges were also grappling with much broader ethical concerns regarding medical research. The trial court sought a historical framework of medical standards from which to judge the Nazi physicians and attempted to elucidate the scope of medical experimentation undertaken by the Nazis, and other physicians and scientists, during World War II. Finally, the trial court attempted to establish a set of principles of human experimentation that could serve as a code of research ethics.

This chapter focuses on the historical origins of the 10 principles later known as the Nuremberg Code. An attempt is made to place the code in context by analyzing earlier German and non-German medical codes. Significant questions are raised concerning the standing, scope, impact, and enforceability of all of the codes, which may address diverse populations and circumstances. The codes of human experimentation all appear to have been developed in response to specific abuses and perceived needs. In all cases, violations continued to surface after their promulgation. Most of the codes do not distinguish therapeutic from nontherapeutic human experimentation because experimentation carried out in the context of patient care was rarely considered research. All of the codes appear to accept a universal necessity to continue scientific inquiry through experimentation.

The Nuremberg Code was not the first code of human experimentation, nor was it the most comprehensive. Even pre-German codes are more extensive in their concern for the ethics of human experimentation. Perhaps it was the unprecedented nature of the atrocities committed by Nazi physicians that has made the Nuremberg Code the hallmark for all subsequent discourse on the ethics of human experimentation. Because the code was written in response to the acts of a scientific and medical community out of control, it is not surprising that voluntary informed consent was its critical centerpiece and the protection of human subjects its paramount concern.

Early Medical Codes and Ethical Statements
as the Basis for the Nuremberg Code

The Nuremberg Code was based on a convergence of historical documents and circumstances. During the trial, both the prosecution and the defense repeatedly cited and analyzed past experiences and standards of ethical human experimentation. The defense counsel cited examples of widespread misuse of human subjects for research, as well as the existing medical ethics literature.[2]

The prosecution used its two primary medical expert witnesses, Leo Alexander and Andrew Ivy, as the sources for the history and ethical

---

2. Ibid., *Military Tribunal*, Vol. II, Section VIII, I, Medical Ethics, pp. 70-93.

standards of human experimentation.[3] It is particularly important to understand the testimony of these witnesses, for we will see later that they were the primary sources of the principles upon which the Nuremberg Code is based. All of the physician witnesses and defendants at the trial based their views of medical ethics on the history of human experimentation and on historical documents. This section analyzes four historical documents that were well known and undoubtedly influenced the thinking of Ivy and Alexander. These documents are the oaths, codes, and writings of Hippocrates, Percival, Beaumont, and Bernard.

Ivy and Alexander specifically cited Hippocrates as the major foundation for their views on medical ethics.[4] At the trial, Ivy was asked the sources of his belief in the acceptability of human experimentation. He responded:

> I base that opinion on the principles of ethics and morals contained in the oath of Hippocrates. I think it should be obvious that a state cannot follow a physician around in his daily administration to see that the moral responsibility inherent therein is properly carried out. This moral responsibility that controls or should control the conduct of a physician should be inculcated into the minds of physicians just as moral responsibility of other sorts, and those principles are clearly depicted or enunciated in the oath of Hippocrates, with which every physician should be acquainted. According to my knowledge, it represents the Golden Rule of the medical profession. It states how one doctor would like to be treated by another doctor in case he is ill. And in that way how a doctor should treat his patient or experimental subjects. He should treat them as though he were serving as a subject.[5]

Alexander further noted:

> Every professional relationship between the physician and another human being, irrespective of whether the physician treats the pa-

---

3. Andrew Conway Ivy, M.D., Ph.D., was a professor of physiology and pharmacology. From 1946 to 1953, Dr. Ivy was vice president of the University of Illinois in charge of the Chicago Professional Colleges. He was a consultant to the U.S. Secretary of War and the U.S. Chief Counsel for War Crimes of the Nuremberg Tribunal at the request of the American Medical Association. Leo Alexander, M.D., was a professor of psychiatry and neurology and a colonel, U.S. Army Reserves. Dr. Alexander served as a consultant to the U.S. Secretary of War and the U.S. Chief Counsel for War Crimes during the Doctors' Trial, and he examined many of the survivors of the Nazi medical experiments.

4. See A. C. Ivy, "The History and Ethics of the Use of Human Subjects in Medical Experiments," *Science* 108 (1948): 1-5; L. Alexander, "Ethics of Human Experimentation," *Psychiatric Journal of the University of Ottawa* 1(1976): 40-46; L. Alexander, "Limitations in Experimental Research on Human Beings," *Lex et Scientia 3* (1966): 8-24.

5. *Military Tribunal*, Vol. II, Direct Examination; Trial transcript, pp. 9029-9324; Ivy, "History and Ethics."

tient, examines him or performs an experiment upon him with his
permission, is bound by the principles laid down in the Hippocrates
oath.[6]

It is interesting, but not surprising, that both Leo Alexander and Andrew Ivy cite the Hippocratic oath as the basis of their views on medical
ethics. The Hippocratic oath was written (probably not by Hippocrates)
some time between 470 and 360 B.C.E. It has had profound significance
for the general ethos of medical practice and medical ethics.[7] It explicitly
states that the physician should work to the best of his ability for the
good of his patients:

> I will follow that system of regimes which, according to my ability
> and judgment, I consider for the benefit of my patients, and abstain
> from whatever is deleterious and mischievous.[8]

The primary thrust of the Hippocratic oath, and its most critical
point, is the obligation to benefit the patient. During the Hippocratic period, however, benefit to the patient was determined by the physician; today's medical ethicists are concerned with benefit as determined by the
patient or the patient's proxy.[9]

The most striking problem, however, with using the Hippocratic oath
as the foundation for the Nuremberg Code on human experimentation is
that it does not deal with research. The oath deals with patients, not with
experimental human subjects. Benefit to the patient is most problematic in
the area of human experimentation, particularly in nontherapeutic re-

---

6. Alexander, "Ethics of Human Experimentation," 41. Dr. Alexander cites the
Hippocratic oath in a section entitled "Medical-Ethical (Hippocratic)
Requirements." This paper was written to republish his original memoranda to the
U.S. Chief of Counsel for War Crimes at Nuremberg in December 1946.

7. See P. Carrick, *Medical Ethics in Antiquity* (Hingham, Mass.: D. Reidel/
Klüwer, 1985); pp. 69-94, for a discussion of the Hippocratic tradition. The
Hippocratic oath is reprinted in 0. Temkin and C. Temkin, eds., *Ancient Medicine:
Selected Papers of Ludwig Edelstein* (Baltimore: Johns Hopkins University Press,
1967).

8. Ibid.

9. There is a certain irony in even discussing the Hippocratic tradition in the
context of Nazi medical experimentation. The Jews of Cos, the city in Crete where
Hippocrates was born and where he taught his beliefs on medicine, were
assembled in 1944, perhaps at the very site where Hippocrates had once sat, and
shipped to the Auschwitz and Buchenwald concentration camps. They arrived at
the train station in Germany in 1944 and were divided into groups to be killed and
others to be interned for concentration camp work. It was the very heirs of
Hippocrates, Nazi *physicians,* who made those selections. Many of these same
physicians probably took the Hippocratic oath on graduation from medical school.
This poignant irony was pointed out by Prof. William Seidelman of McMaster
University, Ontario, Canada, in his unpublished manuscript "An Inquiry Into the
Spiritual Death of Dr. Hippocrates."

search, where there is no claim of benefit for the subject at all. The risks to the subject are balanced against the benefits to society at large. In addition, no discussion of the principle of informed consent is found without the oath. This is particularly relevant in that consent is believed by many to be the key principle of the Nuremberg Code (see Chapter 12 of *Nazi Doctors* for a discussion of the importance of informed consent to the Nuremberg Code and the ethics of human experimentation). It is also of interest that during the Hippocratic period, animals were considered sacred and human autopsies were outlawed. This is important because the Nuremberg Code explicitly states that animal experimentation should be done before humans become subjects. Alexander and Ivy confused therapeutic treatment of patients with nontherapeutic experimentation on prisoners and thus incorrectly cited Hippocrates as the source for the ethics of human experimentation.

Medicine had hardly advanced, with regard to effective therapies, from the time of Hippocrates until the end of the eighteenth century.[10] During the intervening centuries, human experimentation was performed in an uncontrolled, unscientific manner. Reports of medical experiments on condemned criminals in ancient times and of human vivisection are now well documented.[11] Some of these early examples of human experimentation focused on the use of variolation vaccinations. In England in 1721, condemned prisoners at Newgate Prison were offered a pardon if they participated in inoculations.[12] Perhaps the earliest evidence of experimentation on children dates from 1776, when Edward Jenner inoculated an 8-year-old boy with cowpox material.[13] It should be noted that up to the nineteenth century, almost all medical practice may be considered uncontrolled, unstandardized, and innovative therapeutics or, quite simply, human experimentation of a purely empirical nature.

One of the earliest codes to include specific directives with respect to research ethics was written by Thomas Percival, an English physician, in 1803. Percival's code of medical ethics was the source for the first American Medical Association Code of Ethics in the United States in 1847. Andrew Ivy, as the representative of the American Medical Associa-

---

10. For a complete discussion of the historical aspects of human experimentation, see N. Howard-Jones, "Human Experimentation in Historical and Ethical Perspectives," in *Human Experimentation and Medical Ethics,* F. Bankowski and N. Howard-Jones, eds., (Geneva: XVth CIOMS Council for International Organization of Medical Sciences Round Table Conference, 1982), pp. 453-495.

11. Ibid.; see also C. Bernard, *Principes de la Médecine expérimentale* (Paris: Presses Universitaires de France, 1947), and John Scarborough, "Celsus on Human Vivisection at Ptolemaic, Alexandria," *Clio Medica* 11 (1976): 25-38.

12. James Johnston, *Abraham Lettson, His Life, Times, Friends and Descendants* (London: Heinemann, 1933), pp. 186-188.

13. E. Jenner, *An Inquiry Into the Cause and Effects of the Variolae Vaccine.* (London: S. Low, 1789).

tion at the Nuremberg Tribunals, was well aware of the Association's Code and its roots in the English Code of Percival. It is of interest that the first American Medical Association Code of Ethics does not identify human experimentation as a distinct area of concern.[14]

While Percival's code deals primarily with the clinical practice of medicine, it does include specific directives to the physician who is planning to perform human experiments. Percival notes:

> Whenever cases occur, attended with circumstances not heretofore observed, or in which the ordinary modes of practice have been attempted without success, it is for the public good, and in especial degree advantageous to the poor (who, being the most numerous class of this society, are the greatest beneficiaries of the healing art) that new remedies *and new methods of chirurgical treatment* should be devised but, in the accomplishment of the salutary purpose, the gentlemen of the faculty should be *scrupulously and conscientiously governed by sound reason, just analogy, or well-authenticated facts.* And no such trials should be instituted without a previous consultation of the physicians or surgeons according to the nature of the case.[15]

Percival's code clearly states the need to devise new remedies and new, innovative therapies. In his view, this research must be based on conscientious and scrupulous reasoning and careful investigation of facts, and action should be taken only after consultation with one's fellow physicians. The focus, then, of this early guide to research ethics is on good methodology and competent investigators. While both are crucial, there is no mention in Percival's code of the need for the protection of human subjects, nor is there any discussion of consent at all.

Some have cited the code of William Beaumont in 1833 as the oldest American document dealing with the ethics of human experimentation.[16] Beaumont was a physician who carried out extensive nontherapeu-

---

14. See H. Beecher, *Research and the Individual Human Subject* (Boston: Little, Brown, 1970), pp. 219-225, for a discussion of the American Medical Association codes of 1846, 1847, 1946, 1949, 1958, 1966, and 1967. Also see the *Archives of the American Medical Association Proceedings* of the National Medical Conventions held in New York in May 1846 and in Philadelphia in May 1947, printed for the American Medical Association by T. K. and D. G. Collins Printers, Philadelphia (1847). The first American Medical Association code to deal specifically with human experimentation was promulgated in 1946.

15. Percival's code is cited in Beecher, *Research,* p. 218 (emphasis added). Also see S. Reiser, A. Dyck, and W. Curran, eds., *Ethics in Medicine: Historical Perspectives and Contemporary Concerns* (Cambridge, Mass.: Massachusetts Institute of Technology Press, 1977), pp. 18-25, and T. Percival, *Medical Ethics,* 3rd ed. (Oxford: John Henry Parker, 1949), pp. 27-68.

16. See Beecher, *Research,* pp. 219-220. Also see K. Wiggers, "Human Experimentation as Exemplified by the Career of Dr. William Beaumont," *Alumni Bulletin,* School of Medicine and Affiliated Hospitals, Western Reserve University

tic experiments with his patient, Alexis St. Martin. St. Martin had suffered an accidental gunshot wound to his abdomen that, in healing, had left an open fistula tract. Beaumont utilized this tract to study the physiology of the stomach. In an attempt to justify his human experiments, Beaumont set forth a set of principles to guide the researcher.

William Beaumont's code includes the following points:

1. There must be recognition of an area where experimentation in man is needed. . . .

2. Some experimental studies in man are justifiable when the information cannot otherwise be obtained.

3. The investigator must be conscientious and responsible . . . for a well-considered, methodological approach is required so that as much information as possible will be obtained whenever a human subject is used. No random studies are to be made.

4. The voluntary consent of the subject is necessary. . . .

5. The experiment is to be discontinued when it causes distress to the subject. . . .

6. The project must be abandoned when the subject becomes dissatisfied.[17]

Beaumont's code resembles Percival's in claiming that human experimentation is needed, and that the investigator must be conscientious and responsible and must use a sound methodological approach. Of particular importance, however, is its further statement that the voluntary consent of the subject is necessary and that the project should be abandoned if the subject is distressed by it. These requirements reflect the fact that Beaumont's subject was not a prisoner but an alert, competent adult, so that consent would seem to be a prerequisite to enlisting his cooperation.

The influential French physiologist Claude Bernard wrote extensively on experimental medicine, including the guidelines governing human experimentation. His work was known to both Ivy and Alexander.[18]

(September 1950), pp. 60-65, where other authors and scientists have noted that "the ethical principles . . . of William Beaumont gradually grew into an unwritten code consonant with the moral dictates and laws of all civilized countries." Also see R. Numbers, "William Beaumont and the Ethics of Human Experimentation," *Journal of the History of Biology* 12 (1979): 113-135, which questions Beaumont as the source for the ethics of human experimentation in the United States as well as the ethics of Beaumont's human experimentation with patient Alexis St. Martin.

17. The text of Beaumont's code as found in Beecher, *Research*, p. 219 (selections by the author).

18. See note 4.

In his famous text, *An Introduction to the Study of Experimental Medicine*, published in 1865, Bernard lays down his principles for the ethical pursuit of human experimentation:

> It is our duty and our right to perform an experiment on man whenever it can save his life, cure him or gain him some personal *benefit*. The principle of medical and surgical morality, therèfore, consists in never performing on man an experiment which might be harmful to him to any extent, even though the result might be highly advantageous to science, i.e., to the health of others. . . . Christian morals forbid only one thing, doing ill to one's neighbor. So, among the experiments that might be tried on man, those that can only *harm* are forbidden. Those that are innocent are permissible, and those that may do good are obligatory.[19]

Bernard's writings suggest a merging of patient care, innovative therapy, and therapeutic experimentation. He appears to exclude any nontherapeutic research by demanding the personal benefit of the subject. In the context of medical care, he believes that it is imperative to perform scientifically vigorous experimentation in order to gain that benefit. The benefit, however, is to be determined by the physician.

The limits of acceptable research condoned by Bernard can be surmised from the following two cases. He supported the use of dying patients in human experimentation that caused no suffering. He also endorsed the administration of the larvae of intestinal worms to a condemned woman with the goal of postmortem examination. These cases seem to call into question Bernard's prohibition of nonbeneficial experimentation.[20]

The codes of Hippocrates, Percival, Beaumont, and Bernard are all concerned with a physician's responsibility to benefit the patient/subject. While Hippocrates deals only with the physician-patient relationship, Percival addresses innovative therapies, Beaumont covers nontherapeutic experimentation, and Bernard focuses on the scientific method and therapeutic research. Beaumont and Bernard are also concerned with acceptable experimental risk. Only Beaumont provides any discussion of voluntary consent as a necessity for human experimentation.

Alexander and Ivy had read the works of Hippocrates, Percival, Beaumont, and Bernard. Beyond these documents, Alexander was most interested in American statements and court decisions on cases involving the use of new medical or surgical techniques and the administration of new and unproven drugs. Alexander cites several reviews and cases as impor-

---

19. See C. Bernard, *An Introduction to the Study of Experimental Medicine,* trans. Henry Copley (New York: Macmillan, 1927), pp. 101-102. The original volume was published in Paris in 1865 and was entitled *Introduction à l'Étude de la Médicine Experimentale* (emphasis added).

20. See Howard-Jones, "Human Experimentation," p. 458.

tant foundations for his ethical formulations.[21] These law review articles
and cases identify the liability of the physician who subjects a patient to
experimental methods of treatment without making a full disclosure of the
material facts so that the patient may assume or reject the risk. The law
review articles also specify the legal responsibility for human experimentation involving risk to life without compensating social or scientific interests.[22]

Ivy and Alexander, as medical experts at the Nuremberg trial, were
also cognizant of some of the prewar German literature on the ethics of
human experimentation. Alexander specifically cites a German book by
Ebermayer, written in 1930, as an influence on his views of the ethics of
human experimentation.[23] Insofar as the German physicians on trial at
Nuremberg claimed that the ethics of their human experimentation must
first be judged on the basis of German standards and codes, it is relevant
to examine the nature of medical ethics and the ethics of human experimentation in prewar Germany.

The Ethics of Human Experimentation
in Pre-Nuremberg Germany

The earliest piece of legislation in Germany concerning the ethics of
human experimentation was a directive issued on December 29, 1900, by
the Prussian Minister of Religious, Educational and Medical Affairs. This
document may, in fact, be the first reported regulatory action relating specifically to the field of human experimentation (see the discussion in
Chapter 8 of *Nazi Doctors*). The directive reads:

> I. I wish to point out to the directors of clinics, polyclinics and similar estab-
> lishments that medical interventions for purposes other than diagnosis,
> therapy and immunization are absolutely prohibited, even though all other
> legal and ethical requirements for performing such interventions are ful-
> filled if:
>   1. The person in question is a minor or is not fully competent on other
>   grounds;
>   2. The person concerned has not declared unequivocally that he consents
>   to the intervention;

---

21. See Alexander, "Limitations in Experimental Research with Human Beings,"
15.

22. See *Pratt v. Davis*, 79 NE 562 (1906); Consent as Condition of Right to
Perform Surgical Operations; *American Law Reports* 76 (1942): 562-571; E. H.
Smith, "Antecedent Grounds of Liability in the Practice of Surgery," *Rocky
Mountain Law Review* 14 (1942): 233-293; and W. R. Arthur, "Some Liability of
Physicians in the Use of Drugs," *Rocky Mountain Law Review* 17 (1945): 131-162.

23. L. Ebermayer, *Der Arzt in Recht* (Leipzig: Georg Thieme, 1930), pp. 1-287. As
cited in 4 Alexander, "Limitations in Experimental Research with Human Beings."

3. The declaration has not been made on the basis of a proper explanation of the adverse consequences that may result from the intervention.

II. In addition, I prescribe that:
1. Interventions of this nature may be performed only by the director of the institution himself or with his special authorization;
2. In every intervention of this nature, an entry must be made in the medical case-record book, certifying that the requirements laid down in Items 1-3 of Section I and Item 1 of Section II have been fulfilled, specifying details of the case.

III. This directive shall not apply to medical interventions intended for the purpose of diagnosis, therapy, or immunization.[24]

The 1900 Prussian directive was issued, at least in part, in response to a public debate in the German daily press, Parliament, and the courts about the permissibility of human experimentation. Much of the debate focused on the "Case of Neisser." Albert Neisser, a professor of dermatology and venereology in Breslau, had conducted experiments in 1892 on the possibility of immunizing healthy persons against syphilis by inoculating them with serum from known syphilis patients. Four children served as healthy controls and were inoculated with syphilis serum. Three adolescent female prostitutes were similarly injected and contracted syphilis. Consent was not obtained from any of the subjects or their legal guardians. Legal and legislative debate ultimately led to the 1900 "Instructions to the Directors of Clinics, Out-Patient Clinics and Other Medical Facilities."[25]

The Prussian directive explicitly prohibits nontherapeutic research on minors or incompetents. This may be the first document dealing with the ethics of human experimentation that specifically recognizes the need for the protection of uniquely vulnerable populations such as minors or incompetents. The document further demands unequivocal consent and a proper explanation of the possible adverse consequences of the research. This recognition of voluntary informed consent as fundamental to ethically sound experimentation is a much more refined notion of the protection of human subjects than is seen in earlier documents. If research is to be carried out according to the directive, then it can only be done by the director of the institute or with special supervision. Furthermore, all experiments must be entered into a medical record book, along with documentation of how the requirements for human experimentation were met. This 1900 Prussian document is critical in the history of the development of human experimentation guidelines in that it not only states the substantive

24. *Centralblatt der gesamten Unterrichtsverwaltung in Preussen* pp. 188-189 (1901). This informal translation was prepared by the Health Legislation Unit of the World Health Organization.

25. See B. Elkeles, "Medizinische Menschenversuche gegen Ende des 19. Jahrhunderte und der Fall Neisser," *Medizin Historisches Journal* 20 (1985): 135-148.

standards for the ethical conduct of research, but also contains specific procedural mechanisms to ensure responsibility for the experimentation.

One of the defenses raised at the Nuremberg trial by the Nazi physicians was the relativism of codes of ethics, especially in regard to human experimentation. The Nazi physicians claimed that standards of ethics of earlier times or other locales could not be considered the standard for Germany, and thus they could not be held accountable to these codes of ethics (see Chapter 13 of *Nazi Doctors* for a discussion of ethical relativism). It is thus most important to look at German regulations from the 1930s on to see what the standards of research ethics were during that period.

Medicine in prewar Germany was a showcase of academic, scholarly, and analytical pursuits (see Chapters 2 and 3 of *Nazi Doctors*). The prewar German Medical Association was a democratic forum with such progressive concerns as hygiene and public health. Germany had legislated compulsory health insurance for workers. Questions of medical ethics and malpractice were handled through the German Medical Association and the Reich Chamber of Physicians. Physicians were licensed by the Ministry of Education and the Reich Health Office in the Minister of Interior, which had been established in 1876 by the German Imperial Reich and was responsible for drafting legislation and policy, compiling health statistics, carrying out research, and publishing information.

Criticism of the German medical profession for alleged unethical conduct became widespread in the 1920s. Such criticism was unparalleled in other countries at that time, especially as the German criticism appeared in the daily press.[26] A paper appearing in 1931 written by Alfons Stauder, a member of the Reich Health Office, described the state of medical research as

> naked cynicism; placing the lives of small children on the same level as those of experimental animals (rats), dubious experiments having no therapeutic purpose; science sailing under false colors; crimes against the health of defenseless children; lack of sensibility; mental and physical torture; martyrization of children in hospitals; the worst forms of charlatanism; disgustingly shameful abominations in the name of science run mad; horrors of the darkest middle ages, outstripping the infamous deeds of the inquisition and the hangman; social injustice; discrimination between the rich and the poor.[27]

---

26. An extensive discussion regarding public concern about human experimentation in prewar Germany is found in Howard-Jones, "Human Experimentation," pp. 470-473.

27. See A. Stauder, *Die Zülassigkeit ärtzlicher Versuche an gesunden und Kranken Menschen Münchener Medizinische Wochenschrift* 78 (1931): 107-112, as it appears in Howard-Jones, "Human Experimentation."

Further criticisms were lodged by Friedrich Müller in 1930 in referring to the increased number of medical pharmaceuticals being "thrown onto the market and advertised." Müller accused hospitals of working for the chemical industry and big business.[28] On March 14, 1930, the Reich Health Council held a session to discuss "the permissibility of medical experiments on healthy and sick subjects." The two speakers were Friedrich Müller of Munich and Alfons Stauder of Nuremberg. Müller postulated several principles that should guide human experimentation. Müller's principles included the agreement of the patient, the weighing of consequences, planning, and competent and responsible investigation. Stauder, while acknowledging that abuses existed, suggested that it was the physician's duty to cure patients and that without human experimentation, medical progress would cease.[29]

An important and interesting regulation was promulgated in Germany in 1931 by the Reich Minister of the Interior. It consisted of guidelines for medical experimentation with humans that were probably set down by the Reich Health Council at the urging of Dr. Julius Moses. Moses practiced general medicine in Berlin from 1920 to 1932 and was a member of Parliament for the Social Democratic Party. In 1930, Dr. Moses alerted the public to the deaths of 75 children caused by pediatricians in Lübeck in the course of experiments with tuberculosis vaccinations.[30] In his role as physician/legislator, Moses was in a unique position to respond to these abuses. The 1931 Reich Minister's guidelines are also important because they were recognized and cited during the Nuremberg tribunal as a standard of ethics for the practice of human experimentation during the Nazi period.[31]

There was a great deal of controversy at the trial and in subsequent writings regarding the legal force of the 1931 document. This controversy surfaced during the trial, where Ivy cited the 1931 regulations and the defense counsel claimed that they had no force of law.[32] The International

---

28. See F. Müller, *Die Zülassigkeit ärtzlicher Versuche an gesunden und Kranken Menschen Münchener Medizinische Wochenschrift* 78 (1931): 104-107, as cited and discussed in Howard-Jones, "Human Experimentation," pp. 471-472.

29. See Howard-Jones, "Human Experimentation," p. 472.

30. See further discussion in C. Pross and A. Gotz, eds., *Der Wert des Menschen Medizin in Deutschland 1918-1945* (Berlin: Hentrich, 1989), pp. 92-93. I would like to thank Professor Ezraim Kohack, Boston University Department of Philosophy, for translation of this German document. Dr. Moses perceptively warned in 1932: "Thus in the name of the National Socialist 'Third Reich Empire,' a medical doctor would have the following mission, in order to create a 'new noble humanity': only those who can recover would be healed. The sick who cannot recover, however, are dead weight existences, human refuse, unworthy of living and unproductive. They must be destroyed and eliminated. So in a word, the physician would become an executioner!"

31. See *Military Tribunal*, Vol. II, p. 83.

Office of Public Hygiene in Paris, which had the task of monitoring national and international laws and regulations on health under the Rome Arrangement of 1907, did not cite the 1931 guidelines as part of their monitoring of legislation, and there is no mention of the 1931 guidelines in the Bulletin of the Office between 1931 and 1932.[33] This is of particular interest in that there are numerous reports of items on legislation relating to the quality of milk, standards for bread, and hygienic standards for housing, but not on the German guidelines for experimentation. Several authors have claimed that the 1931 Reich Guidelines constituted a valid, enforceable law up to 1945.[34] Others have claimed that the Reich guidelines were only recommendations and did not have legal force.[35] Independent of their legal standing, however, they are useful in understanding prewar German principles concerning the acceptable limits of human experimentation.

These guidelines were issued in a Reich Circular on February 28, 1931, and were entitled, "Regulations on New Therapy and Human Experimentation." This German document contains almost all of the points subsequently cited in the Nuremberg Code. Some would even argue that the guidelines are even more inclusive and formalistic than the Nuremberg Code in that they demand complete responsibility of the medical profession for carrying out human experimentation. The document explicitly states that it is the individual physician and the chief physician who are responsible for the well-being of the patient or subject. The 1931 Reich Circular states:[36]

> The Reich Health Council [*Reichsgesundheitsrat*] has set great store
> on ensuring that all physicians receive information with regard to

32. See Trial Transcript testimony and cross examination of Dr. Andrew Ivy, June 13,1947, pp. 9141-9145 and 9170-9171.

33. Personal communication, Mr. Sev Fluss, chief of the Health Legislation Unit of the World Health Organization.

34. See S. Fluss, "The Proposed Guidelines as Reflected in Legislation and Codes of Ethics," in Seidelman, "An Inquiry," where Fluss states that the 1931 guidelines "appear to have remained in force until 1945." Also see F. Fischer and H. Breuer, German Research Society, Federal Republic of Germany, "Influence of Ethical Guidance Committees on Medical Research. A Critical Appraisal," in *Medical Experiments and the Protection of Human Rights* (Geneva: XIIth CIOMS Round Table, 1989), which states that the 1931 guidelines were "valid up to 1945." Also see H. Sass, "Reichsrundschreiben 1931: Pre-Nuremberg German Regulation Concerning New Therapy and Human Experimentation," *Journal of Medicine and Philosophy* 8 (1983): 99-111. Sass states that the guidelines "remained binding in Germany even during the period of the Third Reich."

35. See Howard-Jones, "Human Experimentation," which notes that "These guidelines were recommendations not having legal force."

36. *Reichsgesundheitblatt* 11, No. 10, (March 1931), 174-175. This is believed to be the first English translation of the 1931 regulations. Published in the *International Digest of Health Legislation* 31 (1980): 408-411.

the following guidelines. The Council has agreed that all physicians in open or closed health care institutions should sign a commitment to these guidelines when entering their employment.

The final draft of the Circular continues with 14 points:

1. In order that medical science may continue to advance, the initiation in appropriate cases of therapy involving new and as yet insufficiently tested means and procedures cannot be avoided. Similarly, scientific experimentation involving human subjects cannot be completely excluded as such, as this would hinder or even prevent progress in the diagnosis, treatment, and prevention of diseases.

   The freedom to be granted to the physician accordingly shall be weighed against his special duty to remain aware at all times of his major responsibility for the life and health of any person on whom he undertakes innovative therapy or perform an experiment.

2. For the purposes of these Guidelines, "innovative therapy" means interventions and treatment methods that involve humans and serve a therapeutic purpose, in other words, that are carried out in a particular, individual case in order to diagnose, treat, or prevent a disease or suffering or to eliminate a physical defect, although their effects and consequences cannot be sufficiently evaluated on the basis of existing experience.

3. For the purposes of these Guidelines, "scientific experimentation" means interventions and treatment methods that involve humans and are undertaken for research purposes without serving a therapeutic purpose in an individual case, and whose effects and consequences cannot be sufficiently evaluated on the basis of existing experience.

4. Any innovative therapy must be justified and performed in accordance with the principles of medical ethics and the rules of medical practice and theory.

   In all cases, the question of whether any adverse effects that may occur are proportionate to the anticipated benefits shall be examined and accessed.

   Innovative therapy may be carried out only if it has been tested in advance in animal trials (where these are possible).

5. Innovative therapy may be carried out only after the subject or his legal representative has unambiguously consented to the procedure in the light of relevant information provided in advance.

   Where consent is refused, innovative therapy may be initiated only if it constitutes an urgent procedure to preserve life or prevent serious damage to health and prior consent could not be obtained under the circumstances.

6. The question of whether to use innovative therapy must be examined with particular care where the subject is a child or a person under 18 years of age.

7. Exploitation of social hardship in order to undertake innovative therapy is incompatible with the principles of medical ethics.

8. Extreme caution shall be exercised in connection with innovative therapy involving live microorganisms, especially live pathogens. Such therapy shall be considered permissible only if the procedure can be assumed to be

relatively safe and similar benefits are unlikely to be achieved under the circumstances by any other method.

9. In clinics, polyclinics, hospitals, or other treatment and care establishments, innovative therapy may be carried out only by the physician in charge or by another physician acting in accordance with his express instructions and subject to his complete responsibility.

10. A report shall be made in respect of any innovative therapy, indicating the purpose of the procedure, the justification for it, and the manner in which it is carried out. In particular, the report shall include a statement that the subject or, where appropriate, his legal representative has been provided in advance with relevant information and has given his consent.

  Where therapy has been carried out without consent, under the conditions referred to in the second paragraph of Section 5, the statement shall give full details of these conditions.

11. The results of any innovative therapy may be published only in a manner whereby the patient's dignity and the dictates of humanity are fully respected.

12. Section 4-11 of these Guidelines shall be applicable, *mutatis mutandis,* to scientific experimentation (cf. Section 3).

  The following additional requirement shall apply to such experimentation:
  (a) Experimentation shall be prohibited in all cases where consent has not been given;
  (b) Experimentation involving human subjects shall be avoided if it can be replaced by animal studies. Experimentation involving human subjects may be carried out only after all data that can be collected by means of those biological methods (laboratory testing and animal studies) that are available to medical science for purposes of clarification and confirmation of the validity of the experiment have been obtained. Under these circumstances, motiveless and unplanned experimentation involving human subjects shall obviously be prohibited;
  (c) Experimentation involving children or young persons under 18 years of age shall be prohibited if it in any way endangers the child or young person;
  (d) Experimentation involving dying subjects is incompatible with the principles of medical ethics and shall therefore be prohibited.

13. While physicians and, more particularly, those in charge of hospital establishments may thus be expected to be guided by a strong sense of responsibility toward their patients, they should at the same time not be denied the satisfying responsibility *[verantwortungsfreudigkeit]* of seeking new ways to protect or treat patients or alleviate or remedy their suffering where they are convinced, in the light of their medical experience, that known methods are likely to fail.

14. Academic training courses should take every suitable opportunity to stress the physician's special duties when carrying out a new form of therapy or a scientific experiment, as well as when publishing his results.

These guidelines on human experimentation were visionary in their depth and scope. The Reich Circular enumerates clear directives concerning the general, technical, and ethical standards of medicine, informed consent, documented justification of any deviation from protocol, a risk-benefit analysis, justification for the study of especially vulnerable populations (such as children), and the necessity to maintain written records. In many ways, these guidelines are more extensive than either the subsequent Nuremberg Code or the later Declaration of Helsinki recommendations (see Chapter 8 of *Nazi Doctors*).

One final piece of German legislation concerning the ethics and limits of scientific experimentation is relevant. On November 24, 1933, the Nazis passed a law to prevent cruelty and indifference of humans toward animals.[37] The law stated that all operations or treatments that were associated with pain or injury, especially experiments involving the use of cold, heat, or infection, were prohibited and could be permitted only under exceptional circumstances. This law, of course, would prevent the use of animals as an alternative to human experimentation. If the 1931 Reich Circular did have any force of law, the guidelines' stipulation that animal experimentation precede any human experimental trials would have been revoked by this 1933 Nazi legislation. Ironically, if this law for the protection of animals were seen as including human beings as a type of animal, most, if not, all Nazi human experimentation would also have been outlawed.[38]

The Nuremberg Trial and Judgment

The Doctors' Trial, Military Tribunal 1, Case 1, United States of America v. Karl Brandt et al., began on December 9, 1946, at the Palace of Justice in Nuremberg. Twenty-three defendant Nazi physicians were indicted for war crimes and crimes against humanity (see Chapter 5 of *Nazi Doctors*). The charges included human experimentation involving unconsenting prisoners. The experiments included military-related studies to test the limits of human endurance to high altitudes and freezing temperatures. Medically related experiments included inoculation of prisoners with infectious disease pathogens and tests of new antibiotics. Various mutilating bone, muscle, and nerve experiments were also performed on unconsent-

---

37. See *Military Tribunal,* Vol. I, p. 71. It is of interest that Hitler himself was a vegetarian.

38. A parallel irony existed in the United States, where the first laws for the prevention of cruelty to children were enacted only after the Society for the Prevention of Cruelty to Animals had succeeded in securing the protection of animals by law. The first case brought on behalf of a child, on April 19, 1874, stated explicitly that the child, being an animal, should be protected. This led to legislation for the protection of children. The American Society for the Prevention of Cruelty to Children was organized in December 1874. See T. Cone, *History of American Pediatrics* (Boston: Little, Brown, 1979), p. 100.

ing prisoner subjects. (Chapter 5 of *Nazi Doctors* includes a complete description of the medical experiments conducted on concentration camp prisoners.)

The question of what were or should be the universal standards for justifying human experimentation recurred throughout the trial. The lack of universally accepted principles for carrying out human experimentation was an issue pressed by the defendant physicians throughout their testimony. The ethical arguments presented by the defendants during the trial as justification for their participation in human experimentation with concentration camp prisoners can be summarized as follows:

1. Research is necessary in times of war and national emergency. Military and civilian survival may depend on the scientific and medical knowledge derived from human experimentation. Extreme circumstances demand extreme action.[39]

2. The use of prisoners as research subjects is a universally accepted practice. The defense counsel cited examples of human experimentation on prisoners throughout the world, with particular emphasis on research conducted in U.S. penitentiaries.[40]

3. The prisoners utilized for human experimentation were already condemned to death. Thus, prisoner involvement in human experimentation actually served the prisoners' best interests by keeping them alive and preventing their certain execution.[41]

4. Experimental subjects were selected by the military leaders or the prisoners themselves. An individual physician thus could not be held responsible for the selections.[42]

5. In times of war, all members of society must contribute to the war effort. This includes the military, civilians, and those who are incarcerated.[43]

6. The Germans physicians involved in human experimentation were only following the German law.[44]

7. There are no universal standards of research ethics. Standards have varied according to time and place. (For further discussion of this ar-

---

39. See *Military Tribunal*, Vol. 11, pp. 1-9.

40. See *Military Tribunal*, Vol. 1, pp. 983-987; Vol. II, pp. 90-93. For a defense of the ethically appropriate use of prisoners for medical research see R. Strong, "The Service of Prisoners," *Journal of the American Medical Association* 136 (1948): 457. Also see M. H. Pappworth, *Human Guinea Pigs: Experimentation on Man* (Boston: Beacon Press, 1967), pp. 61-63. Also see *"Ethics Concerning the Service of Prisoners as Subjects in Medical Experiments,* Report of a Committee Appointed by Governor Dwight H. Greene of Illinois," *Journal of the American Medical Association* 136 (1948): 457-458.

41. See *Military Tribunal*, Vol. II, pp. 9-12.

42. See *Military Tribunal*, Vol. I, pp. 983-984; Transcript, p. 2567.

43. See *Military Tribunal*, Vol. I, pp. 989-992.

44. See *Military Tribunal*, Vol. II, pp. 10-16.

gument of ethical relativism, see Chapter 13 of *Nazi Doctors*.) The defense counsel cited 60 published papers involving human experimentation carried out throughout the world. Many of these experiments involved questionable informed consent, serious consequences, and repeated justification of the research based on the necessity of the data for scientific progress.[45]

8. If the physicians did not participate in the research, they would be putting their own lives at risk and might be killed. Furthermore, if the physicians did not carry out the medical experiments themselves, less skilled nonmedical technicians would perform surgery and medical tests, producing even greater harm.[46]

9. The state determined the necessity for human experimentation. The physicians were just following orders.[47]

10 Sometimes it is necessary to tolerate a lesser evil, the killing of some, to achieve a greater good, the saving of many. That the experiments were useful, the defense claimed, was evident by the use of the data derived from Nazi human experimentation by the United States and Britain in the war against Japan.[48]

11. The prisoners' consent to participation in human experimentation was tacit. Since there were no statements stating that the subjects did not consent, it should be assumed that a valid consent existed.[49]

12. Without human experimentation, there would be no way to advance the progress of science and medicine.[50]

In countering these defenses, the prosecution focused its arguments concerning ethical standards for the conduct of human experimentation on the testimony of the prosecution's two chief medical expert witnesses. It was these witnesses and their testimony that served as the substance for the ethical principles for human experimentation that appear in the final judgment and constitute the Nuremberg Code.

Andrew Ivy's testimony during the trial focused primarily on the ethical standards for the conduct of human experimentation. As a noted physiologist and research scientist, Dr. Ivy cited the Hippocratic tradition as central to his views. In his testimony, he also noted that the United States had specific standards for the ethics of research that were embodied

---

45. See *Military Tribunal*, Vol. I, pp. 991; Vol. II, pp. 72-73, 94-110, 149.

46. There is no evidence that any physician was executed for refusing to participate in Nazi human experimentation. Many unskilled technicians were directly involved in performing human experiments.

47. This "only following orders" claim is a variation on the "Fuerher defense" used by many of the military defendants during the military trials at Nuremberg. See *Military Tribunal*, Vol. I, pp. 980-982; Vol. II, pp. 5-10, 29-30, 50; Transcript, pp. 2566-2571.

48. For this utilitarian argument, see *Military Tribunal*, Vol. I, pp. 64-66, 74-77.

49. See *Military Tribunal*, Vol. II, pp. 53-56.

50. See *Military Tribunal*, Vol. II, pp. 61-70; Transcript, p. 11186.

in the American Medical Association guidelines.[51] The archives of the American Medical Association reveal no evidence of such explicit principles on the ethics of human experimentation prior to December 28, 1946. The guidelines that Dr. Ivy cites in his testimony on June 12-14, 1947 were published 19 days after the prosecution's opening arguments were presented at trial. It appears that Ivy studied the tribunal prosecution's pretrial records and exhibits and then reported his views on the ethics of human experimentation to the American Medical Association's trustees, who subsequently incorporated his guidelines into the *Journal of the American Medical Association.*

These "Principles of Ethics Concerning Experimentation on Human Beings" included three points:

1. The voluntary consent of the individual upon whom the experiment is to be performed *must* be obtained.

2. The danger of each experiment *must* be previously investigated by animal experiments.

3. The experiment *must* be performed under proper medical protection and management.[52]

In cross-examination, the defense readily discovered the lack of universally held or published substantive standards on human experimentation in the United States prior to the published 1946 American Medical Association principles. Thus, the principles of ethics concerning human experimentation could not be held to be relevant prior to 1946.

As the trial was drawing to a close, Dr. Alexander, in consultation with Dr. Ivy, attempted to pull together their testimony into a set of ethical principles that could be utilized by the judges in their final decision. These principles served as the basis for the Nuremberg Code. There remains controversy as to who was the primary author of the final 10-point code. Some writers claim that "the primary compiler of the ten principles of the Nuremberg Code was the physician A. C. Ivy."[53] Still other writers note that "no one knows for sure who formulated those ten points" but conclude that Alexander is the primary author.[54]

---

51. See Dr. Ivy's testimony of June 13, 1947, in Transcript, pp. 9141-9145, 9168; *Military Tribunal,* Vol. II, pp. 82-86.

52. *Journal of the American Medical Association 132* (1946): 1090 (emphasis added).

53. W. Curran, "Subject Consent Requirement in Clinical Research: An International Perspective for Industrial and Developing Nations," in Seidelman, "An Inquiry," pp. 35-79. Curran is the Francis Glessner Lee Professor of Health Law at Harvard University's School of Public Health.

54. E. Deutsch, "Die Zehn Punkte des Nürnberger Ärzteprozesses über die Klinische Forshung am Menschen: der sog. Nürnberger Codex," *Festschrift für Wasserman,* trans. by Jennifer Cizick and Deborah Banford of Boston University. (1985), pp. 69-79. Professor Dr. Erwin Deutsch is the director of the Abteilung für

Dr. Alexander did prepare a memorandum entitled "Ethical and Non-Ethical Experimentation on Human Beings," which he submitted to the United States Chief of Counsel for War Crimes and the court on April 15, 1947.[55] It is not clear if this memorandum was also given to the defense.[56] Alexander proposed six essential requirements for ethically and legally permissible experiments on human beings:

1. Legally valid voluntary consent of the experimental subject is essential. This requires specifically
   a. The absence of duress;
   b. Sufficient disclosure on the part of the experimenter and sufficient understanding on the part of the experimental subject of the exact nature and consequences of the experiment for which he volunteers to permit an enlightened consent.

   In the case of mentally ill patients, for the purpose of experiments concerning the nature and treatment of nervous and mental illness, or related subjects, such consent of the next of kin or legal guardian is required; whenever the mental state of the patient permits (that is, in those mentally ill patients who are not delirious or confused), his own consent should be obtained in addition.

2. The nature and purpose of the experiment must be humanitarian, with the ultimate aim to cure, treat, or prevent illness, and not concerned with methods of killing or sterilization (kienology). The motive and purpose of the experiment shall also not be personal or otherwise ulterior.

3. No experiment is permissible if the foregone conclusion exists, or the probability or the *a priori* reason to believe that death or disabling injury of the experimental subject will occur.

4. Adequate preparations must be made and proper facilities be provided to aid the experimental subject against any remote chance of injury, disability, or death. This provision specifically requires that the degree of skill of all those who are taking an active part as experimenters, and the degree of care which they exercise during the experiment, must be significantly higher than the skill which is considered qualifying and the care which is considered adequate for the performance of standardized medical or surgical procedures, and for the administration of well-established drugs. American courts are very stringent in

---

Internationales und Auslandisches Privatrecht Juristisches Seminar of Göttingen University.

55. See Alexander, "Limitations on Experimental Research with Human Beings," and Alexander, "Ethics of Human Experimentation." Also see F. Bayle, *Croix Gammeé contre Caducée: Les Expériences humaines en Allemange pendant la deuxieme guerre mondiale* (Berlin and Neustadt: Palatinat, 1950), I-XXCII, pp. 1430-1432.

56. See *Die Zehn Punkte,* where Professor Deutsch claims that no published proof exists that any counsel for the defense knew of or utilized this memorandum.

requiring for the permissible use of any new or unusual technique or drug, irrespective of whether this use is experimental or purely therapeutic, a degree of skill and care on the part of the responsible physician, which is higher than that required for the purpose of routine medical or surgical procedures.

5. The degree of risk taken should never exceed that determined by the humanitarian importance of the problem to be solved by the experiment. It is ethically permissible for an experimenter to perform experiments involving significant risks only if the solution, after thorough exploration along all other lines of scientific investigation, is not accessible by any other means, and if he considers the solution of the problem important enough to risk his own life along with the lives of his non-scientific colleagues, such as was done in the case of Walter Reed's yellow fever experiments.

6. The experiment to be performed must be so designed and based upon the results of thorough thinking-through, investigation of simple physico-chemical systems and of animal experimentation that the anticipated results will justify the performance of the experiment. That is, the experiment must be such as to yield decisive results for the good of society and should not be random and unnecessary in nature.[57]

This memorandum contains almost all of the principles that appear in the final 10-point Nuremberg Code. Point 1 is concerned with free, voluntary, and informed consent, as well as proxy consent. It is of interest that the first point of the Nuremberg Code also deals with free, voluntary, and informed consent. (For a discussion of the centrality of informed consent for the Nuremberg Code, see Chapter 12 of *Nazi Doctors*.) The first, point 1 of the Code expands on the substance and procedure of informed consent and suggests the duty and responsibility of the physician to ascertain the quality of the consent. The Code does not address the problem of proxy consent for incompetent subjects. (Chapter 8 of *Nazi Doctors* points out the problems that the Code's absence of provision for proxy consent caused for later international codes such as the Declaration of Helsinki.) Point 2 of the memorandum is concerned with the nature, motive, and purpose of experimentation. This point is subsumed in points 2 and 6 of the Code. Point 3 of the memorandum forbids experiments in which death or disabling injury might occur. This subject is covered in point 5 of the Code. It is interesting that the code qualifies this absolute prohibition by "those experiments where the experimental physicians also serve as subjects." Point 4 of the memorandum is concerned with proper facilities, qualified investigators, and the avoidance of unnecessary injury. These principles are covered in points 4, 7, and 8 of the Code. Point 5 of the memorandum is concerned with risk-benefit analysis. This principle is found in point 6 of the Code. Point 6 of the memorandum deals with the

---

57. See note 55, where the memorandum is reproduced.

scientific merits and experimental design of research. This principle is covered in points 2 and 3 of the Code. Finally, the Code covers two principles that do not appear in the memorandum. These principles, covered in points 9 and 10 of the Code, are concerned with the interruption of the experiment at any time if either the subject or the scientist deems termination necessary.

Dr. Alexander, in a commentary on his own memorandum, notes:

> The judges enlarged these criteria to ten points by dividing my point No. 4 into three separate points, and by adding two provisions for prompt termination of an experiment at the discretion of the investigator or at the request of an experimental subject. These were incorporated in their final judgment as the basic principles which must be observed in order to satisfy moral, ethical and legal concepts with regard to medical experiments. However, they omitted from my original point No. 1 provisions for valid consent in the case of mentally sick subjects to be obtained from the next of kin and from the patient whenever possible, probably because they did not apply to the specific cases under trial.[58]

The closing arguments for the United States were delivered on July 14, 1947, by James McHaney, the chief prosecutor for the Medical Case. This final statement incorporates Alexander's memorandum and Ivy's testimony, foreshadowing the final text of the Code. The statement does not, however, focus on informed consent as a critical prerequisite. Prosecutor McHaney closes:

> It will be seen from this review of the indictment and from the evidence submitted by the prosecution that these defendants are, for the most part, on trial for the crime of murder. As in all criminal cases, two simple issues are presented: Were crimes committed and, if so, were these defendants connected with their commission in any of the ways specified by Law No. 10? It is only the fact that these crimes were committed in part as a result of medical experiments on human beings that makes this case somewhat unique. And while considerable evidence of a technical nature has been submitted, one should not lose sight of the true simplicity of this case. The defendant Rose, who was permitted to cross-examine the prosecution's witness, Dr. A. C. Ivy of the Medical School of the University of Illinois, became exasperated at his reiteration of the basic principle *that human experimental subjects must be volunteers,* that, of course, is the cornerstone of this case. There are, indeed, other prerequisites to a permissible medical experiment on human beings. *The experiment must be based on the results of animal experimentation and a knowledge of the natural history of the disease under study and designed in such a way that the anticipated results will*

---

58. See note 54 and Alexander, "Limitations in Experimental Research on Human Beings," pp. 15-16.

justify the performance of the experiment. This is to say that the experiment must be such as to yield results for the good of society unprocurable by other methods of study and must not be random and unnecessary in nature. Moreover, the experiment must be conducted by scientifically qualified persons in such a manner as to avoid all unnecessary physical and mental suffering and injury. If there is a priori reason to believe that death or disabling injury might occur, the experimenters must serve as subjects themselves, along with the nonscientific personnel. These are all important principles, and they were consistently violated by these defendants and their collaborators. For example, we have yet to find one defendant who subjected himself to the experiments which killed and tortured their victims in concentration camps. But important as these other considerations are, it is the most fundamental tenet of medical ethics and human decency that the subjects volunteer for the experiment after being informed of its nature and hazards. This is the clear dividing line between the criminal and what may be noncriminal. If the experimental subjects cannot be said to have volunteered, then the inquiry need proceed no further. Such is the simplicity of this case.[59]

The final judgment was delivered after the conclusion of the trial on July 19, 1947, by Judge Beals. Although Judge Beals was the presiding judge, the chief prosecutor, Brigadier General Telford Taylor, noted that "the moving spirit on legal and evidentiary problems on the court was Judge Harold Siebring." Taylor also believed that the "10 point code was primarily his work."[60] Of the 23 physicians on trial, 16 were convicted of war crimes and crimes against humanity and 7 were condemned to death. The judgment reviews the evidence of criminal action and, in the final section, addresses the question of the permissibility of medical experimentation and enumerates the 10 principles later to be known as the Nuremberg Code. (Page 2 of *Nazi Doctors* contains the final form of the Nuremberg Code.)

Conclusions

It is impossible to analyze the origins of the Nuremberg Code apart from the historical setting of the atrocities and murders committed in Nazi Germany. It is not surprising that, in the context of a criminal judgment, the judges found the need to go beyond the guilty verdict and to speak to

---

59. See Trials of War Criminals, Closing Argument for the United States of America by James M. McHaney, July 14, 1947, transcript pp. 10718-10796 (emphasis added).

60. Personal communication in letter dated March 6, 1989, signed by Telford Taylor.

the broader norms of medical ethics. The Nuremberg Code is an attempt to provide a natural law based universal set of ethical principles.

The Code was written in direct response to the criminal human experimentation detailed during the Medical Trial. As such, the Code specifically addresses the scope and limits of acceptable, nontherapeutic human experimentation conducted on adult prisoners. Because of the unique characteristics of such a competent yet confined population, the Code is particularly concerned with elements of coercion and duress. Informed consent becomes a fundamental method for ensuring the protection of this special population. The ethical limits of human experimentation on an incarcerated adult population probably remain the same today. The United States federal regulations, however, have added the further restriction that prisoners, because of their particular vulnerability, should be used only if the study cannot be carried out scientifically on a nonprison population. This restriction essentially limits experimentation on prisoners to the study of problems found uniquely in prisoners and can thus be achieved only in the prison setting. Consent remains the hallmark of protection in this population.

It is not known if the judges at Nuremberg actually held the defendant physicians accountable to the standards articulated in the Nuremberg Code. Because the defendants were adjudicated as guilty of murder and crimes against humanity, the subtler stipulations for ethical human experimentation did not need to be invoked. If the judges had held the Nazi physicians to the standards enumerated in the Code, however, it would have been necessary to condemn many other physicians and scientists throughout the world for violations of the ethical limits of human experimentation.

The evidence of widespread, ethically suspect medical research in countries other than Germany must have been most disturbing to the judges at Nuremberg. Throughout the trial, the debate surrounding the historical and existing standards of medical ethics surfaced. The judges soon realized that while there was a significant number of codes and regulations dealing with the standards of human experimentation prior to the Tribunal, there was also significant disparity among them. The Nuremberg Code embodies many of the principles enumerated in the 1931 Reich Circular Guidelines. Despite the existence of these Guidelines, the Nazi physicians were either unaware of their existence or their force of law, or simply chose to disregard them. Whether the status of any of the prewar standards was embodied in medical ethics, statutory, or administrative law, all of these codes were violated. It is possible that the judges at Nuremberg incorporated the Nuremberg Code as part of their legal judgment to ensure its place in common law. It was their hope and vision that, once established in international criminal law, this Code would be widely disseminated and, if followed, would guard against future atrocities. Furthermore, while punishment for violation of ethical codes and principles might be unclear, punishment for violation of international law would have clarity and force. (See Chapter 10 of *Nazi Doctors* for a discussion of the use of the Nuremberg Code in U.S. common law and Chapter 11 for a discussion of the Nuremberg Code in international law.)

If the Nuremberg Code was to be viewed solely as just another ethical framework to guide human experimentation, it would have no greater force than the earlier ethical codes. The Code, as an ethical document, would take its historical place as yet another new code created in response to violations and abuses of medical researchers. Once the Code was established in law, however, it might serve to enforce ethical standards by holding researchers accountable.

As medical research and human experimentation since World War II have become increasingly sophisticated, the specific application of the Nuremberg Code has become problematic. (See Chapter 16 of *Nazi Doctors* for an overview of modern medical research.) Most modern research is therapeutic, involving either competent or incompetent patients as subjects. Even during the Nuremberg trial, however, it was hoped that the ethos and spirit of this international tribunal would establish a universal sense of human experimentation ethics. The judges at the trial probably did not envision the use of the Code for this broader application, as the Nuremberg Tribunal focused solely on competent, unconsenting prisoners. Therefore, the judges had edited out of Leo Alexander's memorandum the recommendation to include incompetent patients and the provision for proxy consent. Alexander, however, clearly believed that the Code would have a broader audience:

> These ten points constitute what is now known as the Nuremberg Code, a useful guide setting the limits for experimental research on human beings. It is evident, of course, that the crimes to which this Code owes its formulation could not have occurred in any country in which the ordinary laws concerning murder, manslaughter, mayhem, assault, and battery had not been suspended in regard to all or certain groups of its citizens and inhabitants. This Code is also unlikely to prevent another dictatorial government from repeating the crimes of the National Socialist Government. Nevertheless, it is a useful measure by which to prevent in less blatant settings the consequences of more subtle degrees of contempt for the rights and dignity of certain classes of human beings, such as mental defectives, people presumably dying from incurable illnesses, and people otherwise disenfranchised, such as prisoners or other inarticulate public charges whose rights might be easily disregarded for the apparently compelling reason of an urgent purpose.[61]

61. See L. Alexander, "Limitations of Experimentation on Human Beings with Special Reference to Psychiatric Patients," *Diseases of the Nervous System* 27 (1966): 61-65, at 62.

The Nuremberg Code articulates a set of principles that must be considered in any ethical use of humans as experimental subjects. These principles set the framework for United States federal regulations as well as the international guidelines. The concerns outlined in the Nuremberg Code include the research setting, the integrity of the investigator, the specifics of voluntary informed consent, the balancing of risks and benefits, and the unique problems of special vulnerable populations.

The exact origin of the Nuremberg Code will probably remain a historical mystery. It appears to have been derived from multiple sources, including the writings of Percival, Beaumont, and Bernard. Early German guidelines on human experimentation were also considered by the framers. Andrew Ivy and Leo Alexander were the primary compilers, who together formulated the points that Alexander ultimately cited in his memorandum to the judges. The judges, in turn, incorporated much, but not all, of the memorandum, added some points of their own, and formalized the final Nuremberg Code in their judgment. The legal judgment delivered at the Nuremberg trial went beyond the simple charges and convictions for war crimes and crimes against humanity. Medical ethics would be forever changed after the Holocaust. The Nuremberg Tribunal attempted to pave the way for a reconstituted moral vision. The source of that vision need not lie solely in a legal framework derived from the criminal law. The Nuremberg Code is prefaced by the judges' statement:

> *All agree,* however, that certain basic principles must be observed in order to satisfy moral, ethical and legal concepts.[62]

It is this vision that makes the Nuremberg Code the cornerstone of modern human experimentation ethics.

In 1949, in their official history of the Medical Trial, two German Medical Commission observers, Mitscherlich and Mielke, quoted the chief U.S. prosecutor, Telford Taylor. General Taylor's statement remains a challenge for those who are interested in the Nuremberg Code, its origin, its source, and its present standing:

> The tribunal judgment will be of profound and enduring value in the field of medical jurisprudence; and the trial as a whole is an epochal step in the evolution of forensic medicine. The trial illustrates, furthermore, how rapidly the focus of activity in international law has moved from the academic lecture hall and toward the courtroom. The Nuremberg proceedings are among the outstanding examples of modern international law in action.[63]

---

62. See *Military Tribunal,* Vol. II, pp. 181-185 (emphasis added).

63. A Mitscherlich and F. Mielke, *Doctors of Infamy* (New York: Henry Schuman, 1949), p. XXVI.

VII.

Into the Future

19

Relevance of Nazi Medical Behavior to the Health Profession Today

Michael J. Franzblau

The lessons that should be learned from a study of the period 1933 to 1945 (the Hitlerian era) are extremely relevant to physicians, medical students, and other health care providers in the United States in 1994.

It is my perception that the issues we face at the present time, namely the implementing of informed consent in its broadest ethical concept, the proposal to ration care, the proposal for physicians to assist in euthanasia, and, finally, the introduction of newer therapies on the basis of advances in medical technology such as gene therapy, cry out for an ethical solution.

A careful historical analysis of the role that physicians played during the Hitlerian era, I think, is an important basis on which to implement strategies in 1994 that will be in the best interests of the patients we serve. It is clearly demonstrated that physicians can be co–opted by a state to act in the best interests of the corporate body rather than the best interests of the individual patients whom we serve.

It is clearly evident that the philosophy of racial hygiene as espoused by the Nazi philosophers had a broad acceptance in the medical community prior to the ascent of Hitler to power. Utilizing the principal of *Gleichschaltung* (unification) it was evident that within an extremely short period of time every professional organization representing physicians and other health care providers came under control of the central government in Berlin. The appointment of a "Medical Reichsführer" for medicine demonstrates the implementation of this policy. This meant that every organization representing physicians was under the control and domination of laws and administrative regulations that were generated by the central government. It became quickly apparent that unless there were blind obedience to the State at every level, it would be difficult, if not impossible, for physicians to practice independently. In addition, medical education was dominated and controlled from Berlin. The curriculum for medical schools was determined; the creation of specific medical study units called *Medizinische Fachschaft* demonstrated very clearly how the Nazi Party philosophy was required to be embraced by every medical student in Germany. At the very same time, it was evident that physicians had suffered economically and were, in some cases, unemployed. Because of the political stresses within Germany at that time, there was an extreme political polarization of physicians. They were being divided into the Socialist and Communist camp on one side and the Nazi Party and ultra nationalists on the other. Finally, there was extreme enthusiasm for the philosophic basis of Nazism, and medicine became integral to the implementation of these policies. The ability to be admitted to medical school, the ability to advance in classes, the ability to graduate and be licensed, all were under the direct control of the central government and unless obedience to the State was demonstrated, then the individual medical student was put at great risk to be able to practice. This had an extremely controlling effect on the free exchange of ideas within medical schools.

As an attempt to implement the principal of *Gleichschaltung* (unification) each individual German State (*Länder*) had a "Medical Führer" appointed who was directly responsible for implementing the laws created by the central German authority. The passage of such laws as the sterilization law, also called "the law for the prevention of genetic diseased offspring," the marital health law, the law to permit castration of criminals, the creation and the implementation of the T4 program in which innocent children as well as mentally ill patients were murdered under the direct supervision of physicians, all indicate the dangers that can accrue to a society in which the fundamental relationship between physician and patient is subordinated to the needs of the State.

I believe that unless the lessons of this period are carefully noted by American physicians practicing in our present milieu one in which increasing economic pressures are forcing doctors to make decisions which may be based on broader economic constraints rather than on the traditional view of the actual best interests of the individual patient, that there are severe risks within our nation for going down the wrong pathway.

It is very dangerous to suggest that the model of a Nazi totalitarian dictatorship can be extrapolated to a democratically constituted society, but it is essential that every effort be made to ensure that individual doctors retain their professionalism, their autonomy and their specific continued responsibility to individual patients. If these concepts are not adhered to, it is my judgment that the practice of medicine will change radically in the United States, and that patients will become subordinate to the needs of a higher authority, namely, the State.

It is for this reason that I feel the teaching from an historical perspective of the events of Nazi Germany is essential in the full education of medical students and other health providers in 1994.

20

Medicine and Human Rights:
A Proposal for International Action

Michael A. Grodin, George J. Annas,
and Leonard H. Glantz

Medical ethics is properly viewed as universal, and use of the art of medicine to benefit individual patients is its core. There is also universal condemnation of physicians who engage in "crimes against humanity" such as torture, killing, and involuntary human experimentation under government auspices. Although one need not be a physician to commit crimes against humanity, physicians who commit such acts betray the central ethos of their profession, which should work assiduously to prevent or punish such conduct. Calls for an international criminal code and an international tribunal to judge those accused of crimes against humanity and war crimes have been heard for the past forty years. Nonetheless, there has been no international criminal court established since the post World War II Nuremberg and Tokyo war crimes trials, and no international codification of crimes against humanity since 1950.[1] A recent United Nations resolution called for an international court to punish war crimes in the former Yugoslavia, but the permanent members of the Security Council oppose the establishment of a permanent international criminal court.

We support those who continue to work for a permanent international criminal court under United Nations auspices designed to punish human rights abuses that can properly be designated crimes against humanity. Nevertheless, we recognize that it may be decades before the in-

---

1. M. Cherif Bassiouni, *Crimes against Humanity in International Criminal Law* (Dordrecht: Martinus Nijhoff, 1992).

NOTE: Grodin, M.A., Annas, G.J., Glantz, L.H. "Medicine and Human Rights: A Proposal for International Action" *Hastings Center Report,* Vol. 23 No. 4 (1993): 8-12 Copyright 1993, *Hastings Center Report.* Copyright 1992 George J. Annas. Reprinted with permission.

ternational community agrees to establish such a tribunal. Rather than waiting for this perhaps ideal approach to materialize, we believe it is time for the physicians and lawyers of the world, as the two major professions dedicated to promoting human welfare and human rights, to take concrete steps to prevent governments from using physicians as instruments of killing, torture, persecution (on racial, political, or religious grounds), and involuntary human experimentation. Such deterrence requires a clear statement of prohibited conduct, a mechanism for punishing those who engage in such conduct and for supporting those who resist.

Historical Context

The 1946-1947 trial of Nazi doctors (the "Doctors' Trial") documented the most notorious example of physician participation in human rights abuses, criminal activities, and murder. Hitler called upon physicians not only to help justify his racial hatred policies with a "scientific" rationale (racial hygiene), but also to direct his euthanasia programs and ultimately his death camps.[2] Almost half of all German physicians joined the Nazi Party.[3] In his opening statement at the Doctors' Trial, General Telford Taylor, the chief prosecutor, spoke to the watershed nature of the trial for the history of medical ethics and law:

> It is our deep obligation to all peoples of the world to show why and how these things happened. It is incumbent upon us to set forth with conspicuous clarity the ideas and motives which moved these defendants to treat their fellow men as less than beasts. The perverse thoughts and distorted concepts which brought about these savageries are not dead. They cannot be killed by force of arms. They must not become a spreading cancer in the breast of humanity. They must be cut out and exposed, for the reasons so well stated by Mr. Justice Jackson in the courtroom a year ago [before the War Crimes Tribunal]: "The wrongs which we seek to condemn and punish have been so calculated, so malignant, and so devastating, that civilization cannot tolerate their being ignored because it cannot survive their being repeated."[4]

Sixteen physician-scientists were found guilty, and seven executed, on the basis of international and natural law. A universal standard of physician responsibility and human rights abuses involving experimentation

2. Robert Proctor, *Racial Hygiene: Medicine under the Nazis* (Cambridge, Mass.: Harvard University Press, 1987); Robert Lifton, *The Nazi Doctors; Medical Killing and the Psychology of Genocide* (New York: Basic Books, 1986).

3. Proctor, *Racial Hygiene*.

4. George J. Annas and Michael A. Grodin, eds., *The Nazi Doctors and the Nuremberg Code: Human Rights in Human Experimentation* (New York: Oxford University Press, 1992).

on humans, the Nuremberg Code, was articulated and has been widely recognized, if not always followed, by the world community.

The Nuremberg Code was a response to the horrors of Nazi experimentation in the death camps—experimentation on a wide scale, without consent, that often had the death of the prisoner-subject as its planned endpoint. The code has ten provisions, two designed to protect the rights of human subjects of experimentation, and eight designed to protect their welfare. The best known is its consent requirement:

> The voluntary consent of the human subject is absolutely essential. This means that the person involved should have legal capacity to give consent; should be so situated as to be able to exercise free power of choice, without the intervention of any element of force, fraud, deceit, duress, overreaching, or other ulterior form of constraint or coercion; and should have sufficient knowledge and comprehension of the elements of the subject matter involved as to enable him to make an understanding and enlightened decision.

Although the Nuremberg Code has not been adopted as a whole by the United Nations, its consent principle did become an important part of the United Nations International Covenant on Civil and Political Rights, which was promulgated in 1966 and adopted by the United Nations General Assembly in 1974. Article 7 of the Covenant states:

> No one shall be subjected to torture or to cruel, inhuman or degrading treatment or punishment. In particular no one shall be subjected without his free consent to medical or scientific experimentation.[5]

Most physicians would, of course, be shocked at having anything they do to patients be considered "torture or cruel, inhuman or degrading treatment." They would thus view the Covenant's provisions much the same way they might view the Nuremberg Code: as a criminal law document not applicable to anything done by physicians. But this is a mistake, and only helps to protect aberrant physicians by marginalizing their actions as nonmedical in nature and therefore of no concern to the medical profession. As Jay Katz has noted, both torture and involuntary human experimentation are assaults on bodily integrity[6]— in their disregard of that integrity, torture and involuntary human experimentation become virtually indistinguishable.

---

5. United Nations General Assembly, *United Nations International Covenant on Civil and Political Rights* (New York: United Nations, 1974).

6. Jay Katz, "Human Experimentation and Human Rights." Paper presented at the University of St. Louis Law School, 18 March 1993.

The World Medical Association

In late 1946, 100 delegates from thirty-two national medical associations met in London to form the world's first international medical organization. The World Medical Association (WMA) was created to promote ties between national medical organizations and doctors of the world. Its objectives were:

1. To promote closer ties among the national medical organizations and among the doctors of the world by personal contact and all other means available.

2. To maintain the honour and protect the interests of the medical profession.

3. To study and report on the professional problems which confront the medical profession in the different countries.

4. To organize an exchange of information on matters of interest to the medical profession.

5. To establish relations with, and to present the views of the medical profession to the World Health Organization, U.N.E.S.C.O., and other appropriate bodies.

6. To assist all peoples of the world to attain the highest possible level of health.

7. To promote world peace.[7]

In September 1947, shortly after the final judgment at the Doctor's Trial in Nuremberg, the first official meeting of the WMA was held in Paris. The WMA formulated a new physician oath to promote and serve the health of humanity. This was followed by a discussion of the "principles of social security." Key principles adopted included:

1. Freedom of physician to choose his location and type of practice.

2. All medical services to be controlled by physicians.

3. That it is not in the public interest that doctors should be full-time salaried servants of government or social security bodies.

4. Remuneration of medical services ought not to depend directly on the financial condition of the insurance organization.

5. Freedom of choice of patient by doctor except in cases of emergency or humanitarian considerations.[8]

Thus, one of the WMA's first acts was an attempt to protect the welfare of physicians themselves, which, of course, is perfectly consistent with its original objectives. The "principles of social security" were designed to support the personal and financial welfare of physicians rather

---

7. T. C. Routley, "Aims and Objects of the World Medical Association," *World Medical Association Bulletin* 1, no. 1 (1949): 18-19.

8. Routley, "Aims and Objects," p. 19.

than the security of their patients. The quest for a fee-for-service private practice mode is in striking contrast to a social obligation model that almost all industrialized countries ultimately adopted: universal health care entitlement based on social welfare.

To the WMA's credit, however, one of the first issues discussed by the 1947 general assembly was the German "betrayal of the traditions of medicine." The assembly asked, Why did these doctors lack moral or professional conscience and forget or ignore the humanitarian motives and ideals of medical service? How can a repetition of such crimes be averted? and acknowledged the "widespread criminal conduct of the German medical profession since 1933." The WMA endorsed "the judicial action taken to punish those members of the medical profession who shared in the crimes" and it "solemnly condemned the crimes and inhumanity committed by doctors in Germany and elsewhere against human beings." The assembly continued: "We undertake to expel from our organization those members who have been personally guilty of the crimes . . . We will exact from all our members a standard of conduct that recognizes the sanctity, moral liberty and personal dignity of every human being."[9]

Nonetheless, consistent with its physician protection goals, the WMA focused more on physicians' rights than on patients' rights. Through its Declaration of Helsinki in 1964, for example, it endorsed shifting the focus of protection of the human subjects in medical research away from protecting human rights through informed consent. The 1964 Declaration divided research into two types: research combined with professional care and nontherapeutic research. Consent was required for the latter. But as to the former, the subject was transformed into a patient, and consent was simply urged:

> If at all possible, consistent with patient psychology, the doctor should obtain the patient's freely given consent after the patient has been given a full explanation.[10]

The Declaration of Helsinki thus undermined the primacy of subject consent in the Nuremberg Code and replaced it with the paternalistic values of the traditional doctor-patient relationship.[11]

Although the WMA has also issued a number of noble statements condemning physician involvement in torture and capital punishment, it has largely acted as do other professional societies. Its primary interest is the members' welfare, with a secondary objective of issuing lofty "ethi-

---

9. Editorial, *World Medical Association Bulletin* 1, no. 1 (1949): 3-14.

10. World Medical Association, *Declaration of Helsinki* (Helsinki: World Medical Association, 1964).

11. George J. Annas, "The Changing Landscape of Human Experimentation: Nuremberg, Helsinki, and Beyond," *Health Matrix: Journal of Law-Medicine* 2, no. 2 (1992): 119-40.

cal" statements. However, it must be recognized that with the exception of barring membership of the Japanese and German medical communities following World War II, the WMA has never sought or exercised any authority to identify, monitor, or punish either physicians or medical societies who violate its ethical principles. The WMA's inability or lack of desire to act in ways that demonstrate its commitment to these human rights certainly is exemplified by its handling of the Hans-Joachim Sewering scandal.

The Sewering Affair

Hans-Joachim Sewering is a former member of the Nazi Party and the Nazi shock troops known as the SS.[12] During World War II he was a physician at the Schönbrunn Institute for the Handicapped in the city of Dachau. During his tenure at the institute he transferred at least one fourteen-year-old girl with epilepsy to Eglfing-Haar Hospital — three weeks later, in late 1943, this physically healthy girl was dead.[13] Of 275 children who were admitted to Eglfing-Haar from 1940-1942, 213 were killed.[14]

In 1992 Sewering was elected president-elect of the WMA. This was the culmination of a political-medical career during which he held a series of distinguished medical society positions. He is a past member of the German Federal Physician Chamber (GFPC) and has been a German delegate to the WMA since 1959 and its treasurer for twenty years.

Sewering's election to the presidency of the WMA provoked public protests. The president of the German Federal Physician Chamber, fully aware of Sewering's past, came to his defense. Additionally, André Wynen, the secretary general of the WMA, stated that "the German Federal Physician Chamber has our full confidence because if we doubt them on this, we are questioning the entire profession's ethics." This again shows that the WMA has neither the inclination nor the desire to judge the ethics of individual physicians or medical societies. Wynen further explained that "we must accept that the young people of that time had the right to make mistakes."[15]

Following the challenge to his successful campaign to become president-elect of the WMA, Sewering acknowledged his Nazi past but claimed

---

12. Sewering's Nazi Party membership number was 1.858.805 and his SS membership number was 143.000.

13. Michael Kater, *Doctors under Hitler* (Chapel Hill: University of North Carolina Press, 1987), p. 3.

14. Hugh Gregory Gallagher, *By Trust Betrayed: Patients, Physicians and the License to Kill in the Third Reich* (Orlando: Holt & Co., 1990), p. 133.

15. Marc Fisher, "German Doctor's Nazi Past Debated; AMA Seeks New Leader for World Body," *Washington Post*, 19 January 1993.

no knowledge of or involvement in the euthanasia program. In January 1993 four nuns still living at the Schönbrunn Institute, who had worked there during the war, substantiated that from 1940 to 1944 more than 900 mentally and physically handicapped patients were sent to specific "healing centers." The nuns acknowledged that they knew the patients would be exterminated at these centers as so-called "unworthy lives" and that Sewering, despite his denials, must also have known.[16]

Even following Sewering's 23 January withdrawal, the GFPC continues to support him. At the 135th Council of the WMA (April 1993) Karsten Vilmar, the president of the German Federal Physician Chamber, called for a criminal law standard for judgment rather than an ethical one, thereby abrogating any role for physicians in judging the conduct of their colleagues. Vilmar stated:

> Germany in 1993 differs in a decisive way from Germany before 1945 in that it has been a constitutional state for more than forty years now. A state in which it is not up to medical associations or other organizations to pass judgment, but to courts of law. And it is a fundamental principle of the rule of law that only someone who has been finally convicted by a court of law can be considered guilty.[17]

Following receipt of information documenting Sewering's past, Dr. James Todd, executive vice-president of the American Medical Association (AMA), requested a full explanation from the German Federal Physician Chamber. The Chamber responded that the charges against Sewering had been extensively covered in the European press and were so well known that they did not require further notification of WMA members. The AMA called on the WMA to amend the nominating form for all WMA officers to require "verification by the national medical association that the candidate is an individual of impeccable character signed by the Association President and Chief Executive Officer."[18] The AMA also recommended that the WMA set up an ethics committee to help it address ethical issues. The AMA believes that such "strong measures" have brought "this issue to conclusion." We do not share this view.

These events follow an earlier controversy regarding the WMA's admission of the Medical Association of South Africa and its refusal to take a strong stand against apartheid, a crime against humanity.[19] We believe

---

16. Marc Fisher, "German Doctor Quits International Post: Physician's Nazi Past Forces Withdrawal," *Washington Post*, 24 January 1993.

17. Karsten Vilmar address presented to the 135th Council of the World Medical Association, Istanbul, Turkey, 4-7 April 1993.

18. Personal communication, Dr. James S. Todd, 16 April 1993.

19. Winfried Beck, "The World Medical Association and South Africa," *Lancet*, 24 June 1989, pp. 1441-42.

these experiences require one to conclude that the WMA does not represent and cannot enforce the ethics of the world medical community.

A Permanent Nuremberg Court

The 1992 report of the British Medical Association's working party on the participation of doctors in human rights abuses documents physician involvement in crimes against humanity throughout the world.[20] Physicians have been directly involved in the torture of prisoners, as well as involved in indirect activities that facilitate torture. Physician involvement includes the examination and assessment of "fitness" of prisoners to be tortured, and the monitoring of victims while being tortured, the resuscitation and medical treatment of prisoners during torture, as well as falsification of medical records and death certificates after torture. The report documents examples of physician involvement in psychiatric "diagnosis" and commitment of political dissidents, forcible sterilizations, and supervision of amputation and other corporal punishments. Countries implicated span the globe and include the former Soviet Union, the United States, China, India, and South Africa, as well as countries in the Middle East, and Central and South America. The working party notes the existence of international law and codes of ethics, but acknowledges the lack of enforcement and inability to monitor compliance.

The theme of the report is that neither medical associations nor international law have been effective in preventing physician involvement in human rights abuses. This supports our view that we need an international tribunal with authority to judge and punish the physician violators of international norms of medical conduct. Without such a tribunal, we are left where we began before Nuremberg: international norms of medical conduct are relegated solely to the domain of ethics. Without the possibility of judgment and punishment, there is no international law worthy of the name, only international ethics.[21]

M. Cherif Bassiouni, Robert Drinan, Telford Taylor, and others have argued eloquently and persuasively that we need a permanent international tribunal to judge and punish those accused of war crimes and crimes against humanity.[22] Nonetheless, the international political will to form and support such a "permanent Nuremberg" is lacking. We believe that the arguments for a permanent international medical tribunal are every bit

---

20. Working Party, British Medical Association, *Medicine Betrayed: The Participation of Doctors in Human Rights Abuses* (London: Zed Books, 1992).

21. Telford Taylor, *The Anatomy of the Nuremberg Trials* (New York: Knopf 1992).

22. Bassiouni, *Crimes against Humanity*; Annas and Grodin, *Nazi Doctors and the Nuremberg Code*; Taylor, *Anatomy of the Nuremberg Trials*.

as compelling as those for a permanent Nuremberg, and that the establishment and support of such a body is justified not only for its own sake, but also as a model for the broader international tribunal itself. The courts of individual countries, including the United States, for example, have consistently proven incapable of either punishing those engaged in unlawful or unethical human experimentation, or compensating the victims of such experimentation, primarily because such experimentation is often justified on the basis of national security or military necessity.[23]

The medical profession is perhaps the best candidate to take a leading role here because it has an apolitical history, has consistently argued for at least some neutrality in wartime to aid the sick and wounded, and has a basic humanitarian purpose for its existence. Physician acts intended to destroy human health and life are a unique betrayal of both societal trust and the profession itself. It should also be emphasized that it is much easier for governments to adopt inherently evil and destructive policies if they are aided by the patina of legitimacy that physician participation provides.

An International Medical Tribunal

Medicine and law are often viewed as opponents; but in the promotion of human rights in health care they have a common agenda. This common agenda should permit international cooperation among medical and legal organizations to form and support an international medical tribunal. Ideally, such a body should be established with the sanction and authority of the United Nations, and efforts to establish such a body within the U.N. should be of the highest priority.

On the other hand, given the competing political agendas of the members — especially in the World Health Organization, where the re-election of the Secretary General was embroiled in a continuing political controversy — failure to win U.N. approval and support should not doom this project. Although such sanction *is* required to give the tribunal the authority to punish with criminal penalties, it is not required to give the tribunal the power to hear cases, develop an international code, and publicly condemn the actions of individual physicians who violate international standards of medical conduct. The establishment and support of such a tribunal is a worthy project for the world's physicians and lawyers. In addition, such international organizations as Amnesty International and Physicians for Human Rights have special monitoring and reporting roles to play, but as advocacy organizations they are inappropriate bodies to adjudicate responsibility. The WMA has proven itself incapable of playing any meaningful role.

---

23. Annas and Grodin, *Nazi Doctors and the Nuremberg Code.*

We suggest that as a beginning, the establishment of such an international medical tribunal be put on the agenda of all medical and legal associations around the world. Since the tribunal must be both authoritative and politically neutral, no one country or political philosophy can be permitted to dominate it, either by having a disproportionate representation on the tribunal, or by disproportionately funding it. The tribunal itself should be composed of a large panel of distinguished judges. When specific cases need to be heard, three members would be selected to hear the case. Recruiting judges (without which the court would have little credibility) will require a commitment from governments to permit the jurists selected to take time off from their full-time judicial duties to hear these cases. Governments must fund the tribunal's infrastructure.

Ideally this tribunal should be under the jurisdiction of the United Nations and itself have criminal jurisdiction. Yet even without criminal jurisdiction, the tribunal could hear individual cases brought to it, adjudicate these cases based on international law, publicize the proceedings and results widely, and refer decisions for further action to relevant professional organizations and the board or agency responsible for licensing the physician or physicians involved. Accused physicians would be notified and given every opportunity to appear and present a defense. Without an international extradition agreement, however, attendance could not be compelled. The trial should nonetheless proceed with appointed defense counsel, if the defendant chooses not to appear, because punishment is not the only goal. A major goal is to deter crimes against humanity through publication of their brutality and through international condemnation of them.

An Interim Proposal

Waiting, wishing, and even working for the formation of an international medical tribunal is an insufficient response to continuing medical complicity in human rights violations. Immediate steps can be taken at the level of national medical licensure boards (and state boards in countries with political subdivisions having medical licensing authority) to articulate specific rules denouncing physicians who commit crimes against humanity. Those involved in such crimes would lose their license to practice medicine (or be ineligible to obtain one if they were not yet physicians) and be prohibited from practicing medicine anywhere in the world. Licensing agencies themselves can enter into a compact or agreement to adopt and enforce these rules and goals.

A central registry of physicians who have been found to have participated in war crimes, or against whom substantial allegations of such crimes have been made, should be established. This registry would also be a repository of evidence, such as affidavits and sworn testimony, that could be used by licensing agencies. Prior to licensing physicians, licensing agencies should query the central registry. The creation and use of such a registry is especially important in instances where countries authorize and use physicians to violate human rights, whose activities would otherwise go unnoticed and unpunished. While this licensing sanction is not as strong as one might wish for, it puts physicians on notice that they will be "imprisoned" in their own country should they wish to continue to practice their professions.

Keeping the Faith

Physicians who use their special skills and knowledge to violate human rights not only violate the rights of their victims, but betray their obligation to their profession. The standing of the entire profession suffers when physicians act as agents of the state to destroy life and health. Physicians themselves will benefit from the articulation of clear international standards that prohibit the use of physicians by the state to violate human rights. There is also currently no place where crimes against humanity involving physicians can be adjudicated, and no organization dedicated to preventing such crimes that has the purpose, will, and authority to act. Supporting an international compact and a tribunal can be both a symbolic and practical act that can help prevent governmental subversion of medical skills and authority and thus help foster human rights.

VIII.

Conclusions

21

Lessons We Have Learned?

Lisa Sowle Cahill

The enormity and intransigence of human perversity, and the suffering of the innocent which it never fails to perpetrate, are an occasion of the mortal sin of despair. In a subtle and familiar form, this despair appears as an averting of the eyes, a slight turning of the attention, a semi-conscious distancing of our own circumstances from those we painfully contemplate, so that compassion welling up from our shared humanity may not require of us full consciousness of misery's profundity and of our moral bondedness to its victims.

This conference has required its participants to confront evil and to look its victims full in the face. It has also shown us that the circumstances of Nazi evil's origin were as often scientific bias, ideological banality, professional self-serving, and moral vacuity, as they were any demonic grand design easily proclaimed impossible against the moral scenery of our own place and time. On the contrary, analogies are all too readily drawn between Nazi medicine and more recent scientific and social rationalities which are likewise biased by group self-interest and narrowed to cost-benefit calculations.

The contributors to this conference present us with at least four tasks whose accomplishment, we may hope, will fortify us against either the trivialization or the demonization of the Nazi experience, and so against the repetition of its sins:

1) The primordial moral task is to *listen*. As we learn from Eva Kor's powerful and humane testimony, only the "survivors" fully understand the Holocaust. Our first duty is to hear their experience on its own terms, to hear it humbly and compassionately. To try immediately to harness it to our own purposes is only to "objectify" the Holocaust victims again. As Arthur Caplan warns, it is tempting to reach for the Nazi analogy on any number of human rights issues, such as abortion, embryo research, fetal research, genetic therapy, euthanasia, AIDS research, and other drug research. Yet to learn "lessons" and apply them must be a second and derivative move. We have no right to draw a "moral" from the story of the survivors or to draw analogies for our own lives (or, more likely, for those of our

opponents) until we have registered the magnitude and the dignity of each life destroyed.

2) If the second move, instructive application, is then to be accomplished honestly, it is critical that we apply the Nazi analogy to current issues by means of *nuanced and careful analysis*. As Jay Katz and others have noted, it was distinctive of the Jews under the Nazi regime to be designated "scientifically" as belonging to a category which as such was destined for extinction. Caplan notes that differences in specific cases of biomedical practice are important; we must ensure that apparent similarities of circumstance really have the same sorts of *causes* before we will know what practical or policy remedy to pursue.

I would also add that it is important to ascertain whether what appear to be similar present situations of practice are really likely to lead to *consequences* similar to the Nazi practice. Are the social conditions which permitted A to lead to Z in Nazi Germany present in our day, too? The "slippery slope" argument is a valid one, but it calls for caution and precision in the application.

Further, we may also turn around Caplan's quite proper call for awareness of differences, and take a hard look at similarities from which we think we are protected *because of* certain clear dissimilarities. This goes back to the ease of averting our eyes from danger and misery in our own day and time. Benno Müller-Hill observes that the idolatry of science which perverted Nazi medicine and society is paralleled by an idolatry of economics in the United States. People are marginalized in employment, insurance, medical care, on a supposedly value-free and objective economic criterion—which is only a rationalization for self-interest and prejudice. There is a focus in our analogical analysis on the medical profession because it once provided the route to disaster in Germany. What are other professions and social institutions where the same kind of evil can be embedded and disguised as a beneficent and efficient rationality?

3) We need to build a stronger and broader *public forum* for this discussion of social morality. The present conference, which is ecumenical and interdisciplinary, takes place on a Catholic university campus and is presented by an institute representing moral and social concerns of the Society of Jesus. The Catholic tradition, as exemplified in its one-hundred-year-old tradition of social encyclicals, stands for a confidence in reasonable public discourse and movement toward consensus out of a plurality of religious, political, and moral traditions. In a similar vein, Michael Grodin has developed the point that the Nuremberg court appealed across pluralism to natural law, and to an international standard of justice. In coming together here, both the co-sponsors and the participants of this conference have demonstrated that a variety of traditions and interests can indeed cooperate in seeking greater moral insight and agreement about which social practices

are harmful and wrong, and which contribute to human flourishing and promote the moral bonds of person to person and group to group.

Unfortunately, however, our society often allows itself to be paralyzed by pluralism. Perhaps due in part to a legitimate wariness of dogmatism and tyranny, we seem to lack confidence that we can make any significant progress whatsoever toward substantive and policy-guiding agreement on crucial moral issues (whether euthanasia, abortion, fetal research, infertility therapies, health care reform, or genetic therapy). We resort, therefore, to merely procedural solutions, especially to investing the process of giving information and obtaining consent with absolute and all-sufficient moral importance. It is easier and in the short run less divisive to steer clear of any judgments about or limits on the morality of that to which various "self-determining" individuals are giving consent, and whether their decisions build up or tear down the common good and the right of all to participate in and benefit from it.

"Free and informed consent" is a major and certainly indispensable legacy of the Nuremberg Trials (Grodin, Katz). Yet avoidance of the substantive issues can produce a pluralism of practice with no other limit than consent. We need to have a public conversation, not only about the value of choice (and how best to guarantee it), but about the worth and priority of the goods chosen, and whether other goods are being neglected in the selection process. When we consider the Mengele twin research and Grodin's examples of Nazi experiments, we realize all too readily that much Nazi "medicine" was sadistic and pointless, and that even if consent had been given, its projects still would have been immoral. We might ask now, for example, whether if some individuals choose euthanasia, or eugenic improvements for their children, will this have negative effects on others or on the moral quality of the social fabric?

Moreover, many so-called free choices are made under the pressure of social forces and expectations that induce individuals to consider only a limited range of options, and to weigh them with an uncritically accepted value. (George Annas once authored an article in the *Hastings Center Report* called "Fairy Tales Surrogate Mothers Tell.") Recalling the case of the German nurses described by Susanne Hahn, we are well advised to inquire whether by staking too much of our moral capital on free choice and "personal" decision-making, we are co-opted into social practices which we have not fully examined, and which may lead us places we do not want to go. Such co-optation will happen when people are as naively obedient as the German nurses, but it may also happen if we despair of our ability as a society even to undertake together reasonable, civil, ethical analysis of issues on which there is initially wide disagreement.

4) We have a mission as *educators* of others, through conferences such as the present endeavor, as well as through more limited community lectures

or panels, courses in high schools, colleges, medical schools, nursing schools, and even schools in other disciplines (like economics) which run the risk of monopolizing the culture's moral vocabulary or of assimilating the language of the disciplines that do.

*   *   *   *   *

To return to my first point, the foundational aim of such education should be to teach us to hear in their own voices the survivors of the Holocaust (as well as other victims of hegemonic ideologies). The foundation of the human moral sense is empathy and compassion—to be able to identify with the "other" and to stand in her or his shoes. Michael Grodin remarked that in the minds of the Nazi murderers, the victims were not individuals at all. Thus, we would do well to take the experience of the Holocaust on its own terms, and teach those we help to educate not immediately to rewrite that experience to make sense in their own or our own moral universe. To learn the lessons of the Holocaust is essentially to break the boundaries of our own worldview, and then to realize that our "own" world is not as we imagined it, but dangerously close to one that we deplore. The hope of our redemption is nourished by a true memory and an open-eyed recognition, not preeminently of evil, but of the humanity we share with the victims and with the oppressors alike.

Appendix:

Documents

Appendix: Documents

The Oath of Hippocrates

"I swear by Apollo, the physician, by Aesculapius, Hygeia, and Panacea, and I take to witness all the gods, all the goddesses, to keep according to my ability and to my judgment the following oath: To consider dear to me as my parents him who taught me this art; to live in common with him and if necessary to share my goods with him; to look upon his children as my brothers, to teach them this art if they so desire without fee or written promise; to impart to my sons and to the sons of the master who taught me and the disciples who have enrolled themselves and have agreed to the rules of the profession, but to these alone, the precepts and the instruction. I will prescribe regimen for the good of my patients according to my ability and my judgment and never to harm anyone. To please no one will I prescribe a deadly drug, nor give advice which may cause his death. Nor will I give a woman a pessary to procure abortion. But I will preserve the purity of my life and my art. I will not cut for stone, even for patients in whom the disease is manifest; I will leave this operation to be performed by practitioners (specialist in this art). In every house where I come I will enter only for the good of my patients, keeping myself far from all intentional ill-doing and all seduction, and especially from the pleasures of love with women or with men, be they free or slaves. All that may come to my knowledge in the exercise of my profession or outside of my profession or in daily commerce with men, which ought not to be spread abroad, I will keep secret and will never reveal. If I keep this Oath faithfully, may I enjoy my life and practice my art, respected by all men in all times, but if I swerve from it or violate it, may the reverse be my lot."

Charter of the International Military Tribunal

Nuremberg — 1945

II. Jurisdiction and General Principles

Article 6. The Tribunal established by the Agreement referred to in Article 1 hereof for the trial and punishment of the major war criminals of the European Axis countries shall have the power to try and punish persons who, acting in the interests of the European Axis countries, whether as individuals or as members of organizations, committed any of the following crimes.

The following acts, or any of them, are crimes coming within the jurisdiction of the Tribunal for which there shall be individual responsibility:

a. CRIMES AGAINST PEACE: namely, planning, preparation, initiation, or waging of war of aggression, or a war in violation of international treaties, agreements or assurances, or participation in a common plan or conspiracy for the accomplishment of any of the foregoing;

b. WAR CRIMES: namely, violations of the laws or customs of war. Such violations shall include, but not be limited to, murder, ill-treatment or deportation to slave labor or for any other purpose of civilian population of or in occupied territory, murder or ill-treatment of prisoners of war or persons on the seas, killing of hostages, plunder of public or private property, wanton destruction of cities, towns or villages, or devastation not justified by military necessity;

c. CRIMES AGAINST HUMANITY: namely, murder, extermination, enslavement, deportation, and other inhumane acts committed against any civilian population, before or during the war; or persecution on political, racial or religious grounds in execution of or in connection with any crime within the jurisdiction of the Tribunal, whether or not in violation of domestic law of the country where perpetrated.

Leaders, organizers, instigators and accomplices participating in the formulation or execution of a common plan or conspiracy to commit any of the foregoing crimes are responsible for all acts performed by any persons in execution of such plan.

Article 7. The official position of defendants, whether as Heads of State or responsible officials in Government Departments, shall not be considered as freeing them from responsibility or mitigating punishment.

Article 8. The fact that the Defendant acted pursuant to order of his Government or of a superior shall not free him from responsibility, but may be considered in mitigation of punishment if the Tribunal determine that justice so requires.

Article 9. At the trial of any individual member of any group or organization the Tribunal may declare (in connection with any act of which the individual may be convicted) that the group or organization of which the individual was a member was a criminal organization.

After receipt of the Indictment the Tribunal shall give such notice as it thinks fit that the prosecution intends to ask the Tribunal to make such declaration and any member of the organization will be entitled to apply to the Tribunal for leave to be heard by the Tribunal upon the question of the criminal character of the organization. The Tribunal shall have power to allow or reject the application. If the application is allowed, the Tribunal may direct in what manner the applicants shall be represented and heard.

Article 10. In cases where a group or organization is declared criminal by the Tribunal, the competent national authority of any Signatory shall have the right to bring individuals to trial for membership wherein before national, military or occupation courts. In any such case the criminal nature of the group or organization is considered proved and shall not be questioned.

Article 11. Any person convicted by the Tribunal may be charged before a national, military or occupation court, referred to in Article 10 of this Charter, with a crime other than of membership in a criminal group or organization and such court may, after convicting him, impose upon him punishment independent of and additional to the punishment imposed by the Tribunal for participation in the criminal activities of such group or organization.

Article 12. The Tribunal shall have the right to take proceedings against a person charged with crimes set out in Article 6 of this Charter in his absence, if he has not been found or if the Tribunal for any reason, finds it necessary, in the interest of justice, to conduct the hearing in his absence.

Article 13. The Tribunal shall draw up rules for its procedure. These rules shall not be inconsistent with the provisions of this Charter.

Permissible Medical Experiments
(Nuremberg Standards, 1947)

The great weight of the evidence before us is to the effect that certain types of medical experiments on human beings, when kept within reasonably well-defined bounds, conform to the ethics of the medical profession generally. The protagonists of the practice of human experimentation justify their views on the basis that such experiments yield results for the good of society that are unprocurable by other methods or means of study. All agree, however, that certain basic principles must be observed in order to satisfy moral and legal concepts:

1. The voluntary consent of the human subject is absolutely essential. This means that the person involved should have legal capacity to give consent; should be so situated as to be able to exercise free power of choice, without the intervention of any element of force, fraud, deceit, duress, over-reaching, or other ulterior form of constraint or coercion; and should have sufficient knowledge and comprehension of the elements of the subject matter involved as to enable him to make an understanding and enlightened decision. This latter element requires that before the acceptance of an affirmative decision by the experimental subject there should be made known to him the nature, duration, and purpose of the experiment; the method and means by which it is to be conducted; all inconveniences and hazards reasonably to be expected; and the effects upon his health or person which may possibly come from his participation in the experiment.

The duty and responsibility for ascertaining the quality of the consent rests upon each individual who initiates, directs, or engages in the experiment. It is a personal duty and responsibility which may not be delegated to another with impunity.

2. The experiment should be such as to yield fruitful results for the good of society, unprocurable by other methods or means of study, and not random and unnecessary in nature.

3. The experiment should be so designed and based on the results of animal experimentation and a knowledge of the natural history of the disease or other problem under study that the anticipated results will justify the performance of the experiment.

4. The experiment should be so conducted as to avoid all unnecessary physical and mental suffering and injury.

5. No experiment should be so conducted where there is an *a priori* reason to believe that death or disabling injury will occur; except, perhaps, in those experiments where the experimental physicians also serve as subjects.

6. The degree of risk to be taken should never exceed that determined by the humanitarian importance of the problem to be solved by the experiment.

7. Proper preparations should be made and adequate facilities provided to protect the experimental subject against even remote possibilities of injury, disability, or death.

8. The experiment should be conducted only by scientifically qualified persons. The highest degree of skill and care should be required through all stages of the experiment of those who conduct or engage in the experiment.

9. During the course of the experiment the human subject should be at liberty to bring the experiment to an end if he has reached the physical or mental state where continuation of the experiment seems to him to be impossible.

10. During the course of the experiment the scientist in charge must be prepared to terminate the experiment at any stage, if he has probable cause to believe, in the exercise of the good faith, superior skill, and careful judgment required of him, that a continuation of the experiment is likely to result in injury, disability, or death to the experimental subject.

Declaration of Tokyo

(World Medical Association, 1975)

It is the privilege of the medical doctor to practice medicine in the service of humanity, to preserve and restore bodily and mental health without distinction as to the person's comfort and to ease the suffering of his or her patients. The utmost respect for human life is to be maintained even under threat, and no use made of any medical knowledge contrary to the laws of humanity.

For the purpose of this Declaration, torture is defined as the deliberate, systematic, wanton infliction of physical or mental suffering by one or more persons acting alone or on the authority of any authority, to force another person to yield information, to make a confession, or for any other reason.

1. The doctor shall not countenance, condone or participate in the practice of torture or other forms of cruel, inhuman or degrading procedures, whatever the offense of which the victim of such procedures is suspected, accused or guilty, and whatever the victim's beliefs or motives, and in all situations, including armed conflict and civil strife.

2. The doctor shall not provide any premises, instruments, substances or knowledge to facilitate the practice of torture or other forms of cruel, inhuman or degrading treatment or to diminish the ability of the victim to resist such treatment.

3. The doctor shall not be present during any procedure during which torture or other forms of cruel, inhuman or degrading treatment is used or threatened.

4. A doctor must have complete clinical independence in deciding upon the care of a person for whom he or she is medically responsible. The doctor's fundamental role is to alleviate the distress of his or her fellow men, and no motive, whether personal, collective or political, shall prevail against this higher purpose.

5. Where a prisoner refuses nourishment and is considered by the doctor as capable of forming unimpaired and rational judgment concerning the consequences of such a voluntary refusal of nourishment, he or she shall not be fed artificially. The decision as to the capacity of the prisoner to form such a judgment should be confirmed by at least one other independent doctor. The consequences of the refusal of such nourishment shall be explained by the doctor to the prisoner.

6. The World Medical Association will support, and should encourage, the international community, the national medical associations and fellow doctors, to support the doctor and his or her family in the face of threats or reprisals resulting from a refusal to condone the use of torture or other form of cruel, inhuman or degrading treatment.

United Nations Principles of Medical Ethics (1982)

*The General Assembly**

Desirous of setting further standards in this field which ought to be implemented by health personnel, particularly physicians, and by government officials,

1. Adopts the Principles of Medical Ethics relevant to the role of health personnel, particularly physicians, in the protection of prisoners and detainees against torture and other cruel, inhuman or degrading treatment or punishment set forth in the annex to the present resolution;

2. Calls upon all Governments to give the Principles of Medical Ethics, together with the present resolution, the widest possible distribution, in particular among medical and paramedical associations and institutions of detention or imprisonment in an official language of the state;

3. Invites all relevant inter-governmental organizations, in particular the World Health Organization, and non-governmental organizations concerned to bring the Principles of Medical Ethics to the attention of the widest possible group of individuals, especially those active in the medical or paramedical field.

Principles of Medical Ethics Relevant to the Role of Health Personnel, particularly Physicians, in the Protection of Prisoners and Detainees against Torture and other Cruel, Inhuman or Degrading Treatment or Punishment.

Principle 1

Health personnel, especially physicians, charged with the medical care of prisoners and detainees have the duty to provide them with protection of their physical and mental health and treatment of disease of the

---

* Preamble of the resolution has been edited.

same quality and standard as is afforded to those who are not imprisoned or detained.

Principle 2

It is a gross contravention of medical ethics, as well as an offense under applicable international instruments, for health personnel, particularly physicians, to engage actively or passively, in acts which constitute participation in, complicity in, incitement to or attempts to commit torture or other cruel, inhuman or degrading treatment or punishment.

Principle 3

It is a contravention of medical ethics for health personnel, particularly physicians, to be involved in any professional relationship with prisoners or detainees the purpose of which is not to solely evaluate, protect or improve their physical and mental health.

Principle 4

It is a contravention of medical ethics for health personnel, particularly physicians:

a) To apply their knowledge and skills in order to assist in the interrogation of prisoners and detainees in a manner that may adversely affect the physical or mental health of such prisoners or detainees and which is not in accordance with the relevant international instruments.

b) To certify, or to participate in the certification of, the fitness of prisoners or detainees for any form of treatment or punishment that may adversely affect their physical or mental health and which is not in accordance with the relevant international instruments, or to participate in any way in the infliction of such treatment or punishment which is not in accordance with the relevant international instruments.

Principle 5

It is a contravention of medical ethics for health personnel, particularly physicians, to participate in any procedure for restraining a prisoner or detainee unless such a procedure is determined in accordance with purely medical criteria as being necessary for the protection of the physical or mental health or the safety of the prisoner or detainee himself, or his fellow prisoners or detainees, or of his guardians, and presents no hazard to his physical or mental health.

Principle 6

There may be no derogation from the foregoing principles on any grounds whatsoever including public emergency.

Chronology

1933

Jan. 30 President Paul von Hindenburg appoints Adolf Hitler as Chancellor.

Feb. 27 Reichstag Fire.

Feb. 28 Leading communists arrested
Constitutional rights "temporarily" suspended (until 1945!).

Mar. 23 Reichstag passes the Enabling Act.
First concentration camp set up at Dachau.

Apr. 1 One-day boycott of Jewish stores.

Apr. 7 Law for the Restoration of the Professional Civil Service removes "non-Aryan" civil servants.

Apr. 20 "Non-Aryans" and "enemies of the state" who are doctors may be excluded from practice.

May 2 Trade unions dissolved.

May 10 Public book burnings.

June 1 "Marriage loans" for young couples to encourage production of babies.

July 14 One-party state established.
Law for the Prevention of Progeny of Hereditary Disease mandates the sterilization of patients with hereditary diseases like epilepsy, schizophrenia, manic depressive illness, and feeble-mindedness.

July 20 Concordat signed with the Roman Catholic Church.

1934

Apr. 24 People's Court set up for cases of high treason.

June 30 Night of the Long Knives. Nazis murder opponents within and outside the party.

Aug. 2 Death of President von Hindenburg.
Hitler becomes Head of State and commander-in-chief of the Armed Forces.
181 Genetic Health Courts and Appellate Health Courts to decide cases dealing with sterilization established in this year.

1935

Mar. 11 Nazi race hygienists and civil servants plan the sterilization of the "Rhineland bastards"—the children born after the French occupation in 1923 to German women who had had sexual relationships with African soldiers.

Mar. 16 Reintroduction of military draft.

May 21 No Jews allowed in military.

July 26 Marriages between Aryans and non-Aryans stopped by order of Justice Minister Frick.

Sept. 15 Nuremberg Laws, Reich Citizenship Law, and the Law for the Protection of German Blood and German Honor announced.

Oct. 18 Addendum to the sterilization law forbids marriages between "hereditary ill" and "healthy" people. Also forces the abortion of children of the "hereditary ill" up to the sixth month of pregnancy.

1936

Feb. 5 Ministry of the Interior establishes information system on patients in mental hospitals.

Mar. 7 German army marches into the Rhineland.

Aug. 1 Opening of the Olympic Games in Berlin.
Temporary removal of anti-semitic signs.

Oct. 18 Goering put in charge of the Four-Year Economic Plan.

Oct. 26 Hitler and Mussolini of Italy sign the Rome-Berlin Axis.

1937

Spring Sterilization of the "Rhineland bastards" begins.

July 16 Buchenwald concentration camp opens.

July 24 Jews separated from other guests at health resorts.

1938

Mar. 12 German army occupies Austria.

Apr. 26 Decree on the Reporting of Jewish Assets.

June 15 Arrest of all "previously convicted Jews."

July 6 Evian Conference attended by thirty-two nations does not help Jewish refugees.

July 23 Announcement that Jews will need identity cards beginning in 1939.

July 25 Jewish doctors will only be allowed to treat Jewish patients.

Aug. 17 Jews required to insert "Sara" or "Israel" into their names.

Sept. 29 Munich Conference gives Sudetenland to Germany.

Sept. 30 Jewish physicians lose their licenses.

Oct. 5 Jewish passports marked with "J."

Oct. 26 17,000 Polish Jews expelled from Germany.

Nov. 1 Jewish children removed from non-Jewish schools.

Nov. 9 *Kristallnacht* ("Night of Broken Glass").

Dec. 13 Compulsory expropriation of Jewish industries and shops.

1939

Jan. 30 Hitler predicts that Jews will be "exterminated" in the event of another war.

Mar. 15 Germany takes over the rest of Czechoslovakia.

Aug. 18 Beginning of child "euthanasia" in Germany as doctors must report the birth of newborns with deformities.

Aug. 23 Nazi-Soviet Pact.

Sept. 1 German invasion of Poland. Beginning of World War II.
Order allowing for the "mercy killing" of adults backdated to begin on this date.

Oct. 1 Questionnaires go to mental hospitals beginning the process of marking patients for "euthanasia."

Oct. 15 First gassing of Polish mental patients in Posen.

Nov. 23 Polish Jews must wear the Star of David.
Interior Ministry ordered all newborn twins to be registered with the Public Health Office for genetic research beginning in this year.

1940

Apr. 9 German army invades Denmark and Norway.

Apr. 30 Ghetto set up for the Jews of Lodz, Poland.

May 10 German army invades the Netherlands, Belgium, and France.

June 22 France surrenders.

Nov. 15 Ghetto set up in Warsaw.

1941

Mar. 7 German Jews used as forced laborers.

Apr. 6 German army invades Yugoslavia and Greece.

June 22 German army invades the Soviet Union

July 8 Jews in Baltic States forced to wear the Star of David.

July 31 Goering's letter to Heydrich talks about the Final Solution.

Aug. Due to public protests led by Catholic Bishop Count von Galen, the killing of mental patients is stopped. Resumes later but in a less centralized manner.

Sept. 15 Jews throughout Germany have to wear the Star of David.

Sept. 2 First gassing experiments in Auschwitz.

Oct. 10 Theresienstadt Ghetto is set up.

Oct. 14 Deportation of German Jews to Lodz Ghetto begins.

Dec. 7 Japanese bomb Pearl Harbor.

Dec. 8 Chelmno death camp, the first one, opens.

Dec. 11 Germany declares war on the United States.

1942

Jan. 15 First group of Lodz Ghetto residents transported to Chelmno.

Jan. 20 Heydrich presides over the Wannsee Conference.

Jan./Feb. First experiments on prisoners in low pressure chambers in Dachau.

Mar. 16 Belzec death camp opens.

May 1 Sobibor death camp opens.

June 1 Treblinka death camp opens.
French and Dutch Jews must wear the Star of David.

June 23 Auschwitz opens as death camp and work center.

July 28 Jewish resistance organization set up in Warsaw.

Aug. 15 Cold shock experiments on prisoners begin in Dachau.

Dec. 16 Himmler orders the "final solution of the Gypsy question."

1943

Feb. 2 German Sixth Army surrenders at Stalingrad.

Apr. 19 Uprising in Warsaw Ghetto begins.

May 16 Warsaw Ghetto destroyed.

May 30 Josef Mengele becomes camp doctor at Auschwitz.

1944

June 6 D-Day in Europe.

July 20 Attempted assassination of Hitler.

Oct. 23 Paris liberated.

Nov. 26 Himmler orders the destruction of Auschwitz.

1945

Jan. 26 Soviet troops liberate Auschwitz.

Feb. 4 Yalta Conference begins.

Apr. 11 U.S. troops liberate Buchenwald.

Apr. 15 British troops liberate Bergen-Belsen.

Apr. 25 U.S. and Soviet troops meet at the Elbe River.

Apr. 30 Hitler commits suicide.

May 8 V-E Day.

Aug. 15 V-J Day.

Nov. 22 Beginning of the Nuremberg Trials.

Dec. 9, Trial of the first U.S. Military Court in Nuremberg known as
1946 the Nuremberg Doctors Trial begins.

July 19, Sentences are passed on the Nazi doctors guilty of crimes
1947 against humanity.

The Auschwitz/Mengele Twins[1]

Of the 1500 sets of twins used in the experiments, these are the known survivors (1994).

(*Adler*), Marc Berkowitz,
(*Adler*) Florence (*Franceska*), USA

Back, Anton (*Anchie*), CANADA
Back, Izidor (*Srulie*), CANADA

Bash, Mordechai, ISRAEL
Bash, Shmuel, ISRAEL

(*Baum*), Miriam Shteinhoff, ISRAEL
Baum, Yizchak, ISRAEL

Blau, Haya (*Vera*), ISRAEL
Eitan, Rachel, ISRAEL

(*Blyer*), Edith Balderman, ISRAEL
(*Blyer*), Yiczhak Efrat, ISRAEL

(*Blyer*), Moshe (Mickey) Offer, ISRAEL
*Blyer, Tibi, died in Auschwitz

(*Braver*), Yehudit (*Agyt*) Gheto, ISRAEL
*Triplet sister, died of pneumonia
*Triplet sister, died in Auschwitz

(*Brichta*), Mordechai Alon, ISRAEL
(*Brichta*), Yoel Alon, BELGIUM

(*Brown*), Kalman Baron, ISRAEL
(*Brown*), Yehudith Keren, ISRAEL

(*Bryer*), Ychudith Mayer, ISRAEL
Twin brother, ISRAEl

(*Csengbery*). Lea Haber, ISRAEL
(*Csengbery*). Yehudit Barnea, ISRAEL

(*Czuker*), Lea Berkman, ISRAEL
(*Czuker*), Irena Shtronwasser. ISRAEL

(*Deitch*), Rachel (Rose) Markovitz, ISRAEL
(*Deitch*), Hana Faiger, ISRAEL

(*Dunst*), Lili Wiser, ISRAEL
Dunst, Therese, died after liberation.

(*Ekstein*), Sarah Shahar, ISRAEL
(*Ekstein*), Leah Gamado, ISRAEL

---

*Deceased
**Sibling is still searching for this twin/triplet
†Relative is still searching for these twins
Names in italics were used at Auschwitz. Names in parentheses are no longer used.

---

1. Courtesy of Eva (Moses) Kor, Terre Haute, Ind.

†*Ferg, Ita*, sought by sister Lee Feig Breur.

†*Feig, Esther*, sought by sister.

Frankovitz, Morris, USA
**Frankovitz, Jacob, died of cancer, 1979.*

Fridman, Zahava, ISRAEL
(*Fridman*), Olga Smadar, ISRAEL

Fuggel, Ezra, ISRAEL
*Fuggel, Menashe, died in ISRAEL, 1986.

(*Fux*), Yona Lux, ISRAEL
(*Fux*), Miriam, WEST GERMANY

Goldental, Alexander, ISRAEL
Goldental, Arny, HUNGARY

(Grenbaum) Varda (Bertha) Sax. ISRAEL.
(Grenbaum) Yolanda Yosef. ISRAEL.

(Grossman) Vera Krighel. ISRAEL.
(Grossman) Olga Solomon. ISRAEL.

Gutman, Menahem (Mencsel), ISRAEL
***Gutman, Yoel*. missing since liberation.
*Triplet sister, presumed dead.

(*Guttman*), Rene Slotkin, USA
(*Guttman*), Irene Hizme, USA

(*Hadl*), George Heimler, USA
(*Hadl*), Paul Heimler, USA

(*Herman*), Czvi Weisel, ISRAEL
*Twin sister, died in Auschwitz

Heller, Stephanie, AUSTRALIA
Annetta, AUSTRALIA

(*Herman*), Czvi Weisel, ISRAEL
*Twin brother, died in ISRAEL. 1984

(*Herman*), Ruth Fast, ISRAEL
(*Herman*) Shoshana Nesher, ISRAEL

(*Herskovic*). Perle Pufeles. USA
(*Herskovic*), Helen Rapaport, USA

†*Hornung*, Henry sought by father Samuel Hornung.
†*Hornung*, Victor, sought by father.

(*Huffman*), Olga Adler, ISRAEL
*Twin sister, died after liberation.

(*Kaff*), Vera Weissman, ISRAEL
(*Kaff*), Miriam (*Maria*) Rott, ISRAEL

Klein, Bela. ISRAEL
*Twin brother died in Auschwitz

Klein, Otto. SWITZERLAND
**Klein, Frank (Ferene)*, died in USA, 1986

(*Kleinman*), Peter (*Josef*) Green-field, ISRAEL
**Kleinman. Martha, disappeared before liberation, #A-4931

(*Kupas*), Hava (*Eva*) Shaked, ISRAEL
(*Kupas*), Moris Zalmanowitz, USA

(*Lazarovitz*), Ethel Yoshovich, ISRAEL
Lazarovitz, Yiczhak, ISRAEL

(*Lebowitz*), Lulu Pasternak, ISRAEL
(*Lebowitz*), Hava (*Eva*) Kreener, ISRAEL

(*Levinger*), Rachel Zehira, ISRAEL
(*Levinger*), Piroska, ISRAEL

(*Levinstein*), Lili Birkenfeld, RU-MANIA
*Levinstein, Herman, died of leukemia in Israel.

Lieberman, Gota, ISRAEL
*Twin sister, deceased.

(*Lipshitz*), Zeipora Milstein, ISRAEL
*(*Lipshitz*), Elimeleck, died of cancer, 1986.

Lorenczy, Menashe (*Shandor*), ISRAEL
(*Lorenczy*), Icora Gluck, USA

Lowy, Leo. CANADA
Lowy, Miriam, CANADA

Malek, Elias, USA
Malek, Jacob, USA

Malek, Slomo (*Solomon*), ISRAEL
(*Malek*), Yehudith Feig, ISRAEL

(*Marmorshtein*), Martha Goldstein, ISRAEL
(*Marmorshtein*), Valeria Bimel, USA

(*Meyer*), Ahuva (*Luba*) Brill, ISRAEL
Meyer, Moshe (*David*), ISRAEL

(*Mintz*), Rivka Vered, ISRAEL
*Twin sister, died in Auschwitz from tuberculosis.

Moskowitz, Elizabeth, ISRAEL

(*Mozes*), Eva Kor, USA
(*Mozes*), Miriam Zaiger, ISRAEL
*(Died in 1993)

Reichenberg, Efraim, ISRAEL
Reichenberg, Tibi, died in Auschwitz

†*Rosen, Eva,* sought by cousin Gilda R. Dangot.
Rosen, Helen, sought by cousin.

(*Rosenbaum*), Yehudith Yaguda. ISRAEL
*Rosenbaum, Ruth, died in Auschwitz.

Sainer, Ilan, ISRAEL
Novomkova, Hana, CZECHOSLOVAKIA

(*Sattler*), Rolme (*Vera*) Lengyel, HUNGARY

(*Sattler*), Gardony (*Magda*) Tiborne, HUNGARY

(*Schlesinger*), Yael (*Martha*) Elboyeem, ISRAEL
*Twin siter, died in Auschwitz.

Schlesinger, Harry, USA
(*Schlesinger*), Ducy Gluck, USA

(*Seiler*), Susan (*Sarah*) Vigorito, USA
*Seiler, Channah, died in Auschwitz.

Shwartz, Yaakov, ISRAEL
(*Shwartz*), Elizabeth (*Bozsi*) Parid, USA

Shwartz, Yehuda, ISRAEL
*Shwartz, Eva, died in Auschwitz.

(*Solomon*), Charlote Malter, ISRAEL
(*Solomon*), Rosalia Marmostein, ISRAEL

(*Solomon*), Shaul Almog, ISRAEL
(Solomon), Slomo Almog, USA

Somogyi, Peter, USA
(*Somogyi*), Thomas Simon. CANADA

(*Shpigel*), Magda Zalikovich, ISRAEL
(*Shpigel*), Czvi, ISRAEL

(*Stern*), Hedva Katz, ISRAEL
(*Stern*), Lea Firestein, ISRAEL

Taub, Zerah, ISRAEL
Taub, Yizchak, ISRAEL

(*Vigozcka*), Rachel Vachtel, ISRAEL
(*Vigozcka*), Sarah Lushek, ISRAEL

(*Vitssan*), Yuppy (*Yan*) Oobelman, ISRAEL
*Twin brother, died in Auschwitz.

(*Wasserman*), Tova Kupel, ISRAEL
(*Wasserman*), Frida Koh, ISRAEL

Weiss, Yonatan (Boandy), ISRAEL

Weiss, Mayer (Bela), ISRAEL

(*Zawer*), Miri Sheinberger, ISRAEL

(*Zawer*), Sarah Tigherman, ISRAEL

General Bibliography

Alexander, Leo. "Medical Science under Dictatorship." *New England Journal of Medicine* 241, no. 2 (July 14,1949) 39-47.

Amir, Amnon. "Euthansia in Nazi Germany." (Ph.D. Diss. State University of New York, Albany, 1977)

Anderson, Ian. "Americans hushed up wartime experiments on Humans" *New Scientist* 119 (Aug. 18,1988) 22.

Angell, Marcia. "The Nazi hypothermia experiments and unethical research today." *New England Journal of Medicine* 322 (May 17 1992) 1462-1464.

Annas, George and Grodin, Michael. *The Nazi Doctors and the Nuremberg Code.* Oxford: Oxford University Press, 1992.

Arendt, Hannah. *Eichmann in Jerusalem: a report on the banality of evil.* New York: Penguin Books, 1977.

Aziz, Philippe. *Doctors of Death.* Geneva: Ferni Pub., 1976.

Blady Szwajger, Adina. *I remember nothing more: The Warsaw Children's Hospital and the Jewish Resistance.* New York: Pantheon Books, 1990.

Baird, Robert and Rosenbaum, Stuart. *Euthanasia: The Moral Issues.* Buffalo: Prometheus Books, 1989.

Bassiouni, M. Cherif. *Crimes against Humanity in International Criminal Law.* Dordrecht: Martinus Nijhoff, 1992.

Berger, Robert L. "Nazi Science—The Dachau Hypothermia Experiments" *New England Journal of Medicine.* 322 (May 17, 1990) 1435-1440.

Bernadac, C. *Devils' Doctors: Medical Experiments on Human Subjects in the Concentration Camps.* Geneva: Ferni Pub., 1978.

Boozer, Jack. "The Political, Moral and Professional Implications of the 'Justifications' by German Doctors for Lethal Medical Actions 1938-45." *Remembering for the Future, Volume II.* Oxford: Pergamon Press, 1989.

Borkin, Joseph. *The Crime and Punishment of I.G. Farben. The Startling Account of the Unholy Alliance of Adolph Hitler and Germany's Great Chemical Combine.* New York: Free Press, 1978.

Brackman, Arnold C. *The Other Nuremberg: The Untold Story of the Tokyo War Crimes Trials.* London: Collins, 1989.

Briffault, Herma, ed. *The Memoirs of Doctor Felix Kersten.* Garden City, N.Y.: Doubleday, 1947.

British Medical Association. *Medicine Betrayed: The Participation of Doctors in Human Rights Abuse.* London: Zed Books, 1992.

Byman, Beryl. "Bitter Fruit: The Legacy of Nazi Medical Experiments," *Minnesota Medicine,* 62 (1989) 582-586.

Caplan, Arthur, ed. *When Medicine Went Mad: Bioethics and the Holocaust.* Totowa, N.J.: Humana Press, 1992.

Caplan, Arthur. "The Meaning of the Holocaust for Bioethics." *Hastings Center Report.* 19 (Jul/Aug. 1989) 2-3. "The End of a Myth? Four Verdicts on Nazi Doctors," "Malevolent Medicine." *Dimensions 5,* no. 2 (1990) 13-18.

Cocks, Geoffrey. *Psychotherapy in the Third Reich.* New York: Oxford University Press, 1985.

Cohen, Elie Aron. *Human Behavior in the Concentration Camp.* New York: W.W. Norton, 1953.

Conot, Robert E. *Justice at Nuremberg.* New York: Harper & Row, 1983.

Deitrich, Donald J. *Catholic Citizens in the Third Reich: Psycho-Social Principles and Moral Reasoning.* New Brunswick, NJ: Transaction Books, 1988.

Dorian, Emil. *The Quality of Witness: A Romanian Diary 1937-1944.* Philadelphia: Jewish Publication Society of America, 1982.

Eisenberg, Azriel. *Witness to the Holocaust.* New York: Pilgrim Press, 1961.

Eitinger, Leo. *The psychological and medical effects of concentration camps and related persecutions on survivors of the Holocaust: A research bibliography.* Vancouver: University of British Columbia Press, 1985.

Falstein, Louis, ed. *The Martyrdom of Jewish Physicians in Poland.* New York: 1963.

Gallagher, Hugh. *By Trust Betrayed. Patients, Physicians and the License to Kill in the Third Reich.* New York: Holt and Co., 1990.

Gordon, Noah. *The Death Committee.* New York: McGraw-Hill, 1969.

Haas, Alpert. *The Doctor and the Damned.* New York: St. Martin's Press, 1984.

Haas, Peter J. *Morality after Auschwitz: The Radical Challenge of the Nazi Ethic.* Philadelphia: Fortress, 1988.

Haller, Mark H. *Eugenics.* New Brunswick, N.J.: Rutgers University Press, 1984.

Heston, Leonard. *The Medical Casebook of Adolf Hitler: His illnesses, doctors, and drugs.* New York: Stein and Day, 1980.

Hunt, Linda. *Secret Agenda: The United States Government, Nazi Scientists and Project Paperclip. 1944-1990.* New York: St. Martin's Press, 1991.

International Auschwitz Committee. *Nazi Medicine: Doctors, Victims and Medicine in Auschwitz.* New York: Fertig, 1986.

Jakobovits, Immanuel. *Jewish Medical Ethics; A comparative and historical study of the Jewish religious attitude to medicine and its practice.* New York: Philosophical Library, 1959.

Kater, Michael. *Doctors under Hitler.* Chapel Hill: The University of North Carolina Press, 1989.

Katz, Jay. *Experimentation with Human Beings; the authority of the investigator, subject, professions and state in the human experimentation process.* New York: Russell Sage Foundation, 1972.

Kessel, Joseph. *The Man with the Miraculous Hands.* New York: Ayer Company, 1961.

Klee, Ernst. *Was sie taten, was sie wurden: Ärtze, Juristen und andere Beteiligte am Kranken oder Judenmord.* Frankfurt a.M.: Fischer, 1986.

Klee, Ernst. *"Euthanasie" im NS-Staat. Die "Vernichtung lebensunwerten Lebens."* Frankfurt a.M.: Fischer, 1993.

Klein, Dennis, ed. Special Issue, "Malevolent Medicine," *Dimensions,* Vol. V, no. 2 (1990).

Koonz, Claudia. *Mothers in the Fatherland: Women, the family and Nazi politics.* New York: St. Martin's Press, 1986.

Lagnado, L.M., and Dekel, S.C. *Children of the Flames: Dr. Josef Mengele and the Untold Story of the Twins of Auschwitz.* New York: William Morrow, 1991.

Lapon, Lenny. *Mass Murderers in White Coats: Psychiatric Genocide in Nazi Germany and the United States.* Springfield, MA: Psychiatric Genocide Institute, 1986.

Laska, Vera, ed. *Women in the Resistance and the Holocaust.* Westport, CT: Greenwood Press, 1983.

Landman, J.P. *Human Sterilization: The History of the Sexual Sterilization Movement.* New York: Macmillan, 1932.

Lehndorff, Hans. *Token of a Covenant.* Chicago: H. Regnery Co., 1964.

Letulle, Claude. *Nightmare Memoir: Four Years as a Prisoner of the Nazis.* Baton Rouge: Louisiana State University Press, 1987.

Lifton, Robert Jay. *The Nazi Doctors: Medical killing and the psychology of genocide.* New York: Basic Books, 1986.

Maretzki, Thomas W. "The documentation of Nazi Medicine by German Medical Sociologists: A review article." *Social Science and Medicine* 29 (1989) : 1319-1330.

Meier, Levi. *Jewish Values in Bioethics.* New York: Human Sciences Press, 1986.

Mendelsohn, John. *Medical Experiments on Jewish Inmates of Concentration Camps.* New York: Carland Publishers, 1982.

Micheels, Louis. *Doctor #117641: A Holocaust Memoir.* New Haven: Yale University Press, 1989.

Mitscherlich, Alexander, and F. Mielke. *Doctors of Infamy, the Story of Nazi Medical Crimes.* New York: H. Schuman, 1949.

Müller-Hill, Benno. *Murderous Science: Elimination by Scientific Selection of Jews, Gypsies and Others in Germany 1933-1945.* Oxford: Oxford University Press, 1988.

Nadav, Daniel. *Julius Moses (1868-1992) und die Politik der Sozial hygiene in Deutschland.* Tel-Aviv: Gerlingen, 1985.

Nazi Conspiracy and Aggression. A collection of Documentary Evidence. Presented Before the International Military Tribunal at Nuremberg Germany. Washington, D.C.: U.S.G.P.O., 1946.

Nyiszli, Miklos. *Auschwitz: A Doctor's Eyewitness Account.* New York: Frederick Fell, 1960.

Olczak, Hanna. *Mister Doctor: The Life of Janusz Korczak.* London: 1965.

Perl, Gisella. *I Was a Doctor in Auschwitz.* New York: International Universities Press, 1948.

Posner, Gerald L. and John Ware. *Mengele: The Complete Story.* New York: McGraw-Hill, 1986.

Post, Stephen G. "The Echo of Nuremberg: Nazi Data and Ethics." *Journal of Medical Ethics.* 17 (May 1991) 42-44.

President's Commission for the Study of Ethical Problems in Medicine and Biomedical and Behavioral Research. *Protecting Human Subjects.* Washington, D.C.: U.S.G.P.O., 1981.

Proctor, Robert. *Racial Hygiene: Medicine under the Nazis.* Cambridge: Harvard University Press, 1988.

Pross, Christian. "Breaking through postwar corruption of Nazi Doctors in Germany." *Journal of Medical Ethics.* 17 (Dec. 1991) 13-16.

Roland, Charles. *Courage Under Siege: Starvation, Disease and Death in the Warsaw Ghetto.* New York: Oxford University Press, 1992.

Rosner, Fred. *Modern Medicine and Jewish Ethics.* New York: Yeshiva University Press, 1991.

Saller, K. *Die Rassenlehre des Nationalsozialismus in Wissenschaft und Propaganda.* Darmstadt: Progress-Verlag, 1961.

Schneider, William H. *Quality and Quantity: The Quest for Biological Regeneration in 20th Century France.* Cambridge University Press, 1990.

Scwarberg, Gunther. *The Murders at Bullenhuser Damm: The S.S.Doctor and the Children.* Bloomington: Indiana University Press, 1984.

Seidelman, William E. "Mengele Medicus: Medicine's Nazi Heritage." *Milbank Quarterly.* 66 no. 2 (1988) 221-239.

Sereny, Gitta. *Into That Darkness: From Mercy Killing to Mass Murder.* New York: McGraw-Hill, 1974.

Sheldon, Mark. "Nazi Data: dissociation from evil." *Hastings Center Report.* 20 (May/Jun 1990) 44-45.

Shelley, Lore. *Criminal experiments on human beings in Auschwitz and war research laboratories: twenty women prisoners' accounts.* San Francisco: Mellon Research University Press, 1991.

Stepan, Nancy Leys. *The Hour of Eugenics.* Ithaca, N.Y.: Cornell University Press, 1991.

Taylor, Teleford. *The Anatomy of the Nuremberg Trials.* New York: Knopf, 1992.

Tushnet, Leonard. *The Uses of Adversity.* New York: T. Yoseloff, 1966.

Trials of War Criminals Before the Nuremberg Military Tribunals Under Control Council Law 10. Washington, D.C.: U.S. Government Printing Office, 1950.

Weber, Matthais. *Ernst Rüdin: Eine kritische Biographie.* Heidelberg: Springer Verlag, 1993.

Wechsberg, Joseph. *The Murderers Among Us.* New York: McGraw-Hill, 1967.

Weindling, Paul. *Health, Race, and German Politics between National Unification and Nazism, 1870-1945.* Cambridge: Cambridge University Press, 1989.

Weinreich, Max. *Hitler's Professors: The Part of Scholarship in Germany's Crimes Against the Jewish People.* New York: YIVO, 1946.

Wertham, Fredric. *The German Euthanasia Program.* Cincinnati: Hayes, 1988.

Contributors

GEORGE J. ANNAS: Edward R. Utley Professor of Health Law and Director of the Law, Medicine, and Ethics Program at Boston University Schools of Medicine and Public Health, and co-author with Michael Grodin of *The Nazi Doctors and the Nuremberg Code*.

ROBERT L. BERGER: A Holocaust survivor, a surgeon in the New England Deaconess Hospital and Harvard Medical School, as well as lecturer on the Dachau Hypothermia Experiments.

LISA SOWLE CAHILL: Ethicist and Professor of Theology at Boston College and author of the forth-coming work *Love Your Enemies: Discipleship, Pacifism, and the Just War Theory*. She has served as Associate Editor of *Medicine and Philosophy and Religious Ethics*, as well as a board member of *Ethics and Reproduction*.

ARTHUR L. CAPLAN: Former Director of the Center for Biomedical Ethics at the University of Minnesota, and presently Director of the Center for Bioethics at the University of Pennsylvania. He is author of *When Medicine Went Mad: Bioethics and the Holocaust*.

DONALD J. DIETRICH: Chair, Department of Theology at Boston College and author of *Catholic Citizens in the Third Reich: Psycho-Social Principles and Moral Reasoning* as well as *God and Humanity in Auschwitz: Jewish-Christian Relations and Sanctioned Murder*.

MICHAEL J. FRANZBLAU: A Clinical Professor of Dermatology and Lecturer in the Department of the History of Health Sciences at the University of California at San Franscisco School of Medicine. He has a special interest in the historical development of medicine in Germany from the time of Bismarck on, and teaches a course to medical students entitled "Historical Perspectives in Medicine: Ethical Values in Health Care: Lessons from the Nazi Period."

LEONARD H. GLANTZ: Associate Director of the Boston University School of Public Health.

MICHAEL A. GRODIN: A medical ethicist, Associate Professor of Philosophy, Medicine and Public Health and Associate Director of the Law, Medicine and Ethics Program at Boston University Schools of Medicine and

Public Health. He is co-author with George Annas of *The Nazi Doctors and the Nuremberg Code.* Dr. Grodin is also co-author of a text published by Oxford University Press entitled *Children as Research Subjects: Science, Ethics, and Law.*

PETER J. HAAS: Associate Professor of Jewish Thought and Literature in the Religious Studies Department of Vanderbilt University and author of *Morality After Auschwitz: The Radical Challenge of the Nazi Ethic.*

SUSANNE HAHN: Administrator of the German Hygiene Museum in Dresden where she recently helped organize the exhibit "Unter anderen Umstanden: Zur Geschicte der Abtreibung" (*Under Other Circumstances: The History of Abortion*), 2 July-31 December 1993. She is author of *Krankenplege in der Zeit der faschistischen Diktatur in Deutschland (1933-1945).*

NAT HENTOFF: Critic and essayist for *Village Voice.* He is author of *Boston Boy, Black Anti-Semitism and Jewish Racism* and more recently, *Free Speech for Me—But Not for Thee.*

MICHAEL H. KATER: Distinguished Research Professor of History at York University, Toronto, Ontario (Canada). In 1985-86, he was the Jason A. Hannah Visiting Professor of the History of Medicine at McMaster University in Hamilton, Ontario. He has published widely in the history of modern German medicine, including the monograph *Doctors Under Hitler* for which he has been awarded the Hannah Medal of the Royal Society of Canada.

JAY KATZ: Elizabeth K. Dollard Professor Emeritus of Law, Medicine, and Psychiatry, and Harvey L. Karp Professorial Lecturer in Law and Psychoanalysis at Yale University. His work, *Experimentation with Human Beings* (1972) is considered the classic text in the field.

EVA KOR: Survivor of Mengele's Twin Experiments and Founder and President of C.A.N.D.L.E.S. (Children of Auschwitz Nazi Deadly Lab Experiments Survivors). She lectures widely in the area of Holocaust Education.

VERA LASKA: An Auschwitz survivor and Professor of history at Regis College (Weston, MA). She is also the editor of a collection entitled *Women in the Resistance and in the Holocaust,* in which the testimony of Dagmar Hájková and Hana Housková appears.

JOHN J. MICHALCZYK: Boston College Conference organizer, documentary filmmaker, and author of five texts on European film, notably André Malraux, Costa-Gavras, and Ingmar Bergman. His film *The Cross and the Star: Jews, Christians and the Holocaust,* deals with Christian anti-semitism.

BENNO MÜLLER-HILL: Professor at the Institute of Genetics at the University of Cologne where he works on problems of Molecular Biology and the History of Science. He is the author of *Murderous Science: Elimination by Scientific Selection of Jews, Gypsies and Others in Germany 1933-1945*.

DANIEL S. NADAV: Research Fellow at the Institute of German History at Tel Aviv University and Chairman of the Section for Medicine in the era of National Socialism. He is also author of *Julius Moses and the Politics of Social Hygiene*.

ROBERT N. PROCTOR: Professor of the History of Science at Penn State University and author of *Racial Hygiene: Medicine Under the Nazis*. He is currently serving as Scholar in Residence at the U.S. Holocaust Research Institute, U.S. Holocaust Memorial Museum (Washington, D.C.).

CHARLES G. ROLAND: Professor of Medical History who currently holds the Jason A. Hannah Chair History of Medicine at McMaster University in Hamilton, Ontario (Canada). He is the author of *Courage Under Siege: Starvation, Disease and Death in the Warsaw Ghetto 1940-1943*, for which he received the Hannah Medal of the Royal Society of Canada.

PETER STEINFELS: Former editor of *Commonweal* and current Religious Editor of *The New York Times*, as well as author of *The Future of Individualism*.

Index